The Structure of English

The Structure of English

Phonetics, Phonology, Morphology

THOMAS E. MURRAY
Kansas State University

ALLYN AND BACON
Boston ✦ London ✦ Toronto ✦ Sydney ✦ Tokyo ✦ Singapore

Editor-in-Chief, Humanities: *Joseph Opiela*
Series Editorial Assistant: *Brenda Conaway*
Production Administrator: *Rowena Dores*
Editorial-Production Service: *Denise Hoffman*
Copyeditor: *Susan Freese*
Composition Buyer: *Linda Cox*
Manufacturing Buyer: *Louise Richardson*
Cover Administrator: *Linda Knowles*
Cover Designer: *Suzanne Harbison*

A Division of Paramount Publishing
160 Gould Street
Needham Heights, Massachusetts 02194

Library of Congress Cataloging-in-Publication Data

Murray, Thomas E. (Thomas Edward)
The structure of English : phonetics, phonology, morphology / Thomas E. Murray.
p. cm.
Includes index.
ISBN 0-205-16053-0
1. English language—Phonetics. 2. English language—Phonology. 3. English language—Morphology. I. Title.
PE1135.M8 1994
421'.5—dc20 94-188
CIP

Printed in the United States of America

10 9 8 7 6 5 4 3 2 1 99 98 97 96 95 94

For C.D.R.-M. (B.A., J.D., D.A.D., N.B.D. W.G.A.S.),
who has taught me nothing about linguistics
but a lot about living

Contents

Preface: To the Teacher

If, like me, you are a linguist who works in a department of English, one of the courses you teach most frequently is called The Structure of English (or something similar to that). Your students in that course are undergraduates—typically, a mixture of English majors trying to satisfy the departmental requirement in language study and education majors trying to fulfill the state's requirement for certification. Your task, in any case, is to create a course that these students find meaningful and useful. How do you do that? What do you teach? And what books do you use?

Between 1990 and 1992, I conducted an informal, nationwide survey in which I asked colleagues just these questions. The answers were very predictable. Nearly everyone focused on syntax and/or grammar for a good part of the course, for example (though with approaches ranging from traditional to transformational), and many also devoted some time to dialects and usage (especially if no other course covered such material). A few even discussed the semantics, pragmatics, and/or history and development of the language. Nearly *all* the teachers I queried, however, included brief sections on phonetics, phonology, and morphology, usually at the beginnings of their courses: Since spoken language is first and foremost *sound,* those teachers wanted their students to approach the sounds and sound patterns of English before anything else and then to learn how those sounds combine into meaningful grammatical units.

The answers to my How do you do that? question were also very uniform. Though nearly everyone recognized the need to have their students memorize the International Phonetic Alphabet (IPA) and basic definitions of such terms as *allophone, morpheme,* and *complementary distribution* (all the while studying copious examples, of course), all similarly agreed that memorization alone is not enough, that real learning has not occurred unless students can actually apply what they have memorized to unique situations. To *know* linguistics, in other words, is to be able to *do* linguistics, and rightly so. But most students—usually at the hands of well-intentioned junior high school teachers who stressed activities such as parsing, traditional sentence diagramming, and conjugating verbs—believe *doing* language exercises to be boring and meaningless. So the colleagues I polled also recognized the need to overcome these long-standing stereotypes and infused their subject matter with large doses of something that would capture and hold students' attention.

Now for the last question: What books do you use when you teach courses in the structure of English? Here I was surprised to discover that most colleagues used a book with which neither they nor their students were completely happy, used no books at all (choosing instead to create their own materials), or used bits and pieces of several different books. Why? Because no one book on the market dealt adequately and exclusively with phonetics, phonology, morphology, *and* whatever other limited subject(s) the teacher may want to address in the course. One book may take an approach to syntax that seems all wrong. Another may not discuss dialects and usage. Still another may attempt to do *too* much, and so several chapters on neurolinguistics, artificial intelligence, language acquisition, historical linguistics, and the like go unused. The list of reasons goes on and on but is ultimately unimportant. The point is that for most of us, no good, single textbook exists for courses in the structure of English.

This book is not meant to be a panacea; in fact, no panacea is possible, simply because so many teachers take such varied approaches and do so many different kinds of things in their classes. But the book *does* introduce students to those subjects that seem to be a part of most courses called The Structure of English—phonetics, phonology, and morphology. And it *does* provide numerous examples and illustrative exercises designed to get students interested in and thinking critically about the English language. And perhaps most important for you, the teacher, it *does* allow plenty of time for other subjects to be covered. (Having used the material successfully for more than a decade, I have found that it most often consumes about 3 to 4 weeks of a standard 15-week semester but that it can be tailored to fit both shorter and longer periods than that.)

There are several other things you should know about this book before you use it. First, I have tried to keep the language as informal as possible without being irritatingly chatty. As we have all learned (on one side of the desk or the other), students have a difficult enough time mastering the inescapable jargon of linguistics without having to endure a prose style that is stuffy and pedantic, on the one hand, or patronizing and condescending, on the other. In this book, as in my own classes, I try to talk *to* the students rather than preach *at* them, *over* them, or *down* to them.

Second, because I believe in challenging rather than frustrating students, I have included answers to all the exercises, and because I want the users of this book to understand those answers, I have, when necessary, explained how I derived them. Thus, your students have an immediate, built-in measuring device that will let them know how well they have mastered the material at hand. (By the way, the exercises—both those scattered throughout the text and especially those that conclude Chapters 1, 2, and 3—do not just review the material that has preceded them; the exercises also frequently teach applications of the material and even introduce new concepts. So encourage your students to actually do the necessary work before they look at the answers.)

Third, because I intend this book to be an introduction suitable for undergraduates who have had little or no previous training in linguistics, I have purposely limited my discussions of some subjects (such as the articulatory apparatus and IPA symbols) to just the most basic, necessary facts and have entirely omitted others from the main portion of the text. (Diacritics, natural classes, the formal linguistic notation of rules, and distinctive features all fall into this category.) But because I also know that some teachers will want their students to go beyond just the basic facts and/or be introduced to precisely the kinds of material that I have omitted, I have also included sections called "For Further Study" that will either introduce or provide more detail on these topics. Any or all of these sections can easily be assigned or ignored.

Fourth, since, as I mentioned earlier, courses in the structure of English tend to be populated largely by students who are majoring in English or in education (the split tends to be about 50-50 in my own course), and since students in one area usually have little or no patience for classroom topics directed primarily to students in the other, I have resisted the strong temptation to continually relate the structure of English either to pedagogy or to the study of literature. This is not a methods book, nor is it a "literature as language" book. Now, make no mistake: Some of the prose and many of the exercises do, in fact, deal explicitly with pedagogical, literary, and other applied concerns, but such concerns are never the *primary* focus of the book. If you need or desire a stronger focus in one area or the other, however, you should be able to address such issues easily in your lectures and classroom discussions.

Finally, you may be somewhat relieved to learn that this text has no companion workbook, answer key, or instructor's manual. As I have already indicated, the workbook and answer key are built-in features, and, of course, you are the one to determine how the book best fits with what you do in class.

I wish you well with your course in the structure of English. If, after using this book, you have suggestions for how it might be improved, please let me know.

Acknowledgments

Three groups of individuals deserve special recognition for the roles that they played in the production of this book. First, I extend my appreciation to Professors John Hagge (Iowa State University), Charles L. Houck (Ball State University), and Anne LeCroy (East Tennessee State University), who reviewed an earlier version of the manuscript for Allyn and Bacon and provided much valuable feedback.

Second, I owe a debt of gratitude to the many good folks I worked with at Allyn and Bacon: Joe Opiela, who served as my editor, and his assistant, Brenda Conaway; my production editor, Rowena Dores; the project coordinator, Denise Hoffman; and perhaps especially my copyeditor, Sue Freese.

Finally, many thanks to the hundreds of students at Kansas State University who have suffered through earlier renderings of this book and have never hesitated to share with me their frank comments on its strengths and especially its weaknesses. If I haven't yet gotten it right, I have no one to blame but myself.

T. M.

Preface: To the Student

You have enrolled in a class called The Structure of English (or something similar to that), which will probably be different from any English course you have ever taken. If you are like most students, when you think of English, you think of reading literature or writing poetry, short stories, or expository essays—all worthy pursuits, to be sure. But in this course, you will study the English *language*—its sounds, how those sounds form patterns and combine into meaningful units, words, sentences, and so forth.

Since you probably already speak, read, write, and understand English fluently, you may be wondering what else you have to learn. After all, don't you know the language just fine? Well, yes and no. While it is true that you *know* English well enough, it is also true that most of what you know is *unconscious* knowledge. Here is a good example: Imagine that you encounter a new word, *blug*. Assuming the word is a noun, how do you spell and pronounce the plural form? Of course, the answer is *blugs*, with the *s* pronounced more like a *z*, but can you explain why? If *blug* were a verb, could you explain why the past tense would be *blugged* (pronounced with no vowel sound between the *g* and the *d*) and the present participle would be *blugging?*

Your course in the structure of English will teach you these kinds of things. In other words, it will help your unconscious knowledge become more conscious, which is especially important if you want to be a teacher of English or even just a more informed reader of literature (though even if you care deeply about neither of these, the material has many other applications and is even interesting in its own right).

To understand the structure of English, you will have to learn some of the formal methods and techniques of the subject of *linguistics*, which is defined as "the scientific study of language." Linguistics is a broad field, encompassing the study of phonetics, phonology, morphology, syntax, semantics, pragmatics, dialects, lexicon, language history and typology, language acquisition, neurolinguistics, psycholinguistics, and many other topics. This book will introduce you to the first three of these: phonetics, phonology, and morphology.

You should realize that your success with linguistics will largely be measured in two ways. First, as is true when you learn any new subject, you will have to memorize some new symbols and terminology. Second and more important, you will have to learn to apply what you have memorized to unique situations. This means that you must learn to think about language in new ways—that is, analytically, logically, and objectively. If you are like my own students, you will be challenged by such thinking and probably find it difficult at times. To help you along, I have included in this book many exercises, all of which *you must actually try to do* (as opposed to just reading through them quickly; besides, the exercises also teach applications of the material and occasionally even introduce new concepts). And so you can receive immediate feedback about the quality of your responses and understand any mistakes you may have made, the correct answers—including, when necessary, explanations of why they are correct and how they were derived—are given following Chapter 3 (see Answers to Exercises). Remember: Memorizing for its own sake is as useless in linguistics as it is in any other discipline; *learning* linguistics means being able to *do* linguistics.

Before you proceed to Chapter 1, I want you to know about one other feature of this book: Whenever I introduce a new term, it will appear in **boldface** type within the text and will also be included in a review list at the end of the chapter in which it appeared. All such terms are listed and defined in the Glossary, which follows the Answers to Exercises. Numerous cross-references within the Glossary help demonstrate the relationships among terms.

Good luck in your study of the structure of English. If, in using this book, you come up with suggestions for how it could be improved, please let me know. The quality of this book is due largely to the numerous suggestions of my own students, so I will certainly take whatever you have to say seriously.

T. M.

The Structure of English Phonetics 1

The English language can be studied in many different ways, including how its dialects pattern, how its words combine into sentences, how its sounds connect into larger units (such as prefixes and suffixes and words), how its speakers use it to carry on various kinds of conversations, how its spoken and written forms differ, and so forth. But underlying nearly all these avenues of study are the basic "building blocks" of English, the smallest elements it contains—its sounds. Those sounds will be the focus of Chapter 1.

Basic Definitions

The study of speech sounds is **phonetics** and is typically divided into **acoustic phonetics** and **articulatory phonetics**. Acoustic phonetics is the study of speech sounds in terms of their physical properties—what those properties are and how they can be measured—and will not concern us further. (Acoustic phonetics is an interesting branch of linguistics but is not necessary for learning and understanding the structure of English.) Articulatory phonetics, however, is the study of speech sounds in terms of how they are produced when we speak and will be our focus in Chapter 1. Since we are concerned just with the structure of the English language, we will study only those sounds that are part of English; but many other kinds of speech sounds also exist and are used in other languages.

The speech sounds that any given language uses are collectively known as its **phonetic inventory**, and no two languages have phonetic inventories that are exactly alike.

Sounds and Spellings in English

In English words, there is a very poor correlation between sounds and spellings, and the sooner you learn to keep the two distinct, the easier phonetics will be for you. Consider the following possibilities:

1. Sometimes different letters or combinations of letters represent the same sound. The words *to, too, two, few, cue, shoe, you,* and *juice,* for example, all have the same vowel sound but are all spelled differently.
2. Sometimes the same letter or combination of letters represents different sounds. The letter *a,* for example, is pronounced differently in each of the following words: *game, mad, father, ball, many, village, dollar, sofa.*
3. Sometimes two letters combine to make a single sound, as with the *-sh* in *show,* the *-th* in *both,* the *ch-* in *chop* and *chef* and *chiropractor,* the *ph-* in *phone,* the *-ou-* and *-gh* in *rough,* the *-oa-* in *boat,* the *-ai-* in *wait,* the *-ea-* in *deaf* and *bead,* the *-ng* in *ring,* and the *-ua-* and *-ee* in *guarantee,* among many others.
4. Sometimes letters are silent, as with the *-gh* in *through,* the *-h-* in *ghost,* the *p-* in *psychology,* the *k-* in *knot,* the *-ps* in *corps,* the *-e* in *rare,* the *w-* in *who,* the *-b-* in *debt,* and the *p-* (and, for many speakers, the *-l-*) in *psalm,* among many others.
5. Sometimes a sound is not clearly represented by any letter. The word *few,* for example, contains three sounds—the "f" sound, the "y" sound, and the "long u" sound. If the *f* represents the "f" sound and the *-ew* represents the "long u" sound, what is left to represent the "y" sound? The same problem occurs with *cue, Hughes, pew, ague, view,* and many other words.
6. Sometimes one letter represents two sounds. Listen carefully as you pronounce the word *box.* How many sounds does it contain? Besides the "b" sound and the "open-mouthed a" sound, there are also the "k" sound and the "s" sound. (If you cannot

hear four distinct sounds, say the word again, slowly, and try to forget that it is spelled with only three letters.) The *b* represents the "b" sound and the *o* represents the "open-mouthed a" sound, so the *x* must represent both the "k" and the "s" sounds. The same kind of phenomenon occurs in words such as *exit* (the *x* again represents both the "k" and the "s" sounds, or, for some speakers, "g" and "z" sounds) and *exempt* (here the *x* represents the "g" and "z" sounds).

All these possibilities cause lots of problems for people who must learn to read and write English, and for many years, these possibilities also caused problems for linguists and others who were studying the phonetics of English. These scholars found that there was simply no easy, consistent way to represent the same sounds with the same symbols.

✦ *EXERCISE 1-1*

There are at least 15 different ways in English to spell the "long e" vowel sound in *be*. How many can you identify in 60 seconds? In 5 minutes? In 10 minutes? Write sample words containing the various spellings in the spaces below, and underline the letters in each that spell the "long e." (You can use a dictionary if you wish, but it probably will not help unless you spend several hours reading through it.)

1. ____________________
2. ____________________
3. ____________________
4. ____________________
5. ____________________
6. ____________________
7. ____________________
8. ____________________
9. ____________________

10. ______________________________

11. ______________________________

12. ______________________________

13. ______________________________

14. ______________________________

15. ______________________________

✦✦✦

An Introduction to the International Phonetic Alphabet

Since the sixteenth century, people have been trying to devise a universal means of solving this problem of sounds and symbols. Numerous phonetic alphabets have been proposed in which a unique, one-to-one correspondence exists between the sounds being described and the characters in the alphabet, with the same symbols aways representing the same sounds. The best known of these, the **International Phonetic Alphabet (IPA),** was created in 1888.

Your major task in Chapter 1 will be to learn one of the forms of the IPA used most often in North America. (It is substantially the same as other forms of the IPA; only a few alternate symbols have been proposed over the years.) To do so, you must learn three different kinds of information: the alphabetic characters themselves, the sounds those characters represent, and the verbal description of each of those sounds (two or three words that will specify how and where in your vocal apparatus each sound is produced).

This task will be much easier than it may appear. You already know most of the IPA characters, for example, because they correspond to the letters of the Roman alphabet that we use in English. And if you have been speaking English all or most of your life, you already know *all* the sounds, since they are the same sounds you use daily when you pronounce English words. Finally, the verbal descriptions may be more challenging, since they will probably be brand new, but there are proven ways to master them, as well (about which you'll learn more later).

The Making of Sounds

As we begin, it will be helpful for you to become familiar with those parts of the head and throat that you use when you speak. Knowing those body parts will help you learn the verbal descriptions when we get to them and, more immediately, will help you understand how you create each speech sound. Figure 1-1 illustrates all the parts of the body discussed in this section.

We can begin with the parts that you are most familiar with—the lips, teeth, and tongue. Say the word *boy* out loud two or three times. Now get ready to say *boy,* but stop short of actually saying it. Notice how, in preparing for the first sound of the word, your two lips press together; that is because they are primarily responsible for making the *b* sound. Now say *four* and *very* a few times, and notice that the initial sound of each requires you to press your top teeth against the outer part of your lower lip. You just cannot pronounce those sounds—at least, not very easily—with your teeth and lips in any other position. Compare the first sound of *four* with the first sound of *thumb,* and notice where your tongue is when you pronounce the sound represented by the *th-*. If you try to hold your tongue anywhere other than between your teeth, you will either pronounce a different word or no word at all. Again, this is because your tongue, in that particular position between your teeth, is primarily responsible for you being able to say that sound.

Other parts of the head that are involved in producing speech sounds may not be as familiar to you. Take the tip of your tongue and place it so that it touches the back of your top teeth; then move it back along the roof of your mouth, just a fraction of an inch. You should be able to feel a hard, bony ridge just behind and parallel to your teeth. (The ridge is more pronounced in some people than in others, but it is definitely there.) This is the **alveolar ridge.** If you say the words *dog* and *ton,* you will notice that, just before you say the initial sound of each, the tip of your tongue comes to rest lightly on your alveolar ridge.

✦ *EXERCISE 1-2*

What other English consonant sounds involve the tip of the tongue being on or very near the alveolar ridge? (*Hint:* There are five such sounds.) Write sample words containing the sounds in the spaces below.

1. ______________________________
2. ______________________________
3. ______________________________
4. ______________________________
5. ______________________________

✦✦✦

Now move the tip of your tongue from your alveolar ridge back across the roof of your mouth, almost as far as you can reach. That entire area is called the **hard palate.** Most of the body of your tongue is very near the hard palate when you say the initial sounds in words such as *show, Jacques, chief,* and *jump* and the final sounds in words such as *push, beige, lunch,* and *budge.* Just behind the hard palate, also on the roof of the mouth, is the **soft palate, or velum,** which feels very soft and fleshy. (Unless your tongue is very long, you will have to locate the velum with the tip of your finger.) Notice how the body of your tongue rises to touch the velum when you pronounce the first sounds in the words *go* and *cool* and the final sound in the word *thing.*

Just above the mouth and behind the nose is a large, open space called the **nasal cavity**; the air you inhale through your nose must pass through this cavity before going on to your throat and lungs. Your nasal cavity performs two very important functions when you speak. First, it acts like a miniature echo chamber and allows your voice to sound more resonant than it would otherwise. Second, it allows you to produce three of the speech sounds used in English—the initial sounds in *more* and *nice* and the final sound in *song.*

If it seems unlikely to you that an empty space in your head could be responsible for the production of these three sounds, try

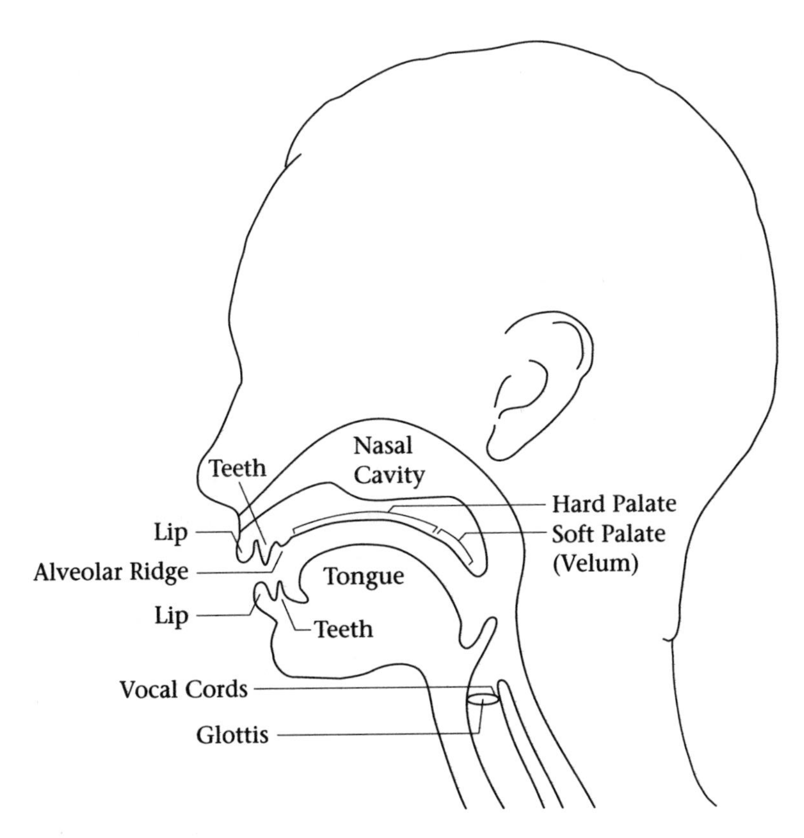

FIGURE 1-1 *Basic Human Vocal Apparatus*

this simple test: First, say *mmmmmm* (a lengthened version of the initial sound in *more*); now pinch your nostrils shut with your fingers, and try to say *mmmmmm* again. You will discover that it is impossible to produce a normal-sounding *mmmmmm,* since the airstream from your lungs can no longer exit your nasal cavity through your nose. With that pathway blocked, you cannot effectively pronounce any of the three sounds described above.

✦ *EXERCISE 1-3*

Pinch your nostrils shut one more time, and say each of the following words: *moat, near, tummy, runner, ringing, roam, sign,* and *long.* Then respond to each of the following questions.

(a) What sounds do you consistently find yourself substituting for those represented by *m, n,* and *ng?*

(b) What resulting words do you find yourself pronouncing?

(c) What does your answer to question (a) imply about the phonetic relationship between the pairs of sounds represented by *m* and *b, n* and *d,* and *ng* and *g,* respectively?

✦✦✦

The last parts of your body that are necessary to speak English are in your throat. Bend your head back so that you are looking up at the ceiling at about a 45 degree angle. Now, using the thumb and first two fingers of one hand, locate your Adam's apple. (It will probably be a bit more pronounced if you are male and less so if you are female.) This structure serves as a protective covering for some very important organs, among which are the **vocal cords** and the **glottis.** The vocal cords consist of two small, parallel bands of muscle that are connected at either end and are somewhat pliable in the middle. (Their length and thickness determine the pitch of your voice: That is, longer, thicker cords produce deeper voices, and shorter, thinner cords produce higher voices.) And the glottis is the opening between the vocal cords when they are relaxed (such as when you breathe). We will explore both the vocal cords and the glottis in greater detail later; for now, suffice it to say that, without one or the other, your speech would sound very different.

FOR FURTHER STUDY
More on the Articulatory Apparatus

The following list identifies 12 additional parts of the body that are involved in the production of speech sounds (see Figure 1-2). (Note that some of these body parts are involved in the production of speech sounds used only in languages other than English.) Three of the terms (**blade, dorsum**, and **tip**) merely identify subdivisions of the tongue, and one other term (**larynx**) includes parts of the body that were introduced in the preceding section. In the list, terms within definitions that occur in boldface type are cross-references to other terms in the list.

- **Blade**—the broad body of the tongue (as distinct from the **tip** and **dorsum**)
- **Bronchi**—the two tubes that connect the lower end of the windpipe to the lungs
- **Diaphragm**—the internal wall of muscle and connective tissue that separates the chest from the abdomen; the diaphragm is connected to the lower ribs, and when it and the **intercostal muscles** (which are located between the ribs) relax, air is forced out of the lungs and through the windpipe to the vocal cords (conversely, when the diaphragm and intercostal muscles flex, the chest expands and air is inhaled into the lungs; thus, the diaphragm and intercostals are necessary for breathing as well as speaking)
- **Dorsum**—the extreme back portion of the tongue

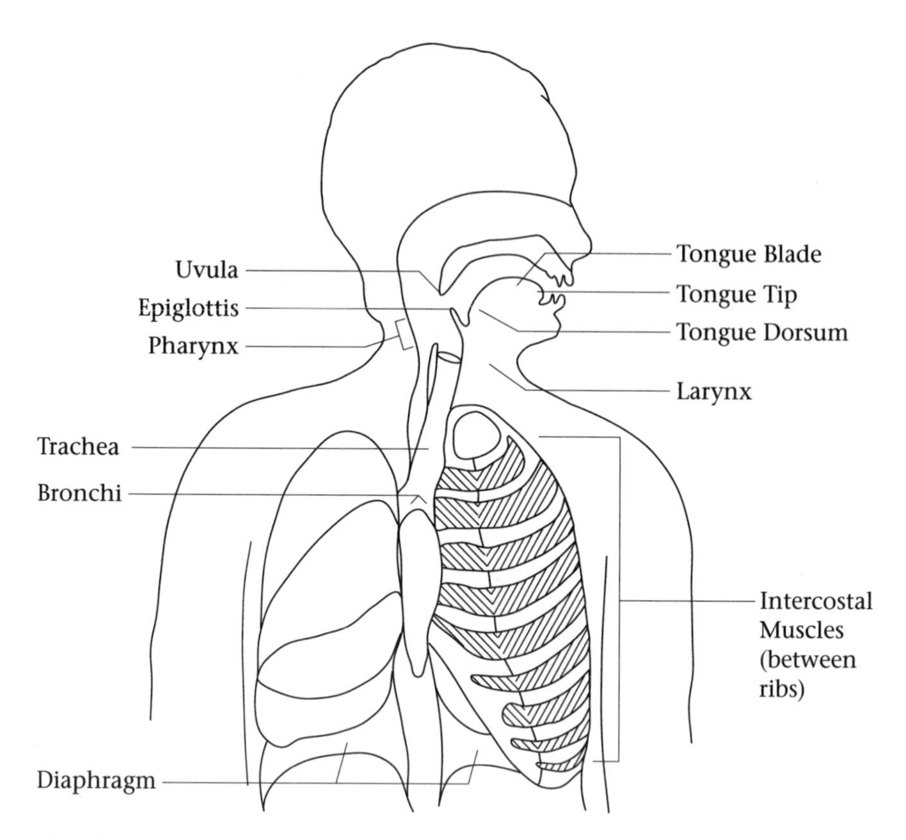

FIGURE 1-2 *More of the Human Vocal Apparatus*

- **Epiglottis**—the small flap of cartilage behind the root of the tongue; the epiglottis is not directly involved in the production of any English speech sounds but plays a major role in Semitic languages such as Arabic (for all humans, the primary purpose of the epiglottis is to close off the opening to the windpipe during swallowing, thus preventing food and drink from entering the windpipe)
- **Intercostal muscles**—the small muscles located between the ribs; when these muscles and the **diaphragm** relax, air is forced from the lungs through the windpipe to the vocal cords
- **Larynx**—the mass of muscle and cartilage located at the top of the windpipe and containing the vocal cords and glottis; commonly called the *voicebox*

- **Pharynx**—the cartilage, muscles, and membranes that connect the back of the mouth to the nasal cavity and **larynx**; the pharynx is not directly involved in the production of any English speech sounds but plays a major role in Semitic languages such as Arabic
- **Tip**—the front end of the tongue
- **Trachea**—the windpipe, which runs from the **larynx** to the **bronchi**
- **Uvula**—the small piece of flesh that dangles from the back of the soft palate (visible if you open your mouth widely and look in a mirror); the uvula is not directly involved in the production of any English speech sounds but plays a major role in languages such as German and (some dialects of) French

Consonants in the International Phonetic Alphabet

It is standard in phonetics to separate consonant sounds from vowel sounds, since all the members of each group have more in common with one another than with any members of the other group in terms of how they are articulated, measured, and described. For that reason (and also because it will be easier for you to learn the IPA if it is subdivided this way), we will go through the consonants first and deal with the vowels later. Keep in mind throughout both sections, however, that you will be learning only those portions of the IPA dealing with English speech sounds; many additional sounds used in other languages also exist.

When the consonants of the IPA are described verbally, three criteria are used. First, **voicing** refers to whether the vocal cords vibrate as the sound is being produced: If they do, the sound is **voiced**; if they do not, the sound is **voiceless.** (If you place your fingers and thumb on either side of your Adam's apple and alternate saying *zzzzzzz* and *sssssss,* you can contrast the vibration with the lack of vibration: *zzzzzzz* is voiced, and *sssssss* is voiceless.)

The second criterion is **place of articulation**, which refers to *where* in the mouth or throat the sound is primarily being produced. To describe English consonants, terms naming seven basic places of articulation are needed:

- **Bilabial**—"two lips"
- **Labiodental**—"lip and teeth"
- **Interdental**—"between the teeth"
- **Alveolar**—"alveolar ridge"
- **Palatal**—"hard palate"
- **Velar**—"velum"
- **Glottal**—"glottis"

Some phoneticians also use three other places of articulation:

- **Dental**—referring to the back of the top teeth
- **Alveopalatal** (or, occasionally, *palatoalveolar*)—referring to the roof of the mouth directly behind the alveolar ridge and just in front of the hard palate
- **Labiovelar**—referring to the simultaneous rounding of the lips and raising of the body of the tongue toward the velum

But these additional places of articulation essentially represent more advanced subdivisions or combinations of the basic seven given earlier; they are not necessary for the study of the basic phonetic structure of English, and so they will not concern us further.

The final criterion is **manner of articulation**, which refers to *how* the sound is being produced. Six manners of articulation are necessary to describe English consonants:

- **Stop**—the airstream is stopped momentarily before being allowed to exit the mouth or nose
- **Fricative**—the airstream is interfered with, though not stopped entirely, and the resulting friction produces sound
- **Affricate**—the airstream is first stopped momentarily and then quickly released with friction, so the result is a combination of a stop and a fricative
- **Nasal**—the airstream is forced into the nasal cavity and exits through the nose
- **Liquid**—the airstream is interfered with, though without friction resulting, so the air merely "flows" smoothly around the tongue and out the mouth

- **Glide**—also sometimes called **semivowel**, since the unobstructed airstream allows an easy "gliding" movement to and between vowel sounds

When giving the verbal description of a particular consonant sound, it is customary to specify these three criteria in the order (1) voicing, (2) place of articulation, and (3) manner of articulation. Thus, for example, you would say "voiced bilabial stop" rather than "bilabial stop voiced," "voiced stop bilabial," or any other combination. (It is not really wrong to specify the criteria in some other order, since all the characteristics of the sound would still be present in the description, but it *would* be unconventional and would probably cause others who use the IPA to wonder how well you actually know it.)

It is also customary to use only the minimum number of criteria necessary to keep each of the consonant sounds distinct from all the others. Because all three nasals and both glides in English are voiced, for example, you need not specify that feature in their various verbal descriptions; it is already implied. So you can say "bilabial nasal" rather than "voiced bilabial nasal," "palatal glide" rather than "voiced palatal glide," and so forth. (Again, it is not really wrong to specify the unnecessary feature, but it *is* redundant.) Similarly, since both affricates happen to be palatal sounds, you can say merely "voiced affricate" and "voiceless affricate" rather than "voiced palatal affricate" and "voiceless palatal affricate." And since the only glottal fricative is voiceless, you need not specify the feature of voicing for that sound. (There are no voiced glottal fricatives with which to confuse it.) All these guidelines will make more sense shortly, when you know all the characteristics of all the consonant sounds.

Look now at Table 1-1, in which all the places of articulation are listed across the top, one per column, and all the manners of articulation are listed down the left side, one per row. By finding the intersection of any column and any row, you can easily see which consonant sounds have which characteristics. If two sounds have the same place and manner of articulation and differ only in voicing, they occur side by side in the same box, with the voiced sound to the left. (Of the stops, for example, the "b," "d," and "g" represent voiced sounds and the "p," "t," and "k" represent voiceless sounds.)

In the box for "alveolar liquid," notice that two symbols occur—"l" and "r"—but not side by side. That is because both represent voiced sounds and differ only in ways that cannot be expressed in the chart. For that reason, each is given a special name: "l" is called **lateral** (because its articulation involves the airstream passing

TABLE 1-1 *Consonant Chart for English*

Manner of Articulation	*Place of Articulation*						
	Bilabial	**Labiodental**	**Interdental**	**Alveolar**	**Palatal**	**Velar**	**Glottal**
Stop	b p			d t		g k	
Fricative		v f	ð θ	z s	ž š		h
Affricate					ǰ č		
Nasal	m			n		ŋ	
Liquid						(r)	
Glide (semivowel)	w				j	(w)	

Note: In those boxes in which two symbols occur side by side, the symbol on the left always represents a voiced sound.

on either side of the tongue before it exits the mouth), and "r" is called **retroflex** (because its articulation involves the tongue flexing and retracting so that the base is near the velum and the tip is near the alveolar ridge). And notice also that two of the symbols, "r" and "w," occur twice in the chart, once in parentheses and once not. That is because each sound actually involves two places of articulation—for "r," the alveolar ridge and the velum; for "w," the lips and the velum—and can properly be thought of as alveolar/velar and bilabial/velar, respectively. But to keep the verbal descriptions of these sounds as simple and consistent as possible, linguists usually just refer to the "r" as alveolar and the "w" as bilabial.

✦ *EXERCISE 1-4*

Do both (a) and (b).

(a) Specify the verbal descriptions of the sounds represented by the following symbols. (*Note:* You do not need to know what the sounds are to be able to give their verbal descriptions; you must merely be able to read the consonant chart in Table 1-1.)

"p" ______________________

"k" ______________________

"v" ______________________

"s" ______________________

"č" ______________________

"š" ______________________

"g" ______________________

"f" ______________________

"r" ______________________

"ǰ" ______________________

"b" ______________________

"l" ______________________

"j" ______________________________

"t" ______________________________

"h" ______________________________

"w" ______________________________

"d" ______________________________

"θ" ______________________________

"ð" ______________________________

"ž" ______________________________

"z" ______________________________

"m" ______________________________

"n" ______________________________

"ŋ" ______________________________

(b) Supply the IPA symbol for each of the following verbal descriptions.

voiceless bilabial stop ______________________________

bilabial nasal ______________________________

voiceless interdental fricative ______________________________

retroflex ______________________________

voiced palatal fricative ______________________________

voiceless affricate ______________________________

voiced alveolar fricative ______________________________

voiced velar stop ______________________________

voiced labiodental fricative ______________________

voiced bilabial stop ______________________

alveolar nasal ______________________

velar nasal ______________________

voiceless alveolar stop ______________________

bilabial glide ______________________

voiceless palatal fricative ______________________

palatal glide ______________________

voiceless alveolar fricative ______________________

voiceless velar stop ______________________

voiceless labiodental fricative ______________________

glottal fricative ______________________

voiced interdental fricative ______________________

lateral ______________________

voiced alveolar stop ______________________

voiced affricate ______________________

F F F

Very shortly, we will go through the consonant chart (Table 1-1) in some detail. Before doing that, however, you must become familiar with several new terms and a new set of symbols. First, because some of the sounds represented in the consonant chart share certain similarities that the chart does not adequately express, they are typically grouped and given a common name. (We will explore some of these similarities further in Chapters 2 and 3.) All the stops, fricatives, and affricates are known collectively as **obstruents** (characterized by a stoppage or obstruction of the airstream during articulation); all the nasals, liquids, and glides (as well as all the vowels) are known collectively as **sonorants** (characterized by a relatively unobstructed airstream during articulation); and the two alveolar fricatives, the two palatal fricatives, and the two affricates are collectively known as **sibilants** (characterized by the airstream being channeled through a narrow groove along the center of the tongue during articulation, which results in a kind of "hissing" sound).

Second, to keep the characters of the IPA distinct from those of other alphabets and also to indicate that those characters symbolize real speech sounds, linguists enclose them in square brackets ([ ]). The symbol for the voiced bilabial stop, for example, is written like this: [b]. And the symbol for the lateral is written like this: [l]. Even when we use several IPA characters in a row, such as to indicate the many speech sounds that occur in a single word, we begin the string with a left square bracket ([) and end the string with a right one ( ]); for example, the first two sounds of *slow* would be written as "[sl]," and the final three sounds of *exempt* would be written as "[mpt]."

Finally, when a speech sound or series of speech sounds is "translated" into IPA characters (as in the preceding paragraph for clusters of consonant sounds in *slow* and *exempt*), that speech has been **transcribed;** the activity of making that "translation" is referred to as **transcription.** Transcription is one of the most important activities associated with articulatory phonetics.

Table 1-2 presents all the IPA symbols from the consonant chart, their corresponding verbal descriptions, and some sample words that illustrate the sounds they represent. Study this list carefully, pronouncing each of the words several times. As mentioned earlier, thoroughly learning these IPA symbols and verbal descriptions will be your biggest task in this chapter of the book, and your ultimate success in Chapters 2 and 3 will, to a large extent, depend on how good a job you do here.

Several pages ago, it was mentioned that there are proven ways to learn the IPA, especially the various verbal descriptions. The first of these methods, which relies on knowing the various parts of the articulatory apparatus, is simply to *feel* each sound as you say it, noticing whether your vocal chords are vibrating, what position your tongue is in and what shape your mouth forms, what is happening to the airstream as it flows from your throat out through your mouth or nose, and so forth. Then, even if you are not sure of the verbal descriptions of, say, [g], [s], and [m], you should be able to figure them out. With [g], for example, your vocal chords are vibrating, the body of your tongue is being pushed up against your velum, and your

TABLE 1-2 *IPA Characters and Verbal Descriptions of English Consonant Sounds*

Symbol	***Verbal Description***	***Sound Represented***
[b]	voiced bilabial stop	*b*oy, o*b*oe, cra*b*
[p]	voiceless bilabial stop	*p*our, a*p*t, sla*p*
[d]	voiced alveolar stop	*d*ock, a*d*ore, bloo*d*
[t]	voiceless alveolar stop	*t*ime, soli*t*ary, adep*t*
[g]	voiced velar stop	*g*ame, a*g*ree, ba*g*
[k]	voicless velar stop	*c*old, a*c*t, po*k*e
[v]	voiced labiodental fricative	*v*ery, a*v*erage, sho*v*e
[f]	voiceless labiodental fricative	*f*ool, a*f*ter, lau*gh*
[ð]	voiced interdental fricative	*th*y, o*th*er, ba*th*e
[θ]	voiceless interdental fricative	*th*igh, e*th*ereal, ba*th*
[z]	voiced alveolar fricative	*z*oo, o*z*one, bu*zz*
[s]	voiceless alveolar fricative	*s*oup, bla*s*t, mi*ss*
[ž]	voiced palatal fricative	*J*acques, a*z*ure, bei*g*e
[š]	voiceless palatal fricative	*s*ure, mi*ss*ion, ma*sh*
[h]	glottal fricative	*h*ope, a*h*oy
[ǰ]	voiced affricate	*j*ump, bu*dg*et, fu*dg*e
[č]	voiceless affricate	*ch*oke, mat*ch*ing, i*tch*

(continued)

TABLE 1-2 *Continued*

Symbol	*Verbal Description*	*Sound Represented*
[m]	bilabial nasal	*m*y, a*mm*onia, ga*m*e
[n]	alveolar nasal	*n*ice, pia*n*o, su*n*
[ŋ]	velar nasal	i*n*k, so*ng*
[l]	lateral	*l*ow, bui*l*d, ca*ll*
[r]	retroflex	*r*ough, so*rr*y, cho*r*e
[w]	bilabial glide	*w*hy, a*w*ay
[j]	palatal glide	*y*es, *y*o*y*o

airstream is stopping before it exits your mouth; thus, [g] must be voiced, a velar sound, and a stop. As you will see shortly, the same technique can be used for each of the vowel sounds.

The second method, which relies on simple memory, is to make a flashcard for each IPA symbol and its corresponding sound and verbal description. On one side of the card, write the IPA symbol and, if you need to, a sample word containing the sound; on the other, write the corresponding verbal description. (The consonant chart has the same information, of course, but often tends to be memorized as a whole chart rather than as a series of individual sounds and verbal descriptions.)

However you ultimately master the IPA, it is important that you not procrastinate learning the consonants. The vowels will be your next priority, and they will present an all new set of challenges.

One final note about the consonant IPA symbols—and, for that matter, the vowel symbols you are about to learn: When you draw them, do not deviate much from the examples in this book. If you do, you risk drawing either a different IPA symbol (maybe one not even used for English) or some other kind of symbol entirely. For example, if you intend to write the voiced alveolar stop, [d], but instead of the lowercase letter, you produce the uppercase one, [D], you will have symbolized the voiced alveolar flap by mistake. Or if you mean to draw [š], the voiceless palatal fricative, but instead write [ŝ] (with the wedge inverted into a circumflex), you will have produced no IPA symbol at all. The mistake would be a minor one, granted, but it still would be a mistake. Or, again, suppose you intend to draw [a] but instead produce something that looks more like [ə]. As you will soon see, the two symbols represent sounds that are very similar in articulation, and you will have to be very clear about which one you intend in any given transcription. The point is that you should not take chances when you draw IPA symbols: Reproduce them *exactly* as they are drawn in this book.

✦ *EXERCISE 1-5*

For each of the following words, first give the IPA symbol or symbols that represent(s) the sound(s) spelled by the italicized consonant(s); then give the verbal description(s) of the IPA symbol(s). (*Remember:* Do not be fooled by the spellings! You should concentrate on sounds, not letters.)

*sh*rink [ ] ________________________________

cou*gh* [ ] ________________________________

*j*udge [ ] ________________________________

si*ng*er [ ] ________________________________

fi*ng*er [ ] ________________________________

wal*ked* [ ] ________________________________

rou*g*e [ ] ________________________________

*th*ere [ ] ________________________________

u*n*til [ ] ________________________________

but*ch*er [ ] ________________________________

*y*early [ ] ________________________________

o*v*er [ ] ________________________________

hea*r*t [ ] ____________________

shu*cks* [ ] ____________________

mo*th* [ ] ____________________

i*mp*erial [ ] ____________________

el*b*ow [ ] ____________________

hot*d*og [ ] ____________________

cra*z*y [ ] ____________________

*wh*oa [ ] ____________________

*h*earing [ ] ____________________

thou*gh* [ ] ____________________

✦ ✦ ✦

FOR FURTHER STUDY

Additional and Alternate Consonant IPA Symbols

Some phonetics textbooks—usually those discussing the subject at a more advanced level than this one—include three additional English consonant sounds: a **glottal stop** ([ʔ]); a second voiced alveolar stop, known as a **"flap"** ([D]); and a **voiceless bilabial glide** ([ʍ]). The glottal stop is very difficult to hear; it is merely the small burst of air that emits from the glottis when the vocal cords part, for example, in anticipation of a syllable-initial vowel sound. If you say *uh-uh* slowly and deliberately or even if you merely open your mouth and say *ahhhh,* you may hear the glottal stop that precedes the given vowel sound; and if you cannot quite hear it, perhaps you will feel it occur as your vocal cords part and release the airstream that will be used for the vowel. We will not recognize or symbolize the glottal stop in this book, but it *does* occur in many English words.

The flap sound typically occurs when one of the spellings *-t-, -d-, tt-,* or *-dd-* occurs between vowels and does not begin a syllable that contains the main stress of a word. (Some speakers use the flap only for *-t-* and *-tt-* and use [d] for *-d-* and *-dd-*.) You can hear the flap in *latter,* for example (the main stress precedes the *-tt-*), but not in *atone* (the main stress follows the *-t-*). Notice that in *latter* and also in *atom* and probably *ladder* and *Adam,* the consonant sound you pronounce between the vowels is neither a true [t] nor a true [d] but something in between. That something is the flap, so called because, in producing it, the tip of the tongue flaps up against the alveolar ridge before quickly getting into position for the following vowel sound. In this book, however, we will treat the flap as a kind of [d].

The voiceless bilabial glide occurs, for some speakers, initially in words such as *which* and *where* and involves inserting an [h] before the [w]. (Some other speakers pronounce *which* like *witch,* articulate no [h] in *where,* and, in general, do not have a voiceless bilabial glide in their dialect.) Notice that this combination of sounds can be represented just as easily by [hw] as by [ʍ].

Besides these three additional symbols, several alternate characters are sometimes used to represent various consonant sounds. Strictly speaking, these alternates defeat the purpose of an alphabet designed specifically to have a perfect one-to-one correspondence between each of its letters and sounds; but all the symbols are so widely recognized and used, at least in certain parts of the world, that it is easier to maintain the imperfection than to try to legislate change. In fact, as mentioned earlier, some have been incorporated into the consonant chart in Table 1-1, since they are more widely used in North America than their counterparts. A list of these alternate symbols follows:

- Flap [D] (introduced just above)—also represented as [ɾ]
- Voiced palatal fricative [ž]—also represented as [ʒ]
- Voiceless palatal fricative [š]—also represented as [ʃ]
- Voiced affricate [ǰ]—also represented as [dž] or [dʒ]
- Voiceless affricate [č]—also represented as [tč] or [tʃ]
- Palatal glide [j]—also represented as [y]
- Retroflex [r]—also represented as [ɹ]

Vowels in the International Phonetic Alphabet

Just as consonant sounds are specified using the criteria (1) voicing, (2) place of articulation, and (3) manner of articulation, so are vowels described, though using three different criteria. The first, **tongue height**, refers to how high or low in the mouth the body of the tongue is when a vowel is pronounced. In English, we have three options—**high**, **mid**, or **low**. If you alternate saying the words *seed, said,* and *sod* several times, you will be able to feel your tongue move up near the roof of your mouth for the high vowel in *seed,* then lower somewhat for the mid vowel in *said,* and then lower even farther for the low vowel in *sod.*

Tongue advancement, the second criterion, is a measure of how far toward the front or rear of the mouth the tongue is when a vowel is pronounced. Again, there are three options: **front** (say the word *bet,* and notice that your tongue is positioned just behind your teeth), **central** (compare *bet* to *but,* for which your tongue must retract into the middle of your mouth), or **back** (now say *boat,* and notice how far toward the rear of your mouth your tongue has moved).

The final criterion that we will use in this book to measure the articulation of English vowels is **tongue tenseness.** Say the words *beat* and *bit* several times. Notice that, while your tongue does lower slightly when you say the vowel in *bit,* the primary difference between the two is that, for the vowel in *beat,* the muscles in your tongue are flexed, or **tense**; for the vowel in *bit,* they are **lax.**

The conditions under which you must apply these three criteria to specific vowels in naming their verbal descriptions are nearly identical to those you learned for consonants. It is still true, for example, that you should use the minimum number of criteria necessary to differentiate each of the vowels. Since there are two vowels that are both high and front, for example, two more that are mid and front, and two more that are high and back, you must make it clear that one vowel in each of these pairs is tense and the other lax. But because only one vowel is low and front, one other is mid and central, one other is low and central, and one other is low and back, their laxness does not need to be mentioned, just as the tenseness of the one vowel that is mid and back need not be specified.

You should also name the criteria in the order in which they were presented earlier—tongue height first, then tongue advancement, and tongue tenseness last. Thus, you would have *high, back, tense* rather than *back, tense, high* and *mid, front, lax* rather than *lax, mid, front.* The one difference between the verbal descriptions of consonants and vowels is that those of vowels must contain the word *vowel* at the end (or else you will have just a string of adjectives, with nothing for them to modify). *One of the most common mistakes that students make in describing vowels is to omit the word* vowel *from the description.*

In a moment, you will be asked to examine the vowel chart in Table 1-3, but first, you must understand that, among the many people who use phonetics in their work (not just linguists but also speech therapists, drama coaches, language teachers, and so forth), there is some disagreement over how to describe those vowels that are both mid or low and central or back. Some call the vowel in *bought,* for example, low and back; others claim it is mid and back. Similarly, the vowel in *pop* is variously described as low and central or low and back. By their very nature, such vowels are troublesome: The tongue can be in a variety of similar yet different positions and still produce more or less the same vowel sound.

This variety in vowel description is important for at least two reasons. First, if you happen to see a vowel chart in another textbook that differs slightly from the one in this book (Table 1-3) or if your teacher requires you to learn a slightly different chart, you should know that both are legitimate and differ only in ways that are small and essentially unimportant (for our purposes, at least). Second, the different arrangements of some vowel charts—and the fact that some charts include vowels that do not appear in the one in this book—often require that a fourth criterion, **lip rounding,** be used to keep all the vowels distinct from one another. (Your lips are **rounded** for the vowel in *boot* but **unrounded** for the vowel in *bait.*) You will not have to learn this feature in this book, since none of the vowels we are using differ in just that way, but you may well have to learn it elsewhere. (In French, for example, the vowel in *si* is high, front, tense, and unrounded, and the vowel in *rue* is high, front, tense, and rounded.)

Look now at the vowel chart in Table 1-3, which can be read in the same way as the consonant chart earlier. The options for tongue height are arranged one per row along the left side; the options for tongue advancement are arranged one per column along the top; and if two vowel symbols occur in the same box, the one closest to the *outside* of the chart is always tense. (That is, the tense vowels are [i], [e], and [u]; [o] is also tense, but, as mentioned earlier, its tenseness need not be specified.)

TABLE 1-3 *Vowel Chart for English*

Tongue Height	*Tongue Advancement*		
	Front	**Central**	**Back**
High	i ɪ		u ʊ
Mid	e ɛ	ə	o
Low	æ	a	ɔ

Note: In those boxes in which there are two symbols, the one closest to the outside of the chart is always tense.
Diphthongs: [aɪ], [aʊ], [ɔɪ]

The sounds corresponding to all these symbols will be provided shortly, but first, the three pairs of symbols labeled *diphthongs* (noted below the chart) require some explanation. If you say the words *hat* and *lip,* you can hear that the vowel sound of each is *singular* in nature; that is, each contains only one kind of sound. But if you say the words *out, bite,* and *toil,* you will hear that the vowel sound of each, though restricted to one syllable, is composed of two different kinds of sound. These *dual* vowels are called **diphthongs** (literally, "two voices" or "two sounds"), as opposed to the *singular* vowels, which are **monophthongs** ("one voice" or "one sound"). As you will soon see, the verbal descriptions of the diphthongs merely combine the verbal descriptions of the vowel sounds they contain—[aʊ], for example, is a "low, central to high, back, lax diphthong." (The word *to* in the description indicates that, in articulating the sounds, the tongue moves from one area of the mouth *to* another; and, of course, the term *diphthong* occurs at the end of the description rather than *vowel.*)

✦ *EXERCISE 1-6*

Do both (a) and (b). As was true earlier in Exercise 1-4, you do not need to know what the various vowels sound like to be able to give either their symbols or their verbal descriptions; you must merely be able to read the vowel chart in Table 1-3.

(a) Specify the verbal descriptions of the sounds represented by the following symbols.

[i] ____________________

[ʊ] ____________________

[o] ____________________

[ɔ] ____________________

[u] ____________________

[æ] ____________________

[e] ____________________

[ɛ] ____________________

[a] ____________________

[ɪ] ____________________

[ə] ____________________

[aɪ] ____________________

[ɔɪ] ____________________

[aʊ] ____________________

(b) Supply the IPA symbols for the following verbal descriptions.

low, back vowel ____________________

low, central vowel ______________________________

high, front, tense vowel ______________________________

high, back, lax vowel ______________________________

low, front vowel ______________________________

mid, front, lax vowel ______________________________

mid, central vowel ______________________________

high, back, tense vowel ______________________________

high, front, lax vowel ______________________________

mid, front, tense vowel ______________________________

mid, back vowel ______________________________

low, central to high, front, lax diphthong ______________________________

low, back to high, front, lax diphthong ______________________________

low, central to high, back, lax diphthong ______________________________

✦ ✦ ✦

Now consider Table 1-4, which presents all the IPA symbols from the vowel chart, their verbal descriptions, and some sample words to illustrate the sounds they represent. A word of warning about the sample words, however: Because many different English dialects exist—some of which are favored over others, but none of which is a worldwide or even nationwide standard—it is difficult to choose words that all speakers pronounce the same. Table 1-4 contains examples that have as little variation as possible in the United States, but many problems still exist. Most natives of the deep South, for example, pronounce *kind* and *like* as containing [æ] or [a]—in either case, a monophthong—rather than the diphthong [aɪ]. Farther inland in the South and Southeast and also in parts of New England, many people pronounce the diphthong in *house* as [æʊ] rather than

TABLE 1-4 *IPA Characters and Verbal Descriptions of English Vowel Sounds*

Symbol	Verbal Description	Sound Represented
[i]	high, front, tense vowel	ease, keep, be, sleet
[ɪ]	high, front, lax vowel	ignore, thing, rid, slip
[e]	mid, front, tense vowel	able, wait, bake, say
[ɛ]	mid, front, lax vowel	elbow, egg, slept, merry
[æ]	low, front vowel	apt, cat, radical, laugh
[u]	high, front, tense vowel	ooze, loose, rule, shoe
[ʊ]	high, back, lax vowel	put, should, look, pudding
[o]	mid, back vowel	oak, okay, abode, show
[ɔ]	low, back vowel	awful, caught, wrong, law
[a]	low, central vowel	option, cot, father, lob
[ə]	mid, central vowel	undo, but, caption, canoe
[aʊ]	low, central to high, back, lax diphthong	out, round, house, loud
[aɪ]	low, central to high, front, lax diphthong	aisle, like, kind, why
[ɔɪ]	low, back to high, front, lax diphthong	oyster, toil, noise, boy

[aʊ], though in the northern Midwest and especially in Canada, the same diphthong is often pronounced [əʊ]. Many speakers throughout the United States, especially those who are upwardly mobile and under the age of about 45 or 50, do not distinguish between the vowels in *caught* and *cot.* Many natives of the south-central United States, from parts of Arkansas to eastern Tennessee, pronounce *thing* with [æ] as the vowel rather than [ɪ]. Many southerners, especially, treat the vowels of *pin* and *pen* as homophones. And on and on the variation goes, from one geographic region, social class, ethnic group, age group, and even gender to another.

While such variation is interesting and adds a certain richness to the language, it often plays havoc with the minds of students who are learning to transcribe based on the examples of someone who speaks a different dialect than they do. If any of the sample words in Table 1-4 do not illustrate a particular sound as you pronounce it, your teacher can suggest alternates and explain the differences. (The same is true of any of those in Table 1-2 that were used to illustrate the various consonant sounds—dialectal variation affects them, too, though not nearly as often.)

If you have adopted the suggestion to use flashcards for learning the IPA, you can now add 15 more to the total—14 for the vowels and diphthongs already given and 1 for [ɚ], which is the **r-colored schwa** and symbolizes the sounds spelled, for example, by the *-ir-* in *bird,* the *-er-* in *her* and *butter,* the *-ar-* in *cougar,* the *-ear-* in *earth,* the *-or-* in *work,* and the *-ur-* in *hurt.* The r-colored schwa is neither a consonant nor a vowel but combines the mid, central vowel and the retroflex.

✦ *EXERCISE 1-7*

For each of the following words, give the IPA symbol(s) that represent(s) the sound(s) spelled by the italicized letter(s); then give the verbal description(s) of the IPA symbol(s).

j*a*b [ ] ____________________

r*o*t [ ] ____________________

wr*o*te [ ] ____________________

wr*o*ng [ ] ____________________

curi*ou*s [ ] ____________________

b*e*d [ ] ____________________

b*ea*d [ ] ____________________

ab*i*de [ ] ____________________

b*i*d [ ] ____________________

j*ui*ce [ ] ____________________

m*ai*d [ ] ____________________

b*oi*l [ ] ____________________

*a*round [ ] ____________________

b*ou*nd [ ] ____________________

j*ur*y [ ] ____________________

bl*ou*se [ ] ____________________

sh*u*t [ ] ____________________

✦ ✦ ✦

FOR FURTHER STUDY
Additional and Alternate IPA Vowel Symbols

Some phonetics textbooks—usually those discussing the subject at a more advanced level than this one—include four additional English vowel sounds:

- [ʌ]—variously described as a lower, mid, central vowel; a mid, back, lax, unrounded vowel; or a low, central, unrounded vowel
- [ɑ]—a low, back, unrounded vowel
- [ɒ]—a low, back, rounded vowel (books that use both [ɒ] and [ɑ] typically classify [ɔ] as a mid, back, rounded, lax vowel and [o] as a mid, back, rounded, tense vowel)
- [ɨ]—a high, central vowel

The first of these, [ʌ], is extremely similar to the mid, central vowel ([ə]) and is used by some Americans in place of that vowel when it occurs in a syllable containing the main stress of a word. (Thus, it would appear in *cut, rump,* and *bun* and in the first syllable of *butter* and *lumpy* but not in the final syllable of *sofa,* the initial syllable of *appear,* or the medial syllable of *tantamount.*) The [ʌ] is also used to differentiate the vowel sounds in Standard British English pronunciations of *pert* and *bird* (in which the *-r-* is not pronounced, yielding simple [ə]) from those in *putt* ([ʌ]).

The vowels [ɑ] and [ɒ] will probably have to be demonstrated by your teacher. The first, sometimes called the "Harvard *a,*" occurs especially in some New England dialects in words such as *car, yard, heart,* and *bark* (as well as in the first syllable of *Harvard*); the second is also used in some New England dialects but occurs primarily in Standard British English pronunciations of words such as *hot* and *yacht.* Dialects using both vowels usually use [ɑ] when the next sound is [r] and [ɒ] when the next sound is anything else.

Finally, the high, central vowel [ɨ] occurs, for most Americans, in the final syllable of words such as *association, boxes, chieftain,* and *planted* and in the medial syllable of words such as *majesty* and *cabinet* (*cabinet* may also have [ɨ] for the vowel sound in its final syllable)—that is, to indicate an unstressed vowel not followed by [r] in the same syllable. The high, central vowel allows a bit more precision in transcription but is not absolutely necessary for our purposes. (We will substitute [ə] or perhaps [ɪ] for it most places in this book.)

Besides these additional symbols, several alternate IPA symbols have been created to represent some of the vowel sounds:

- [i]—also represented as [ij] or [iy]
- [ɪ]—also represented as [ɩ]
- [u]—also represented as [uj] or [uy]
- [ʊ]—also represented as [ω];
- [e]—also represented as [eɪ], [eɩ], [ey], or [ej];
- [o]—also represented as [oʊ], [oω], or [ow];
- [ɛ]—also represented as [ᴇ]
- [aʊ]—also represented as [aw] or [aω]
- [aɪ]—also represented as [ay], [aj] or [aɩ]
- [ɔɪ]—also represented as [ɔy], [ɔj] or [ɔɩ]

Suprasegmentals

Thus far, we have considered only the primary consonant and vowel sounds of English—the basic "building blocks" that occur in every syllable of every word. These sounds are sometimes referred to as **segmentals.** But, of course, there is more to spoken language than simply connecting these segmentals in meaningful sequences. For example, compare the way you say the word *insult* in the following two sentences:

(a) That remark is an insult to John's intelligence.

(b) Did John just insult Mary?

For most speakers, the *insult* of sentence (a) will be emphasized mainly on the first syllable, and the *insult* of sentence (b), mainly on the second (though the word would be transcribed as [ɪnsəlt] in both sentences).

This emphasis is called **stress,** and it is applied to an entire syllable or word rather than to an individual segmental (though some syllables contain only one segmental, as in *a, oh,* and the initial syllables of *occur, above,* and *abide*). Notice in the following examples how the meaning of the sentence changes simply by altering which word receives the main stress. (In each example, the stressed word is italicized; the implications for meaning are included in brackets.)

(c) *John* [not Harold or Sidney] took Mary to the dance.

(d) John *took* Mary to the dance [they didn't just meet there after arriving separately].

(e) John took *Mary* [not Martha or Sophia] to the dance.

(f) John took Mary *to* the dance [but Harvey took her home].

(g) John took Mary to *the* dance [not just any dance but the senior prom].

(h) John took Mary to the *dance* [not the pep rally or basketball game].

Because stress is a feature not inherently associated with a particular segmental or group of segmentals but instead can be shifted to any syllable or word in the language, it is called a **suprasegmental.** (*Supra* literally means "above" or "on top of.")

✦ *EXERCISE 1-8*

When a speaker stresses a particular word or syllable, he or she must force a proportionately greater amount of air from the lungs, up through the larynx, and out the mouth and nose. This results in the stressed sounds being pronounced more loudly than the sounds that surround them. But something else also typically occurs in coordination with stressed sounds. Reread examples (c) through (h), and see if you can discover what it is. (If not, make up other examples of your own or try this simple experiment: Stand up straight, take a deep breath, and pronounce any vowel sound continuously for several seconds; then, continuing your pronunciation of the vowel sound, suddenly draw your stomach up and in briefly. Because of the extra pressure on your diaphragm and lungs, doing this will force more air out of your mouth. What happens to the vowel sound?)

____

____

____

✦ ✦ ✦

English has several other suprasegmentals besides stress. Compare the meanings of *black birds* and *blackbirds* in the following sentence:

(i) John has seen many black birds in his life, but he's never seen any blackbirds.

The major phonetic difference between *black birds* (which refers to any and all birds that are black) and *blackbirds* (which refers to a particular species of birds) is the slight pause, or **juncture**, that occurs in the former but not the latter. Juncture also accounts for the differences in meaning between the following pairs of words: *White House* (located in Washington, D.C.) and *white house* (any house painted white); *redbird* (the species) and *red bird* (any bird with red coloring); *also* and *all so*.

Now say the following two sentences out loud, and notice how your voice rises and falls as you speak:

(j) John is Mary's boyfriend.

(k) John is Mary's boyfriend?

If you read sentence (j) as a simple statement of fact, the pitch of your voice probably rose slightly on *is* and *-ry's* and fell noticeably on *friend.* In (k), however, which implies some disbelief that John could really be Mary's boyfriend, your voice probably rose slightly on *is,* fell considerably on *Mary's,* rose slightly on *boy,* and rose much higher on *friend.* These patterns of pitch for entire sentences are known as **intonation**, and, as just demonstrated, they, too, are responsible for differences of meaning in two otherwise identical sequences of sounds.

The last suprasegmental that will concern us is **tone**, which is usually defined as variations in pitch that affect the meaning of a single word (not to be confused with *tone of voice,* which combines several suprasegmentals and applies to an entire stretch of conversation). In some languages, such as Mandarin Chinese, tone is so important that—independent of context—the same word can have several different meanings depending just on the particular combination of rising and falling pitches with which it is spoken. (The word *ma,* for example, can mean "mother," "horse," "to scold," or "hemp.") Tone is less important in English but still plays a large role in conveying meaning. Notice how differently you would pronounce the word *yes* in response to a particular question if you wished to communicate to your listener that you were feeling happy, sad, irritated, furious, elated, excited, ashamed, pensive, disgusted, scared, or some other emotion. This array of communicative options would not be so accessible without the suprasegmental variation allowed by tone.

✦ *EXERCISE 1-9*

Answer each of the following questions, using the spaces provided for your answers.

(a) Juncture usually occurs in combination with one or more other suprasegmentals. In each of the following sentences, what besides juncture seems to be responsible for the differences in meaning?

(1) It's also clear now./It's all so clear now.

____

____

____

(2) bluebird/blue bird

____

____

____

____

(b) One suprasegmental not discussed in the previous section is the *rate* of speaking. Clearly, how fast we talk frequently conveys meaning to our listener(s). For sentence (3), explain why a very slow or a very fast rate of articulation would seem appropriate, whereas an average rate would not. For sentence (4), describe the different meanings that would be expressed by slow and fast rates of articulation. And in sentence (5), describe why a slow rate of articulation would be almost impossible to achieve without the speaker sounding ridiculous.

(3) I just won 10 million dollars.

____

____

____

(4) I never want you to do that again.

____

____

____

(5) Let's get out of here fast!

____

____

____

(c) Another suprasegmental not discussed earlier is *volume*. As with how quickly or slowly we speak, how loudly we speak *does* convey meaning. What kinds of emotions are typically represented by the use of greater volume in your speech?

____

____

____

(d) For each of the conversational exchanges that follows, describe the intonation that must be attached to the italicized sentence for it to convey the meaning specified in brackets. (Assume that the two sentences in each pair are spoken by different people.)

(6) "John's so stupid."
"Oh, I don't know." [expressing disagreement]

____

____

____

(7) "Where will I find another one?"
"Search me." [meaning "I don't know"]

____

____

____

(8) "You owe me a hundred dollars."
"Yeah, right." [expressing sarcasm]

____

____

____

(e) Do you think that variation in the pitch of a person's voice can be used to convey meaning? If so, would pitch have to be used in conjunction with any other of the suprasegmentals? Explain your answer.

___

___

___

✦ ✦ ✦

Broad versus Narrow Transcription

When we transcribe *kicked* as [kɪkt], we are essentially claiming that the two [k] sounds are identical—in other words, each is a voiceless velar stop. But if you listen closely, you will notice a small difference in how these supposedly identical sounds are articulated: The first [k] is accompanied by a small burst of air, called **aspiration;** the second [k] is not. That aspiration can be symbolized by adding an extra symbol to the transcription: [kʰɪkt]. Both transcriptions correctly symbolize the pronunciation of *kicked* but in varying amounts of detail. When only the basic sounds of a given word are transcribed and the finer details of articulation are ignored (as in [kɪkt]), the result is **broad transcription;** and when transcription is done to capture the basic sounds of the word *and* the details of how those sounds are articulated (as in [kʰɪkt]), the result is **narrow transcription.** The extra symbols that are used in narrow transcription are called **diacritical marks.**

Here is another example of broad versus narrow transcription: If we transcribe *lip* and *milk* as [lɪp] and [mɪlk], respectively, we have accurately represented the basic sounds of those words but have given no attention to the minor differences in how the [l] sounds differ. If you say the words quickly, however, you will notice that, although the [l] in *lip* is always made with the tip of your tongue firmly against your alveolar ridge, the tip of your tongue frequently does not quite touch the alveolar ridge for the [l] in *milk*. In this case, all that must be done to make the broad transcription of *milk* narrower is superimpose the diacritical mark for *velarization,* [~], on top of the [l], like this: [mɪɫk]. (The [l] in *milk* is said to be *velarized* because the body of the tongue, in anticipating the [k] sound, actually begins retracting to the velum before the [l] has been pronounced.)

In this book, for the most part, you will be expected to do only broad transcription. At times, in Chapters 2 and 3, you will have to pay attention to some of the finer details of articulation, but you will not have to transcribe them. Narrow transcription can be extremely useful in distinguishing between similar kinds of sounds. Technically, for example, the superscript *r* attached to the r-colored schwa is a diacritical mark that helps to refine our notion of how that particular vowel is articulated, but such distinctions, for the most part, are not necessary in an introductory course concerned with the basic structure of English.

FOR FURTHER STUDY

Diacritical Marks and Their Meanings

A list of some of the most common diacritical marks used in narrow transcription in English, along with their meanings and examples of words they occur in, appears in Table 1-5. A segmental (usually a liquid) is said to take on a **voiceless** quality when it immediately follows another voiceless sound (especially a stop) in the same syllable. As noted earlier, a sound is **aspirated** when it is pronounced with a small burst of air, as voiceless stops are when they begin syllables. A **labialized** sound occurs with lip rounding (as in anticipation of a following rounded segmental), and a **velarized** sound occurs with the body of the tongue raised toward the velum (as in anticipation of a following velar segmental). **Dental** sounds are those in which the tip of the tongue touches the back of the upper teeth rather than the alveolar ridge and usually occur when the following segmental in the same syllable is an interdental.

If a sound is **unreleased**, as most final, voiceless stops frequently are, then it is articulated with none of the airstream escaping the mouth or nose. The front of the tongue is raised toward the hard palate if a sound is **palatalized;** velar sounds, especially, may be palatalized when the following vowel is articulated at the high, front portion of the mouth. In English, vowels are usually **nasalized** if the following sound in the same syllable is a nasal; the result is that some of the airstream used to articulate the vowel escapes the nose rather than the mouth. A vowel segmental usually becomes **long** if the following consonant segmental in the same syllable is voiced and/or a fricative. And **syllabic** refers to the ability of a consonant segmental (usually a liquid or nasal following an obstruent) to stand

TABLE 1-5 *Common Diacritical Marks Used in the Narrow Transcription of English*

Diacritical Mark	***Meaning***	***Examples***
[̥]	voiceless	ply [pl̥aɪ], clam [kl̥æm], true [tr̥u]
[ʰ]	aspirated	tin [tʰɪn], cat [kʰæt], pot [pʰat]
[ʷ]	labialized	toward [tʷord], dough [dʷo], show [šʷo]
[~]	velarized	pal [pæɫ], elk [ɛɫk], vulgar [vəɫgɚ]
[̪]	dental	eighth [et̪θ], width [wɪt̪θ], breadth [brɛt̪θ]
[ʔ]	unreleased	kite [kaɪʔt], stop [staʔp], lick [lɪʔk]
[ʲ]	palatalized	key [kʲi], cool [kʲul], gears [gʲirz]
[˜]	nasalized	man [mæ̃n], mango [mæ̃ŋgo], slim [slĩm]
[:]	long	have [hæ:v], loathe [lo:ð], major [me:jɚ]
[̩]	syllabic	puddle [pədl̩], shuffle [šəfl̩], button [bətn̩]

alone as a syllable rather than requiring an accompanying vowel. (As you will see in Chapter 2, the structure of English syllables, broadly transcribed, requires a vowel to be present.)

Kinds of Pronunciation

As an adult speaker of English, you already know that you do not consistently pronounce the same words in the same ways. Consider the word *of,* for example. If you read just that word aloud and then transcribe your pronunciation, you will produce [əv]. But if you imagine yourself in a conversation with someone and you say *of* as part of the sentence *John really got out of bed on the wrong side this morning,* your pronunciation would probably change to [ə]. Or consider the word *don't:* If you say the word by itself, you will pronounce it [dont]; but if you say it quickly in the sentence *I don't know how John does that,* you will probably omit the [t] and run *don't* and *know* together—[dono]—and perhaps even change the vowel—[dəno].

These different ways of pronouncing the same word are completely normal and are practiced by all speakers (even those who claim otherwise). However, these variations can cause problems with the transcriptions of words that are seen rather than heard (as in the exercises in this book, for example). If you are asked to transcribe a particular word from the printed page, which of the possible pronunciations should you use? And when you read others' transcriptions, which of the possible pronunciations should you assume they represent?

To eliminate this kind of confusion, linguists distinguish between a person's **reading pronunciation**—the pronunciation produced when a word is read carefully and by itself—from his or her **connected conversation pronunciation**—the pronunciation produced when a word is spoken naturally as part of a larger chunk of discourse, as it would be in conversation. In this book, unless you are specifically told otherwise, always assume that transcriptions are based on reading pronunciations, and always base your transcriptions on reading pronunciations, as well.

✦ *EXERCISE 1-10*

Transcribe each of the following words or phrases twice—first, using your reading pronunciation, and then, using a connected conversation pronunciation. (To arrive at the latter, imagine yourself saying each word in a sentence to a close friend.)

Word	*Reading Pronunciation*	*Connected Conversation Pronunciation*
working	____________	____________
you	____________	____________
probably	____________	____________

Word	*Reading Pronunciation*	*Connected Conversation Pronunciation*
can	______	______
Sunday	______	______
sandwich	______	______
go to	______	______
give me	______	______
don't know	______	______
should have	______	______
his and hers	______	______
five or six	______	______

✦ ✦ ✦

Coarticulation

Many people believe that connected conversation pronunciations result from laziness, that such pronunciations are wrong, and that they are symptoms that the English language is falling apart. But such opinions are based on naive notions of what language is and how it operates. Speech sounds are not often articulated as a series of isolated events but are pronounced as parts of a larger communicative act. When we speak, we adjust the basic sounds of the language in minute, sometimes almost imperceptible ways to allow them to flow out of our mouths more quickly, smoothly, effortlessly, and efficiently. Such adjustments result from the articulation of one sound influencing and being influenced by the articulation of other sounds near it when it is spoken, processes that are collectively known as **coarticulation** (literally, the overlapping or simultaneous production of speech sounds).

The primary result of most coarticulation processes is **ease of articulation**—that is, speakers have an easier time moving from one sound to the next within and between words. In the sample sentence given in the preceding section, for example—*I don't know how John does that*—the omission of the [t] in *don't* results in the nasal airstream not having to be interrupted and redirected out the mouth. Similarly, you have seen that the [l] in *milk* is frequently velarized in anticipation of the following [k] and so does not come into contact with the alveolar ridge. (Compare the [l] of *luck,* in which no such velarization occurs.) Less obvious, perhaps, is how initial velar stops change their place of articulation to accommodate the frontness or backness of an immediately following vowel. When that vowel is front, as in *gear, cat, get,* and *kick,* we tend to pronounce the preceding [g] or [k] with the back of the tongue at the front of the velum (sometimes nearly as far forward as the hard palate); and when the vowel is back, as in *good, cool, coat,* and *gone,* the back of the tongue typically retracts farther into the mouth, nearer the middle of the velum.

Depending on the specific phonetic result, coarticulation processes are given special names. In **assimilation,** one speech sound comes to resemble another nearby speech sound in one or more of its phonetic characteristics—such as when the [l] of *milk* is velarized. **Deletion** results when a phonetic sound is removed from a particular context, as when the [t] is lost from the connected conversation pronunciation of *don't know*. For **epenthesis** to occur, a consonant or vowel sound must be inserted into the middle of an existing string of sounds. Most people pronounce *sense,* for example, as homophonous with *cents* ([sɛnts]), so the [t] is epenthetic, just as the [k] is in *length* and *strength* ([lɛŋkθ], [strɛŋkθ]). **Epithesis,** on the other hand, describes the phenomenon of an extra consonant sound being added to the end of a word. Many people would pronounce *across* in the sentence *John threw the ball across the field* as [əkrɔst] or *drown* in *Mary'll drown if she goes swimming* as [draʊnd], for example. Finally, **metathesis** is a process in which speech sounds are transposed, or reordered. People who pronounce *pretty* as [pɚdi], *spaghetti* as [pəskɛdi] (typical among young children), *ask* as [æks], or *hundred* as [həndɚd] are metathesizing.

✦ *EXERCISE 1-11*

Do both (a) and (b).

(a) For each of the following words, first provide a broad transcription (if none already exists), and then name the coarticulation process(es) illustrated.

cupboard [kəbərd] deletion

relevant [rɛvələnt] metathesis

incomplete [ɪŋkəmplit] assimilation

pronounce [pə-naʊnts] metathesis and epenthesis

parade [pred] ~~metathesis~~ deletion

warmth [wɔrpθ] epenthesis

length [lɛnθ] ~~deletion~~ assimilation

once [wəntst] epenthesis and epithesis

athlete [æθəlit] epenthesis

used to [justə] ~~metathesis~~ assimilation

dreamt [drɛmpt] epenthesis

suppose [spoz] metathesis

horseshoe [ ] assimilation

(b) Compare each of the following pairs of reading and connected conversation pronunciations, and then specify which coarticulation process(es) has (have) operated to create the connectedness.

Reading	***Connected Conversation***	***Coarticulation Process(es)***
[ɪn maɪ]	[ɪm maɪ]	assimilation
[bɛst we]	[bɛs we]	deletion
[kʊkiz]	[kʊgiz]	
[sɪt daʊn]	[sɪdaʊn]	metathesis

[no hɪm]	[nowɪm]	____________
[nem ɪz]	[nemz]	____________
[maɪ ædvaɪs]	[maɪjəvaɪs]	____________
[old mæn]	[olmæn]	____________
[ɔl raɪt]	[ɔraɪt]	____________
[ɪnkohɛrənt]	[ɪŋkohɛrənt]	____________

✦ ✦ ✦

FOR FURTHER STUDY

Natural Classes of Phonetic Sounds

We have seen that it is possible to categorize any speech sound or category of speech sounds to the exclusion of all others by specifying the phonetic characteristics of that particular sound or class. Thus, we speak of the voiced, bilabial stop, the lateral, and the high, front, lax vowel *sounds* and the *classes* of all voiced stops, all nasals, all obstruents, and all front vowels. And we will see in Chapters 2 and 3 that when processes of sound change operate (whether because of coarticulation or some other process), they most often operate on entire classes of sounds rather than on just individual sounds. All vowels are nasalized when followed by nasal consonants, for example; all voiceless stops are pronounced with extra aspiration (breath) when they begin syllables; all voiced sounds cause the immediately preceding vowel in the same syllable to be articulated with extra length; and so forth. It is because of such generalities that classes of sounds are both interesting and important to linguists, speech pathologists, and others who study the sound systems of languages.

Unfortunately, while terms such as *stop, affricate,* and *mid, central vowel* are sufficient to describe most of the sounds and sound classes of English, they are too general to be used for all the sounds of all the world's languages. (Notice that the names *lateral* and *retroflex* were still necessary to distinguish between the two voiced, alveolar, liquid sounds.) For that reason, linguists have devised a set of more specific, descriptive features, a partial list of which follows. (The list is partial in that it includes only those features necessary to describe English speech sounds; and as you will see, some of the features overlap those you have already learned.) Any sounds that have one or more of these features in common are said to constitute a **natural class** of sounds.

This first group contains the **major class features**, or features that account for differences between the three major classes of segmentals—consonants, vowels, and glides.

- **Consonantal**—describes all sounds made with greater closure in the vocal tract than is needed to articulate glides; includes all obstruents, nasals, and liquids
- **Vocalic**—describes all the vowels
- **Syllabic**—describes all sounds that function as the nuclei of syllables—that is, all vowels and, in narrow transcription, nasals and liquids when they function as syllable nuclei (such as the [l] of *bottle* and the [n] of *button*)
- **Sonorant**—describes all sounds that are "noise free" and can be sung on a single pitch; includes all vowels, glides, nasals, and liquids
- **Nasal**—describes all consonant, vowel, and glide sounds that are made with the velum lowered

The next group are those features that describe the various places of articulation.

- **Anterior**—describes all sounds that are articulated between the alveolar ridge and the hard palate; includes all labials, dentals, and alveolars
- **Coronal**—describes all sounds that are made with the tip or blade of the tongue raised; in English, includes all alveolar, palatal, and interdental sounds
- **High**—describes all sounds produced with the body of the tongue raised—palatals, velars, and all high vowels
- **Low**—describes all vowel sounds made with the body of the tongue lowered from a central position in the mouth

- **Back**—describes all sounds articulated behind the palatal region in the mouth; thus, in English, the back vowels as well as the velar stops and velar nasal but not the glottal fricative, since it is produced outside the mouth

The next group of features describes the various manners of articulation. As you will see, these features allow us to distinguish each of the obstruents.

- **Continuant**—describes all sounds characterized by a free airflow through the mouth; thus, all vowels, fricatives, and glides, as well as [r] and—in English, though not in many other languages—[l], are continuants; but nasals are not, since they are produced with the airflow exiting the nose rather than the mouth
- **Delayed release**—describes all sounds produced with a slow release from a stop articulation—or, in English, the affricates
- **Strident**—describes all fricative and affricate sounds that are made with a relatively greater amount of "noise"—that is, [f], [v], [s], [z], [š], [ž], [č], and [ǰ]
- **Voice**—refers to the state of the glottis and vocal cords during articulation; a closed glottis and vibrating vocal cords produce sounds *with* voice, and an open glottis and nonvibrating vocal cords produce sounds *without* voice
- **Aspirated**—describes all consonant sounds (in English, only voiceless stops) produced with an extra burst of air preceding the following voiced sound; thus, there is a delay in the onset of voicing in that following sound
- **Lateral**—distinguishes lateral liquids from nonlateral liquids

Finally, this last set of features is used (in addition to **vocalic**, listed above with the other major class features) specifically to describe vowel sounds.

- **Round**—describes all vowels produced with lip rounding
- **Tense**—describes all vowels articulated with a more flexed, constricted tongue

- **Reduced**—describes the mid, central vowel [ə] and distinguishes it from the other mid, central vowel used in some dialects of (usually British) English, [ʌ]

These various features are always represented as **binary properties** of language. That is, they are always represented as wholly present or wholly absent. (A sound cannot be only partly lateral, for example, or both lateral and nonlateral.) Binary properties are symbolized by putting both the feature and either a "+" (to indicate the feature's presence) or a "–" (to indicate the feature's absence) in square brackets. The sounds [m], [n], and [ŋ] are [+ nasal], for example, and the sounds [p], [t], [k], [f], [s], [θ], [š], [h], and [č] are [– voice].

Notice that expressing features using a binary system frequently reduces by one-half the number of descriptive features necessary: [– voice] implies [+ voiceless], just as [– sonorant] implies [+ obstruent] and [– tense] implies [+ lax]. Conversely, the lack of certain features lengthens some descriptions: [e], [ɛ], [ə], and [o], for example, must be described as [– high] and [– low] rather than simply as [+ mid], since the feature [mid] does not exist.

A complete definition of a particular sound or class of sounds to the exclusion of all others will require using more than one feature. For example, [n] is [+ nasal], but so are [m] and [ŋ]; to further distinguish [n], we would have to include the feature [+ coronal]. Multiple features are, by convention, included in one oversized set of square brackets and placed immediately below the sound or class they describe, like this:

$$\begin{matrix} \text{n} \\ \begin{bmatrix} +\text{ nasal} \\ +\text{ coronal} \end{bmatrix} \end{matrix}$$

Alternatively, the features of all the sounds of a given language are frequently given in feature matrixes, such as those for English that appear in Tables 1-6 and 1-7. (As you look at the chart for vowels, keep in mind that linguists disagree about how some of those vowels are produced—especially [ɔ] and [a]—and that, consequently, other matrixes may differ from this one regarding which features are assigned to which sounds and may even have to introduce a new feature altogether, such as [round].)

✦ *EXERCISE 1-12*

Do both (a) and (b).

(a) Which single feature distinguishes the sounds in each of the following pairs?

[f]:[v] ______________________________

[i]:[ɪ] ______________________________

[i]:[e] ______________________________

[w]:[j] ______________________________

[l]:[r] ______________________________

[ʊ]:[ɪ] ______________________________

(b) What shared [+] feature(s) make(s) each of the following groups of sounds a natural class?

[f], [s], [z], [č] ______________________________

[l], [n], [w] ______________________________

[a], [æ] ______________________________

[t], [θ] ______________________________

[m], [g], [p] ______________________________

[s], [š] ______________________________

✦ ✦ ✦

TABLE 1-6 *Feature Matrix for English Consonants*

	Consonant																							
Feature	**p**	**b**	**m**	**t**	**d**	**n**	**k**	**g**	**ŋ**	**f**	**v**	**s**	**z**	**θ**	**ð**	**š**	**ž**	**č**	**ǰ**	**l**	**r**	**j**	**w**	**h**
Syllabic	–	–	–	–	–	–	–	–	–	–	–	–	–	–	–	–	–	–	–	–	–	–	–	–
Consonantal	+	+	+	+	+	+	+	+	+	+	+	+	+	+	+	+	+	+	+	+	+	–	–	–
Vocalic	–	–	–	–	–	–	–	–	–	–	–	–	–	–	–	–	–	–	–	–	–	–	–	–
Sonorant	–	–	+	–	–	+	–	–	+	–	–	–	–	–	–	–	–	–	–	+	+	+	+	–
Nasal	–	–	+	–	–	+	–	–	+	–	–	–	–	–	–	–	–	–	–	–	–	–	–	–
Anterior	+	+	+	+	+	+	–	–	–	+	+	+	+	+	+	–	–	–	–	+	+	–	–	–
Coronal	–	–	–	+	+	+	–	–	–	–	–	+	+	+	+	+	+	+	+	+	+	–	–	–

High	-	-	-	-	-	-	+	+	+	-	-	-	-	-	-	-	-	-	-	-	-	+	+	-
Low	-	-	-	-	-	-	-	-	-	-	-	-	-	-	-	-	-	-	-	-	-	-	-	-
Back	-	-	-	-	-	-	+	+	+	-	-	-	-	-	-	-	-	-	-	-	-	-	+	-
Continuant	-	-	-	-	-	-	-	-	-	+	+	+	+	+	+	+	+	-	-	+	+	+	+	+
Delayed Release	-	-	-	-	-	-	-	-	-	-	-	-	-	-	-	-	-	+	+	-	-	-	-	-
Strident	-	-	-	-	-	-	-	-	-	+	+	+	+	-	-	+	+	+	+	-	-	-	-	-
Voice	-	+	+	-	+	+	-	+	+	-	+	-	+	-	+	-	+	-	+	+	+	+	+	-
Lateral	-	-	-	-	-	-	-	-	-	-	-	-	-	-	-	-	-	-	-	+	-	-	-	-
	p	**b**	**m**	**t**	**d**	**n**	**k**	**g**	**ŋ**	**f**	**v**	**s**	**z**	**θ**	**ð**	**š**	**ž**	**č**	**ǰ**	**l**	**r**	**j**	**w**	**h**

TABLE 1-7 Feature Matrix for English Vowels

Feature	Vowel										
	i	ɪ	e	ɛ	æ	u	ʊ	o	ɔ	a	ə
Vocalic	+	+	+	+	+	+	+	+	+	+	+
High	+	+	–	–	–	+	+	–	–	–	–
Low	–	–	–	–	+	–	–	–	+	+	–
Back	–	–	–	–	–	+	+	+	+	–	–
Tense	+	–	+	–	–	+	–	–	–	–	–
Reduced	–	–	–	–	–	–	–	–	–	–	+

Hints for Doing Good Transcription

Learning to transcribe takes time and practice—the more of each, the better. Unfortunately, you must become fairly proficient at transcription as quickly as possible. You may find the following hints helpful:

- Vowel sounds will almost certainly cause you more problems than consonant sounds, so give them extra attention.
- Of the consonant sounds, [r] tends to be the most troublesome, especially when it immediately precedes [l] in the same syllable (as in *girl* [gɚl]) or when it follows a vowel in the same syllable (as in *core* [kor], *beer* [bir], *where* [wɛr], or *lyre* [laɪr]). Resist the impulse to insert an extra vowel before the [l] or [r] in these situations. (A narrow transcription would call for more phonetic detail but not another entire vowel).
- If you have trouble distinguishing between any two sounds, it may help to keep in mind a pair of words that vary *only* by the

sounds in question. For example, the sounds [θ] and [ð] can sometimes be problematic, but hearing them in words such as *thigh* ([θaɪ]) and *thy* ([ðaɪ]) may help you keep them distinct.

- When the spelling *-ing* occurs at the end of a syllable, transcribe it as [ɪŋ], not [iŋ]. There are two reasons that it may sound a bit like [i]: First, English does not distinguish between [i] and [ɪ] before [ŋ], so it is hard to hear the difference; second, in preparing for [ŋ], the tongue begins to tense and rise toward the velum before the [ɪ] is completely articulated. But the resulting vowel is still closer to [ɪ] than [i].
- In words such as *universe, unicorn, ukulele, eulogy, union, Europe, use,* and *uvula,* remember that the initial sound is not a vowel but a palatal glide ([j]).
- In words such as *matter, butter, atom, ladder, Adam,* and others spelled with a *d, t, dd,* or *tt* immediately preceded by the main stress of the word, listen carefully before you transcribe that alveolar sound. (In broad transcription, a good case can be made for using either [d] or [t], and, in fact, many linguists use both.)
- If the spelling of a word that you are transcribing contains a double consonant, such as *rr, ss,* or *tt,* do not be fooled into believing that both letters are necessarily pronounced; in fact, double consonants in transcriptions of English words are extremely rare.
- Back-to-back vowel sounds in transcriptions are also very rare; the vowels are almost always connected with a glide (as in *poet* [powɪt], *jovial* [jovijəl], and *evaluate* [ivæljuwet]).
- Remember that, when doing broad transcription, every syllable of a word must contain a vowel. This is true even in syllables such as the *-ton* of *button* ([bətən]) and the *-tle* of *bottle* ([batəl]) (though when such words are spoken using conversational pronunciations, final vowels are difficult to hear).
- If your teacher insists that you transcribe according to his or her pronunciation and the two of you speak different dialects, do not repeat words to yourself that your teacher has pronounced for you, or you will hear your own pronunciation rather than his or hers; instead, ask your teacher to repeat the words as many times as you need to hear them.

- Whenever you transcribe a word having one or more vowels in unstressed syllables, remember that such vowels are frequently pronounced as [ə].
- When transcribing, forget how the word is spelled. More often than not, spelling will hinder rather than help you in hearing all the sounds the word contains. (A good way to break the habit of thinking about the conventional spelling of a word before or as you transcribe it is to practice transcribing nonsense words—words for which there are no established spellings.)
- When transcribing, remember to draw the IPA characters carefully. They should be printed (never written in cursive script), lowercase (even proper nouns are never capitalized), and enclosed in square brackets. And if they include a wedge (the mark above the "s" in [š], for example), it should always point down.

These hints are no substitute for hard work and lots of practice, but they may help you avoid some of the most common errors students tend to make as they are learning to transcribe.

✦ *EXERCISE 1-13*

Transcribe each of the following words, assuming a connected conversation pronunciation for each word marked with an asterisk.

something ______________________

history ______________________

French ______________________

examination ______________________

sprightly ______________________

arrange ______________________

wherever ______________________

Illinois ______________________

Kleenex ______________________

manual ______________________

alabaster ______________________

binding ______________________

jovial ______________________

bathroom ______________________

absolutely* ______________________

desktop ______________________

billiards ______________________

verify* ______________________

midwestern ______________________

coastal ______________________

revolution* ______________________

regional ______________________

disgusting ______________________

tithe ______________________

extensive ______________________

bulletin ______________________

blustery ______________________

blanket ______________________

Wisconsin ______________________

Indiana ______________________

hue ______________________

hounds ______________________

sideways ______________________

conflict ______________________

steering ______________________

mediate ______________________

woodpile ______________________

opinion ______________________

shoveling ______________________

toiling ______________________

✦ ✦ ✦

Summary and Review

You have had three primary tasks in this chapter of the book:

1. To learn the IPA, including the symbols, the sounds they represent, and their verbal descriptions
2. To learn broad transcription, which will be necessary for studying the phonological and morphological structure of English in Chapters 2 and 3
3. To learn some of the terminology used in the study of phonetics

Regarding the IPA, simple memory is required. As for transcription, nothing substitutes for practice. (This is even something you can do at odd moments during the day, while watching television or listening to the radio.) Finally, following are all the key words and phrases used in Chapter 1; if any look unfamiliar, check the Glossary at the back of the book. (Those marked with asterisks were introduced in the sections marked "For Further Study.")

acoustic phonetics
affricate
alveolar
alveolar ridge
alveopalatal
anterior*
articulatory phonetics
aspirated
aspirated*
aspiration
assimilation
back
back*
bilabial
binary property*
blade*
broad transcription
bronchi*
central
coarticulation
connected conversation pronunciation
consonantal*
continuant*
coronal*
delayed release*
deletion
dental*
diacritical mark
diaphragm*
diphthong
dorsum*
ease of articulation
epenthesis
epiglottis*
epithesis
flap*
fricative
front
glide
glottal
glottal stop*
glottis
hard palate
high
high*
intercostal muscles*
interdental
International Phonetic Alphabet (IPA)
intonation
juncture
labialized*
labiodental
labiovelar
larynx*
lateral
lateral*
lax
lip rounding
liquid
long*
low
low*
major class features*
manner of articulation
metathesis
mid
monophthong
narrow transcription
nasal
nasal*
nasal cavity
nasalized*
natural class*
obstruent
palatal
palatalized*
pharynx*
phonetic inventory
phonetics
place of articulation
r-colored schwa
reading pronunciation

reduced*
retroflex
round*
rounded
segmental
semivowel
sibilant
soft palate
sonorant
sonorant*
stop
stress
strident*
suprasegmental
syllabic*
tense
tense*
tip*
tone
tongue advancement
tongue height
tongue tenseness
trachea*
transcribe
transcription
unreleased*
unrounded
uvula*
velar
velarized*
velum
vocal cords
vocalic*
voice*
voiced
voiceless
voiceless*
voiceless bilabial glide*
voicing

✦ *EXERCISE 1-14*

In the 1960s, the writers of the screenplay for the movie *Mary Poppins* created a new word, *supercalifragilisticexpialadocious*. Transcribe it, using a connected conversation pronunciation as the basis for your work.

✦ ✦ ✦

Exercises for Further Thought and Application

✦ *EXERCISE 1-15*

Numerous well-known people throughout history, including Noah Webster, Charles Darwin, Andrew Carnegie, George Bernard Shaw, and Theodore Roosevelt, have complained about the apparent lack of phonetic logic that underlies English spelling. Shaw, for example, once claimed that the word *fish* could just as easily be spelled *ghoti*. Explain Shaw's claim. (*Hint:* The *-gh* in *rough* would be transcribed [f].)

✦ ✦ ✦

✦ *EXERCISE 1-16*

Along with the many complaints over the lack of apparent phonetic logic that underlies English spelling (as mentioned in Exercise 1-15) have come several attempts at spelling reform; that is, various influential people (such as Noah Webster, for example) have proposed that the spelling system of English be changed so that it more nearly reflects how words are pronounced. Such proposals, however, have had little impact on how English words are actually spelled; in fact, the resistance to spelling reform has usually been substantial. List several reasons why spelling reform in English might encounter such resistance.

✦ ✦ ✦

✦ *EXERCISE 1-17*

Do both (a) and (b).

(a) English contains many so-called spelling pronunciations—words in which the spelling leads the speaker to some pronunciation other than that which is held to be conventional. Many people, for example, are tempted to read the word *epitome* ([əpɪdəmi]) as [ɛpətom] (with the main stress on the first syllable). The *epi-* is misanalyzed phonetically as the same prefix that occurs in *epicenter, epicene, epidemic, epilepsy,* and numerous other words, and *-tome* is then misanalyzed as the word *tome*. For each of the following words, explain how a speaker who is reading it might misanalyze it phonetically and produce the pronunciation indicated. On the last line, which is preceded by an asterisk, list any other words that you consistently turn into spelling pronunciations when you see them on a printed page.

awry ([ɔri], *with main stress on the first syllable*)

____

____

misled ([mɪsəld], *with main stress on the first syllable*)

____

____

democracy ([dɛməkræsi], *with main stress on the first syllable*)

____

____

soften ([sɔftən], *with main stress on the first syllable*)

____

____

Worcester ([worsɛstɚ], *with main stress on the first syllable*)

____

____

*____

(b) Sometimes "wrong" pronunciations become popular or are used by such a large portion of the population that they become perceived as "right." More and more people are pronouncing the *-t-* in *often,* for example, and in several generations, [ɔftən] may be the standard (as it was just a few centuries ago). Check the history of each of the following words in a good desktop dictionary or in *The Oxford English Dictionary,* and note how the current "correct" pronunciation was once actually a spelling pronunciation.

theater ____

____

forehead ____

____

author ____

____

habit ____

____

hospital ____

____

✦ ✦ ✦

✦ *EXERCISE 1-18*

Nearly everyone has had the experience of eating ice cream or anything frozen and then, on trying to talk immediately afterward, not being able to articulate all the speech sounds (because the tongue, when it gets very cold, loses some of its flexibility). Which speech sounds would you expect to have special difficulty with in such situations? Why?

____

____

____

____

____

✦ ✦ ✦

✦ *EXERCISE 1-19*

Do both (a) and (b).

(a) Provide the IPA symbols for each of the following:

any two nasals ______________________________

any three voiceless fricatives ______________________________

any two palatals ______________________________

any two voiceless stops ______________________________

any four nonvocalic sonorants ______________________________

all the sibilants ______________________________

all the bilabials ______________________________

all voiced velar sounds ______________________________

any two nonfricative obstruents ______________________________ all the liquids and glides ______________________________

any three front vowels ______________________________

all the high, back vowels ______________________________

all the low vowels ______________________________

all the central vowels ______________________________

any two diphthongs ______________________________

all the back vowels ______________________________

any three lax vowels ______________________________

any two tense vowels ______________________________

all the mid vowels ______________________________

all the diphthongs ending in the high, front portion of the mouth

____

(b) Specify what articulatory fact(s) each of the following groups of sounds have in common:

[b], [m] ______________________________

[t], [f], [s] ______________________________

[g], [v], [l] ______________________________

[l], [n], [t] ______________________________

[š], [č] ______________________________

[p], [w] ______________________________

[θ], [f] ______________________________

[g], [ŋ] ______________________________

[z], [n], [d] ____________________

[r], [s] ____________________

[i], [u] ____________________

[o], [u] ____________________

[e], [i], [u] ____________________

[a], [æ] ____________________

[ɛ], [ə] ____________________

[æ], [e], [ɪ] ____________________

[ɛ], [o], [ə] ____________________

[ə], [a] ____________________

[ɛ], [ɪ] ____________________

[aʊ], [aɪ] ____________________

✦ ✦ ✦

✦ *EXERCISE 1-20*

Do both (a) and (b).

(a) Specify the number of segmentals in each of the following words (count each diphthong as two segmentals):

ambidextrous ____________________

calamity ____________________

federated ____________________

gargantuan ____________________

jambalaya ____________________

Kalamazoo ____________________

monstrous ______________________________

perceptibly ______________________________

sagaciously ______________________________

victimized ______________________________

(b) Rewrite the following sentence in standard spelling (*Note:* Gaps between groups of IPA characters indicate word breaks, and standard punctuation marks have been used):

> [studənts tɪpɪkli tek korsəz ɪn lɪŋgwɪstɪks fɚ wən əv θri rizənz: Səmtaɪmz səč korsəs fʊlfɪl rikwaɪrmənts əstæblɪšt baɪ ðə stet fɚ tičɚ sɚdəfəkešən; əðɚ taɪmz ðə korsəz fʊlfɪl ə pɚtɪkjəlɚ Iŋglɪš dipɔrtmənt rikwaɪrmənt; ænd stɪl əðɚ taɪmz studənts tek ðə korsəz jəst aʊt ə kjʊrijasədi.]

____

____

____

____

____

____

____

____

____

____

____

____

✦ ✦ ✦

✦ *EXERCISE 1-21*

Using what you know of suprasegmentals, explain the scenarios outlined in (a), (b), and (c).

(a) An old joke has a man saying to a woman, "You look like Helen Brown." The woman responds, "Mister, I look like hell in just about any color."

juncture

(b) Another old joke has one man saying to another, "Since my wife died, I live in misery." The other responds, "You mean you left Illinois?"

stress

(c) Near Boonville, Missouri, just off of I-70, stands the Atlasta Motel. Several advertisements for the establishment proclaim, in large letters, ATLASTA MOTEL.

stress
juncture
intonation

✦ ✦ ✦

✦ *EXERCISE 1-22*

Look again at the transcription in exercise 1-20 (b), and then answer both (a) and (b).

(a) Does the transcription reflect more nearly a connected conversation pronunciation or a reading pronunciation?

____

(b) What must you change in the transcription to gain a stricter reading pronunciation? (You do not need to provide a new transcription; just give a general answer, based on any patterns you notice.)

____

____

____

____

____

____

____

✦ ✦ ✦

✦ *EXERCISE 1-23*

Coarticulation phenomena frequently play havoc with students' spelling, especially if those students spell phonetically (that is, if, being poor spellers, students attempt to model their spelling on how words sound when they are pronounced). Using what you know of the processes of coarticulation, explain each of the following errors.

would of (*instead of* would have) ______________________

____

____

pitcher (*instead of* picture) ________________________________

____

____

alot (*instead of* a lot) ________________________________

____

____

good riddens (*instead of* good riddance) ____________________

____

____

coulda (*instead of* could have) ____________________________

____

____

somethin (*instead of* something) ___________________________

____

____

complain to (*instead of* complained to) ____________________

____

____

drownded (*instead of* drowned) ____________________________

____

____

✦ ✦ ✦

✦ *EXERCISE 1-24*

Do both (a) and (b).

(a) Research has shown that babies learning to speak English tend to acquire their speech sounds in a particular order. Among the consonant sounds, [m], [b], and [p] tend to be learned first, [f] and [v] come much later, and [g] and [k] come near the very end. Among the vowel sounds, [a] usually is learned first, followed by [æ]; [i], [ɪ], and [u] typically are learned only later. (Thus, the tendency for most children to say [mama], [papa], and/or [dædæ] at a fairly early age really has less to do with the child knowing the meanings of those utterances than with the natural course of language acquisition.) Using verbal descriptions, capture the generalities of babies' acquisition of English speech sounds.

____

____

____

____

____

(b) The most common exception to the pattern that you noted in part (a) involves the interdentals: Instead of being learned very early, they tend to be learned very late; in fact, occasionally, children use [f] and [v] for [θ] and [ð] through the first few years of life. Assume that you are a speech therapist faced with having to explain to a child the articulatory difference(s) between the interdentals and labiodentals. How do you explain what must be done with the mouth and tongue to produce [θ] and [ð] rather than [f] and [v]?

____

____

____

____

____

✦ ✦ ✦

✦ *EXERCISE 1-25*

One of the characteristics of language is that it is *symbolic:* There is no natural connection between [b] and the letter *b,* for example, or between [s] and the letter *s.* On a larger scale, there is no good reason that *ball, pencil,* and *flower* describe the things that they do or that the sentence *The dog bit John* marks *John* as the recipient rather than the giver of the bite. Yet some sounds or combinations of sounds seem to be inherently identified with certain images. Answer (a), (b), (c), and (d).

(a) Between [i] and [ə], which do you tend to associate with lightness, airiness, and perhaps happiness and which with heaviness, darkness, and perhaps clumsiness? Speculate why.

____

____

____

____

____

(b) Does the sound sequence [sl], especially at the beginning of a word, connote anything to you? If so, speculate why.

____

____

____

____

____

(c) Does the sound sequence [əmp], especially at the end of a word, connote anything to you? If so, speculate why.

(d) Look at the two diagrams shown below. Which seems more naturally to be named by the nonsense word *loomalah* and which by the nonsense word *kratchak?* Speculate why you made the choices you did.

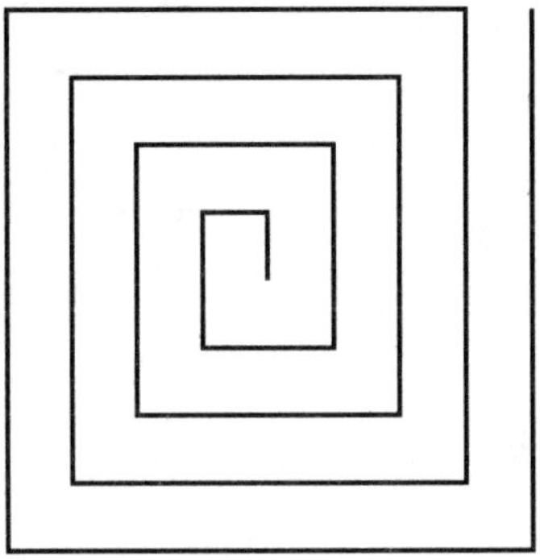

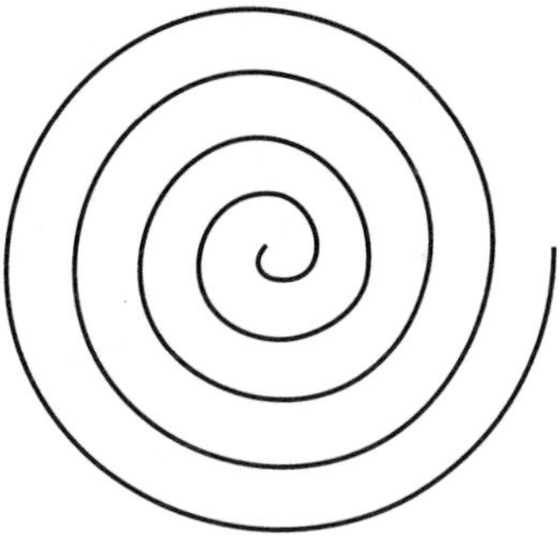

✦ ✦ ✦

✦ *EXERCISE 1-26*

It is a little known fact that before Margaret Thatcher, the former prime minister of Great Britain, assumed office, she took speech lessons to sharpen her mastery of Received Pronunciation (the Standard British English dialect). Yet in the United States, a number of dialectally diverse men have been president; compare, for example, the pronunciation accents of John Kennedy, Lyndon Johnson, Gerald Ford, Jimmy Carter, and Bill Clinton, to name just a few. Comment on the phrase *standard dialect* with respect to how English is spoken in Great Britain versus in the United States. Is it probable that anyone elected president of the United States would ever have to take speech lessons before being inaugurated? (*Note:* You can answer this question even if you have never heard any of the presidents listed earlier speak.)

✦ ✦ ✦

✦ *EXERCISE 1-27*

One of the ways that American novelists typically let readers know that a particular character is poor and/or uneducated is to have the character use pronunciations such as *gonna* (for *going*), *workin'* (for *working*), *fer* (for *for*), *kin* (for *can*), and the like. The method is uniformly successful. Readers always assume that characters using these pronunciations (which are sometimes collectively referred to as *eye dialect*) are poor and/or uneducated—even though all Americans use such pronunciations at one time or another. Comment on this literary practice.

✦ ✦ ✦

✦ *EXERCISE 1-28*

Using what you know of phonetics, explain why so-called tongue-twisters are so difficult to say quickly.

✦ ✦ ✦

✦ *EXERCISE 1-29*

Would it be possible for a language not to rely on phonetics to convey meaning? (*Note:* Do not include written or picture languages or the notion of so-called dead languages—those no longer spoken—in your answer.)

✦ ✦ ✦

✦ *EXERCISE 1-30*

By definition, poetry uses any of a number of well-known devices to convey meaning—including rhyme, meter, various kinds of tropes (figures of speech such as metaphor, simile, and personification), alliteration, assonance, and so forth. Many of these devices rely heavily on articulatory phonetics for the impact they make on the reader or speaker of poetry. Select a poem that you like or know, and read it slowly, noting how the author's purposeful use of phonetics contributes to its meaning. Comment on what you discover.

✦ ✦ ✦

The Structure of English Phonology 2

***Phonology** is the study of sound patterns in a language—which sounds precede or follow which others or begin or end words; what kinds of sounds make up syllables; how the occurrence of one sound in a particular word affects the other sounds around it; how suprasegmentals such as stress affect the segmental sounds with which they occur; and so forth. In this book, we will deal exclusively with the major sound patterns of English, but every language's sounds are patterned in unique and interesting ways.*

Basic Definitions

The central concept in phonology is the **phoneme,** which is a distinctive category of sounds that all the native speakers of a language or dialect perceive as more or less the same. In Chapter 1, for example, you learned that although the two [k] sounds in *kicked* are not identical—the first one is pronounced with more aspiration than the second—they are heard as two instances of [k] nonetheless. The same is true of the [l] sounds in *lip* and *milk*: They are often articulated in slightly different ways but are still regarded as essentially the same sound by speakers of English. Since phonemes are categories rather than actual sounds, they are not tangible things; instead, they are abstract, theoretical types or groups that are only psychologically real. (In other words, we cannot hear phonemes, but we assume they exist because of how the sounds in languages pattern as they are used by speakers.)

Phonemes contrast with **phones**, or actual sounds. Each of the basic sounds from Chapter 1 that is represented in the IPA is a phone, and each of those sounds belongs to a different phoneme. On the other hand, every phoneme contains an infinite number of phones, all of which are similar, though not identical, to one another phonetically. Try this experiment: Say [p] 10 times, 25 times, or 50 times. You have now articulated 10, 25, or 50 [p] phones—no two of which were exactly the same (because of the slightly different amounts of air in your lungs, the varying amounts and consistencies of saliva in your mouth, and so forth); but notice that every instance of [p] *sounded* more or less like all the others. This tells you that all those phones are members of the same phoneme—as opposed, for example, to [p] and [b], which, because they sound quite different, must be members of different phonemes.

Two questions now arise: How do we tell what the phonemes of a language are if they are only theoretical abstractions, and how can we tell what phones go with which phonemes? The answers to both questions are relatively straightforward. Because speakers of a language perceive each phoneme as a category of sounds different from all the other phonemes in the language, phonemes are responsible for differences of meaning in words that vary in the most minimal way—that is, by just one phoneme. Consider *milk* and *silk,* for example: In terms of sounds, the two words are identical except for the initial [m] and [s]. (Any two such words are called a **minimal pair;** when more than two words vary in the most minimal way—as in *bat, mat, sat, pat,* and *rat*—they are called a **minimal set.**) And since the words have different meanings, those different meanings must be traceable to those initial sounds. Therefore, [m] and [s] must belong to different phonemes. On the other hand, if you pronounce *milk* two different ways—once with a velarized [l] and once with an alveolar [l]—of course, the meaning of the word has not changed. The two varieties of [p] must therefore be phones of the same phoneme.

The IPA symbols that you have already learned are used for phonemes as well as phones. The only difference is that, whereas phones are enclosed in square brackets, phonemes are enclosed in slanted lines, or **virgules** (//). When you see a phonetic symbol written like this—[b]—you will know that a particular *sound* is being expressed, and when you see a phonemic symbol written like this—/b/—you will know that a particular *category* of sounds is being expressed. In the broadest of transcriptions, one that attempts to capture only the most basic categories of sound represented in a particular word, phonemes can be used: /kæt/ for *cat,* /kəmpjut/ for *compute,* /hapskač/ for *hopscotch,* and so on. In fact, for our purposes, a broad phonetic transcription and a phonemic transcription are essentially the same in terms of the kinds of information they convey about the basic sounds of a given word.

✦ *EXERCISE 2-1*

Listen carefully as you articulate the /t/'s in the following words, using a connected conversation pronunciation for each; then respond to (a), (b), (c), and (d).

time cat mitten butter stop

(a) How many different ways do you hear the /t/ articulated? Describe them as completely as you can.

(b) As precisely as you can, describe the **phonetic environment** in which each [t] occurs—that is, specify whether each [t] occurs initially, medially, or finally and which sounds or kinds of sounds precede and/or follow it.

(c) Phonemes are sometimes referred to as **underlying forms** because, as theoretical categories, they *underlie* the various phones they contain. Is the figure below a good representation of the relationship between the various phones of /t/ and the underlying /t/ itself? Why or why not?

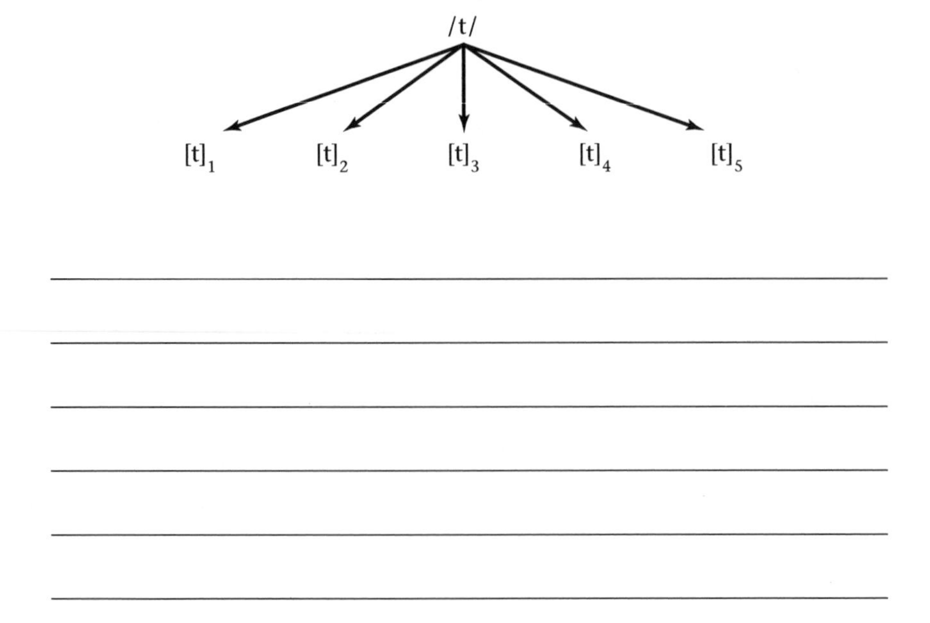

(d) The /t/ in *butter* is frequently described as a *"flap"* (because, as you noted in your answer to (a), the tip of the tongue quickly flaps up against the alveolar ridge during articulation) and is transcribed as [D]. In many dialects, the same flapping sound can be heard in words such as *ladder, atom,* and *adamant.* But the flap is not phonemic in English—no minimal pairs exist in which it contrasts with /t/ or /d/. Given these facts, justify how some linguists transcribe *butter* and *atom* phonemically as /bətɚ/ and /ætəm/ and *ladder* and *adamant* as /lædɚ/ and /ædəmənt/.

____

____

____

✦ ✦ ✦

If you count the number of IPA symbols from Chapter 1, you will see that there are 24 consonants and 11 vowels (excluding the diphthongs and r-colored schwa, each of which is actually a combination of two other sounds). Since each symbol also represents a phoneme, that means English has a **phonemic inventory** of 35 categories of sounds. (That may not seem like many, but some languages have fewer than one-third that number.) Earlier, it was mentioned that phonemes can be distinguished from one another through the use of minimal pairs of words—that, for example, /tæp/ and /tap/ point to the existence of the phonemes /æ/ and /a/, just as /mɪlk/ and /sɪlk/ point to the existence of /m/ and /s/. But what about the /p/ that occurs in *pit* as compared to the /p/ in *keep?* Or the two [k]'s in *kicked?* Or the [l]'s in *lip* and *milk?* Clearly, the differences in each of these pairs of sounds are phonetic rather than phonemic—that is, the differences are *within* rather than *between* categories of sound.

Sounds that have these kinds of differences—in other words, sounds that are merely phonetic variants of the same phoneme—are **allophones.** Notice that any two sounds of a given language represent either two allophones of the same phoneme (if the sounds can be interchanged in words with no resulting change in meaning, such as the [p]'s of *pit* and *keep*) or two different phonemes (if the sounds can*not* be interchanged without a resulting change in meaning, such as the [m] and [s] of *milk* and *silk*).

✦ *EXERCISE 2-2*

Different languages have different phonemic inventories, and their phonemes may also be arranged differently than in English. In Arabic, for example, [b] and [p] are not distinguished as different phonemes; thus, speakers of Arabic can no more easily hear the difference between [b] and [p] than speakers of English can hear the difference between the two [k]'s in *kicked*. Similarly, speakers of French have a difficult time distinguishing between [s] and [θ] and [z] and [ð] (/θ/ and /ð/ do not exist in French.) Speakers of Japanese often cannot hear the difference between [r] and [l] (because /r/ is not in that language). And Americans traveling in Mexico have difficulty distinguishing between /b/ and /β/ (/β/ is a voiced, bilabial fricative), since /β/ is not in the phonemic inventory of English. Respond to the following questions.

(a) What do [b] and [p] have in common phonetically that might cause them to be confused by speakers of Arabic learning English?

___

___

(b) What do [s]/[θ] and [z]/[ð] have in common phonetically that might cause them to be confused by speakers of French who are learning English?

___

___

(c) What do [r] and [l] have in common phonetically that would cause them to be confused by speakers of Japanese who are learning English?

___

___

(d) What do [b] and [β] have in common phonetically that would cause them to be confused by speakers of English?

✦ ✦ ✦

The allophones of a particular phoneme are distributed throughout a language either randomly or in predictable patterns. If they occur randomly and can easily be interchanged with other allophones of the same phoneme, they are in **free variation.** But if they occur in predictable, mutually exclusive phonetic environments—that is, if they always occur in places that other allophones of the same phoneme never occur—they are in **complementary distribution.**

Some examples will help to clarify the concepts *complementary distribution* and *free variation.* Notice again that because the two [k] phones in *kicked* are phonetically similar but not identical, we know that they are allophones of /k/. But are they in free variation or complementary distribution? If you say *kicked* several times, you will notice the predictable pattern that the initial [k] always contains more aspiration than the medial [k]. And if you try to reverse that pattern—pronouncing the first [k] with very little aspiration and the second [k] with considerably more—you will notice that, while such a reversal is possible, it is also very difficult (and not likely to happen unless you consciously do it). So the two allophones of /k/ not only occur predictably but in phonetic environments that do not overlap. Thus, they must be in complementary distribution.

✦ *EXERCISE 2-3*

Do (a), (b), and (c).

(a) Pronounce the following words carefully. Does the pattern established above for the two allophones of /k/ in *kicked* hold true for other words containing /k/ in the initial and medial positions? Does it hold true for allophones of /p/ and /t/, as well? How can you capture what you notice happening in these words in a single descriptive statement?

pour	tipped	likes	cool	ten
clash	keeps	knots	lips	tear
pal	sets	sacks	pokes	cops

(b) Do any of the following words contradict your descriptive statement? If so, how can you modify that statement to include these new words?

appear	contend	accuse	atone	eclair
untold	opinion	compute	perturb	attend
okay	untoward	oppose	acquire	deter

(c) How can you further modify your descriptive statement to include all the following words, as well?

apple	atom	acne	little	ripping
shaker	battle	teeter	open	baker
blatant	opposite	upper	acre	creaking

____

____

____

____

____

✦ ✦ ✦

Now consider the word *stop*. If you say the word several times, you will probably notice that sometimes the final /p/ contains more aspiration and sometimes, less. (In fact, if you end the word with your lips together and do not release the /p/, it contains no aspiration at all.) Since you are not pronouncing *stop* as part of a larger chunk of language that varies from utterance to utterance (for example, *John told Mary to stop the car* versus *Stop and go* versus *When you come to the sign, stop*), the phonetic environment of the /p/ remains constant—it is at the end of the word and preceded by /a/. In other words, we cannot predict when a particular allophone with more or less aspiration is likely to occur, so the allophones of /p/ must be in free variation.

Phonemes occasionally occur in free variation, as well. Do you pronounce *humor* as /hjumɚ/ or /jumɚ/? For the sake of argument, let us assume that you pronounce it both ways (as many people do). And let us further assume that you are just as likely to say /hjumɚ/ on any given occasion as you are to say /jumɚ/—that nothing predisposes you to favor one pronunciation over the other. Your two pronunciations of the word would then be in free variation, since the initial /j/ and /hj/ occur unpredictably and in overlapping linguistic environments. The same free-variation distribution of phonemes occurs in words such as *route* (/rut/ versus /raʊt/), *economics* (/ɛkənamɪks/ versus /ikənamɪks/), *garage* (/gəraž/ versus /gəraǰ/), *depot* (/dipo/ versus /dɛpo/, and *palm* (/palm/ versus /pam/).

✦ *EXERCISE 2-4*

Respond to each of the following questions.

(a) Earlier you learned that the /l/ in *lip* and *milk* is often pronounced two different ways: The body of the tongue is lower, and the tip of the tongue touches the alveolar ridge for the [l] in *lip;* but because the body of the tongue is closer to the velum for the [l] in *milk,* the tip of the tongue often does not touch the alveolar ridge. This latter, velarized [l] is symbolized [ɫ] and also occurs in words such as *bulk, feel, help, sold, fall, real, wilt, bells, tail,* and *mile* but not in *life, low, allow, flap,* and *slow*. This pattern holds true for all speakers of English. What are the allophones of /l/? Are these allophones in complementary distribution or free variation? What are the allophones' phonetic environments?

(b) The stressed vowel in words such as *due, news,* and *Tuesday* is pronounced by some Americans as simply a high, back, tense vowel and by others as a high, back, tense vowel preceded by a palatal glide. Would you analyze this as one phoneme (/u/) with two allophones ([u] and [ju]) or as two separate phonemes (/u/ and /ju/)? Why? In what phonetic environments do both pronunciations occur?

(c) Speakers of English pronounce some of their vowels as more nasalized (the symbol for which is ˜ placed above the vowel) than others. Nasalization can appear with any vowel but only in a certain phonetic environment. Nasalized vowels, for example, occur in *hand, bang, woman* (both vowels), and *thumb* but not in *hat, bar, pass, key,* and *okay* (both vowels). What is the phonetic environment for nasalization of vowels in English? Are nasalization and nonnasalization in complementary distribution or free variation?

(d) In some dialects of English, such as those spoken in Canada and the north-central United States, the diphthongs [əʊ] and [əɪ] are used rather than [aʊ] and [aɪ], respectively, but only in certain words. (This phenomenon is called *raising* because the first element of the diphthong has been raised from a vowel that is low and central to one that is mid and central.) For example, [əʊ] and [əɪ] occur in *out, house, about, mouth, couch, type, Ike, life, bike, mice, ripe,* and *night* but not in *cow, round, gouge, ride, tithe, rise, time, while, pie,* and *choir.* Specify the phonetic environment in which [əɪ] and [əʊ] occur. (You can specify one general phonetic environment for both diphthongs.) Are the raised and unraised diphthongs in complementary distribution or free variation?

____

____

____

____

____

____

____

(e) Why is it impossible for phonemes to occur in complementary distribution?

____

____

____

____

____

____

✦ ✦ ✦

We have already come a very long way in this chapter, and before we move on, you must be sure you thoroughly understand the differences between the following terms (since they will be used throughout the rest of the discussion of the phonological structure of English and even into the discussion of the morphological structure of English in Chapter 3): *phoneme, phone, allophone, complementary distribution, free variation,* and *phonetic environment.*

✦ *EXERCISE 2-5*

You now know that phonemic differences in sound account for corresponding differences of meaning in words (in the minimal pair *lug* and *bug,* for example, the /l/ and /b/ must be responsible for the words meaning different things, since the words are otherwise identical), whereas phonetic differences in sound do not (you could reverse the [k]'s in *kicked* and its meaning would be unchanged). Look again at the discussion and various examples of suprasegmentals in Chapter 1. Are stress, juncture, intonation, and tone phonemic in English? That is, are their variant uses responsible for conveying meaning when we speak? Why or why not?

✦ ✦ ✦

Now that you have learned the basic terminology, we can proceed with a discussion of the phonological structure of English. First, however, a word of caution: We will deal with patterns of *sound* throughout the rest of this chapter, not patterns of *letters*. How a particular sound or sequence of sounds is spelled may be interesting for other reasons, but it will be completely irrelevant to our concerns.

Phonotactics: Some Sound Patterns of English

If you are a native speaker of English or have been speaking it a very long time, you already know intuitively that not just any sequence of phonemes can be an English word, even if all the phonemes are part of the phonemic inventory of the language. For example, though *plam* (/plæm/), while not a word, certainly *could* be a word, *ngobngoboo* (/ŋobŋobu/) could not: It does not sound "Englishy" and is probably impossible for English speakers to pronounce. But why do some sequences of phonemes sound good while some others do not? Simply because part of what you know intuitively about English is its **phonotactics,** or the various constraints governing how its phonemes pattern. *Plam* does not violate any English phonotactics and so sounds like a word, even though it is not; but *ngobngoboo,* just because it *does* violate the phonotactics of English, sounds odd.

You will soon see how the phonotactic restrictions of English greatly limit the kinds of phonemic sequences that can occur at the beginnings and ends of words, but first, let us examine the syllable. If we assume that the English language contains between one and two million words (several recent estimates have fallen in that range) and that many of those words contain two, three, four, or more syllables, we would have to conclude—even allowing for the many frequently occurring prefixes and suffixes, such as *pre-, un-, in-, a-, -ment, -tion,* and *-ly*—that altogether, English has several hundred thousand different syllables, at least. And it may seem unlikely that the basic phonemic structure of all those syllables can be described with a relatively simple formula, but that is exactly the case. Consider the following string of symbols:

(C)(C)(C)V(C)(C)(C)(C)

In this sequence, *C* represents any consonant phoneme, *V* represents any vowel phoneme, and parentheses denote optionality. (In linguistics, it is standard to symbolize that something occurs optionally by enclosing it in parentheses.) In other words, the formula says that every English syllable *must* contain one vowel sound (for our purposes here, diphthongs count as vowels) and that this vowel sound *may* be preceded by one, two, or three consonant sounds and followed by one, two, three, or four consonant sounds.

This description of English syllable structure can easily be tested for validity. Table 2-1 lists several one-syllable constructions and

TABLE 2-1 *The Consonant-Vowel Sequence of Some English Syllables*

Syllable	***Phonemic Transcription***	***Consonant/Vowel Sequence***
state	/stet/	C C V C
lamp	/læmp/	C V C C
widths	/wɪtθs/	C V C C C
re-	/ri/	C V
un-	/ən/	V C
-ness	/nəs/	C V C
a-	/ə/	V
true	/tru/	C C V
crops	/kraps/	C C V C C
stream	/strim/	C C C V C
worlds	/wɚldz/	C V C C C C
stray	/stre/	C C C V
eggs	/ɛgz/	V C C
stripes	/straɪps/	C C C V C C
shirts	/šɚts/	C V C C C

their phonemic transcriptions, as well as a simple statement of the consonant/vowel sequence of each. Granted, only 15 examples out of the many hundreds of thousands possible are provided (feel free to try as many more as you wish), but it is interesting to notice nonetheless that the consonant/vowel sequence never deviates from what the formula predicts: A single vowel (or, again, diphthong) phoneme always occurs and is never preceded by more than three or followed by more than four consonant phonemes.

✦ *EXERCISE 2-6*

Do parts (a), (b), (c), and (d).

(a) For each of the syllables in Table 2-2, provide the phonemic transcription and a simple statement of the structural sequence of consonants and vowels (as in Table 2-1).

(b) Thus far, not one of the syllables that we have examined has completely "filled out" the structural description given earlier—that is, none has had three consonant phonemes followed by a vowel phoneme and four more consonant phonemes. Can you think of any such syllable? (*Hint:* One answer to this question is a word having /s/ as both its first and its last phoneme.)

____

(c) It was noted earlier that, in the discussion of English syllables, diphthongs would count as vowels. Had that not been the case, what would the syllable structure formula have had to look like to accommodate diphthongs? (In your answer, you do not need to introduce any new symbols into the formula; merely use *C*, *V*, and parentheses.)

____

(d) Can every phoneme in English begin a syllable, or is there a phonotactic constraint preventing one or more of them from occurring in that position?

____

✦ ✦ ✦

TABLE 2-2 *The Consonant-Vowel Sequence of Some More English Syllables*

Syllable	***Phonemic Transcription***	***Consonant/Vowel Sequence***
weird		
lumps		
-ry		
-tion		
pre-		
frame		
stride		
elves		
side		
cloud		
oh		
bulk		
streaks		
craft		
them		
quartz		
twelfth		
time		
bold		
search		

Consider now the beginnings of words. Are there phonotactic constraints governing which English phonemes can occur initially? And when consonant clusters occur—that is, when groups of consonant phonemes exist with no intervening vowel phoneme, as in *slip* /slɪp/, *great* /gret/, and *strike* /straɪk/—are there phonotactic constraints governing how those phonemes can pattern? As you discovered in the last part of Exercise 2-6, all but one of the 24 consonant phonemes can begin English words, and a little reflection will tell you that it is possible for all 11 vowel phonemes to occur initially.

As for two-consonant clusters, although 552 possible C-C combinations exist, fewer than 50 actually occur, as depicted in Table 2-3. (Combinations marked with an asterisk occur only in some dialects, and five of the combinations—/bw/, /mr/, /šl/, /ts/, and /št/—occur only in words that have been borrowed relatively recently from other languages.) Notice how some of the initial C-C clusters that sound as though they *could* occur—/fw/ and /pw/, for example—actually do not, resulting in "holes" in our inventory of phoneme sequences. Such holes due to possible but nonoccurring forms are called **accidental gaps.** The gap left by the nonoccurrence of initial /tp/, on the other hand, will probably never be filled, since /tp/ is prohibited by the phonotactic constraints of English. This kind of hole in a language's inventory of phoneme sequences is a **systematic gap.**

✦ *EXERCISE 2-7*

Respond to each of the following questions.

(a) Another textbook, published in 1958,* lists the following combinations as generally possible for initial C-C clusters in English: stop + liquid/glide; voiceless fricative + liquid/glide; and /s/ + voiceless stop/liquid/glide or /m/ or /n/. (Some of these possibilities, such as /pw/ and /fw/, do not actually exist because of accidental gaps.) But Table 2-3 lists some combinations not accounted for by these descriptions. Explain why such discrepancies occur. (*Hint:* You may find a dictionary—one published long after 1958—necessary to answer this question.)

____

____

____

____

*Archibald A. Hill, *Introduction to Linguistic Structures; from Sound to Sense in English* (New York: Harcourt Brace Jovanovich, 1958).

TABLE 2-3 *Initial Consonant-Consonant Sequences in English*

Initial C Phoneme	*Second C Phoneme*	*Sample Words*
/b/	/l/, /r/, /w/, /j/	*blade* /bled/ *break* /brek/ *bwana* /bwanə/ *beauty* /bjuti/
/d/	/r/, /w/, /j/*	*dry* /draɪ/ *dwarf* /dwɔrf/ *due* /dju/
/g/	/l/, /r/, /w/, /j/	*glow* /glo/ *grip* /grɪp/ *Guinevere* /gwɪnəvir/ *gules* /gjulz/
/p/	/l/, /r/, /j/	*play* /ple/ *prime* /praɪm/ *pure* /pjur/
/t/	/r/, /w/, /j/*, /s/	*try* /traɪ/ *twin* /twɪn/ *tune* /tjun/ *tsetse*/tsitsi/
/k/	/l/, /r/, /w/, /j/	*clay* /kle/ *cry* /kraɪ/ *quit* /kwɪt/ *cue* /kju/
/f/	/l/, /r/, /j/	*flow* /flo/ *fry* /fraɪ/ *few* /fju/
/v/	/r/, /j/	*vroom* /vrum/ *view* /vju/
/θ/	/r/, /j/, /w/	*throw* /θro/ *thews* /θjuz/ *thwart* /θwɔrt/
/s/	/l/, /j/*, /w/, /p/, /t/, /k/, /m/, /n/, /f/	*slow* /slo/ *sue* /sju/ *sway* /swe/ *spot* /spat/ *story* /stori/ *scale* /skel/ *smart* /smɔrt/ *snack* /snæk/ *sferics* /sfɛrɪks/
/h/	/w/*, /j/	*which* /hwɪč/ *hue* /hju/
/š/	/l/, /r/, /t/	*schlep* /šlɛp/ *shrimp* /šrɪmp/ *shtick* /štɪk/
/m/	/r/, /j/	*mridanga* /mridaŋgə/ *mew* /mju/
/n/	/j/*	*news* /njuz/

*Occurs only in some dialects.

(b) Label each of the following nonoccurring initial C-C phoneme sequences in English as an *accidental gap* or a *systematic gap*.

/sh/	____________	/ds/	____________
/pt/	____________	/θl/	____________
/gj/	____________	/zg/	____________
/kk/	____________	/ps/	____________
/fw/	____________	/df/	____________

(c) When foreign words are borrowed into a language, their phonemic sequences must often be adapted to the phonotactic constraints of the borrowing language. Explain, then, how this accounts for the silent initial *p-* in words containing the Greek prefix *psycho-* (the *p* is not silent in Greek).

____

____

____

____

____

(d) The text just before this exercise reads, "The gap left by the nonoccurrence of initial /tp/ . . . will probably never be filled, since /tp/ is prohibited by the phonotactic constraints of English." The word *probably* was used in that sentence because not all the words borrowed into English have conformed to its phonotactic constraints. Notice, for example, how comparatively difficult it is to pronounce the initial C-C cluster in *tsetse*. Do you think the phonotactic constraints of English could ever change so that initial /ts/ is *accounted for* rather *an exception?* If your answer is "yes," what evidence can you find that those constraints may already be changing to include /ts/?

____

____

(e) The table listing initial C-C clusters in English may not be comprehensive: New words may have entered the language since the table was compiled, or one or more clusters may simply have been forgotten. Examine the chart closely. Can you think of any additional English C-C clusters?

(f) In English, 13,248 different C-C-C clusters are possible, yet only 8 occur initially. What are they? (*Hint:* After you think of 3 or 4, notice the patterns that are developing and choose your remaining sequences accordingly.) Write a descriptive statement specifying which phonemes can occur in each of the three positions. (Do not simply list the individual phonemes; group them into categories so that the features they share are evident.) How can you be sure that no initial C-C-C-C clusters occur in English?

✦ ✦ ✦

Final consonant clusters are interesting, as well. Again, while 552 C-C sequences can possibly occur at the end of an English word, only about 75 actually do. You can verify this quite easily: Take a piece of graph paper, and list each of the 24 consonant phonemes down the left side and then again across the top, as in the partial model shown in Table 2-4. Using those down the left side as the first consonant of a possible cluster and those across the top as the second, put a checkmark in the box where a row and column intersect if you can think of a word ending with that particular cluster. (The words represented in the chart so far are *apt* /pt/, *picked* /kt/, *rubbed* /bd/, *bagged* /gd/, *laughed* /ft/, *fifth* /fθ/, and *lived* /vd/.)

As for final C-C-C and C-C-C-C clusters, both of which are possible according to the syllable structure formula presented earlier, similarly small numbers occur—for three-phoneme clusters, only about 70 of 13,248 that are possible; for four-phoneme clusters, only

TABLE 2-4 *Partial Sample Grid for Determining Final Consonant-Consonant Sequences in English*

	p	t	k	b	d	g	f	v	θ
p		✓							
t									
k		✓							
b					✓				
d									
g					✓				
f		✓							✓
v					✓				

Note: The first member of the cluster occurs in the left column; the second member occurs in the top row.

9 of 317,952. To determine what the final C-C-C clusters are, you can begin with the chart described in the previous paragraph. As before, let the consonant phonemes in the left column be the first sound of the cluster, those along the top be the second, and those from a separate list be the last. (You will have to write the C-C-C clusters down as you think of them, since your graph is only two-dimensional and you are working with a three-consonant cluster.) You may wish to look first at your list of final C-C clusters, since many of them, if they occur in nouns or verbs, will yield C-C-C clusters when you add /s/. Then simply repeat the method with yet a fourth separate list of consonant phonemes to determine what the final C-C-C-C clusters are.

✦ *EXERCISE 2-8*

Using the method described above (or any other you can devise), determine what the nine final C-C-C-C clusters in English are. Write a statement describing the kinds of consonant phonemes that occur in each of the four positions.

____

____

____

____

____

____

____

____

____

____

____

____

✦ ✦ ✦

Two Kinds of Rules

When most people hear the word *rule,* they probably think of something they should or should not do. Rules exist for all kinds of human activities: When we drive a vehicle, we should not exceed the speed limit; when we eat in a restaurant, we should not put our elbows on the table; when we write a sentence, we should begin the first word with a capital letter and follow the last word with a period, question mark, or exclamation point; when we are at a public meeting and wish to speak, we should usually raise our hand first; and so forth. These kinds of statements are called **prescriptive rules** because they prescribe or dictate behavior. For many people, speaking English is little more than attempting to follow these kinds of rules (do not end a sentence with a preposition, do not split infinitives, do not use double negatives, etc.), which have been declared as "language law" and are enforced by many well-intentioned teachers, parents, and even siblings.

Prescriptive rules have no place in linguistics, which is concerned with the objective study and explanation of language use rather than with its regulation. A large part of that study and explanation, however, relies on first having a complete description of the structure of the language in question. The statement of English syllable structure given earlier is one example of this kind of description, as is the statement you wrote in Exercise 2-7(f) describing the kinds of phonemes that occur in initial C-C-C clusters, as are the statements you wrote in Exercise 2-3 describing when voiceless stops are pronounced with greater aspiration, as are all the phonotactic constraints of English (or any other language) when they are specifically spelled out. Such statements are called **descriptive rules** or sometimes just *rules* (with the word *descriptive* understood). Unless clearly specified otherwise, every time the word *rule* occurs in this book, it refers to a *descriptive,* not a prescriptive, statement.

FOR FURTHER STUDY

Linguistic Notation and Descriptive Rules

It is possible, though not mandatory, to write phonological rules using special linguistic notation. You saw one simplified example of such notation when the syllable structure of English was accounted for by using *C* to represent *consonant, V* to represent *vowel,* and *( )* to represent *optional.* Notice, however, that this rule merely specifies a static portion of the phonological structure of English; it does not describe the kinds of changes that occur when a phoneme yields different allophones in different phonetic environments.

You have seen (and even written) examples of this latter kind of rule. In Exercise 2-3, for example, you produced a series of rules describing when extra aspiration occurs in the articulation of voiceless stops. These kinds of rules can also be written using special linguistic notation. The standard format of such rules looks like this:

A → B / C ___ D

This rule would be read, "A becomes B when it follows C and precedes D." (The arrow represents *becomes;* the slash represents *when* or *in the phonetic environment.*)

Look again at the answers to Exercise 2-3. In part (a), we see that voiceless stops become aspirated when they occur initially in words. This would be symbolized using linguistic notation as follows:

/p/, /t/, /k/ → [p^h], [t^h], [k^h] / ## ___

(The ## represents a *word boundary*—that is, it stipulates that what follows must begin a new word. The symbol *$$* is sometimes used for the same purpose. Similarly, # and *$* are used to represent syllable boundaries.) In part (b), however, we had to modify that basic statement to include voiceless stops that occur at the beginnings of syllables, regardless of whether those syllables occur initially:

/p/, /t/, /k/ → [p^h], [t^h], [k^h] / # ___

(Notice that now only one # occurs in the specification of the environment.) And in part (c), we had to further modify the statement to exclude all syllable-initial voiceless stops except those beginning a syllable that contains the main stress of the word:

/p/, /t/, /k/ → [p^h], [t^h], [k^h] / # ___ V́

(The *V* occurs under the stress mark since, as we saw earlier, every English syllable contains a vowel.)

If you read the "For Further Study" section on natural classes and features in Chapter 1, it may now occur to you that since voiceless stops in English constitute a natural class of sounds and since that class is merely gaining the feature *aspiration* when its members occur in a certain phonetic environment, we could also write the first part of each of these three rules like this:

$$\begin{bmatrix} -\text{ continuant} \\ -\text{ voice} \\ -\text{ delayed release} \end{bmatrix} \rightarrow [+\text{ aspiration}]$$

This is an equally valid, alternate way of representing that voiceless stops become aspirated. Similarly, it is possible to write the last half of the final rule like this:

$$\# \_\_\_ \underset{[+\text{ stress}]}{\text{V}}$$

(The feature [+ stress] written under the *V* indicates that the suprasegmental feature *stress* goes with the vowel.) The entire final version of the rule, written using this alternate method of feature notation, would then look like this:

$$\begin{bmatrix} -\text{ continuant} \\ -\text{ voice} \\ -\text{ delayed release} \end{bmatrix} \rightarrow [+\text{ aspiration}] \ / \ \# \_\_\_ \underset{[+\text{ stress}]}{\text{V}}$$

We will return briefly to this method of feature notation in another "For Further Study" section (see "Distinctive Features," later in this chapter).

✦ *EXERCISE 2-9*

Do both (a) and (b).

(a) In Exercise 2-4(a), you wrote a rule describing that the velarized allophone of /l/ ([ɫ]) consistently occurs following a vowel unless the /l/ begins a syllable. Rewrite that rule using the first of the two methods of linguistic notation described in the preceding section.

(b) In Exercise 2-4(c), you wrote a rule describing that vowels become nasalized if the following sound is a nasal. Rewrite that rule using the first of the two methods of linguistic notation described in the preceding section. (Using the mark ˜ above a vowel indicates that the vowel has been nasalized.)

✦ ✦ ✦

More Sound Patterns of English

As you have already noticed, studying the phonological structure of English does not mean just learning what the sound patterns of the language are; it means being able to figure out what those patterns are for yourself. And there is no foolproof method for doing that kind of work (though later a list of hints will be provided that may make the process a bit easier). Noticing patterns in language is a lot like working a jigsaw puzzle: Luck plays a part, as do patience, experience, and knowing something about the puzzle itself and how its pieces fit together. In this section, we are going to examine some more sound patterns of English, but we will focus as much on method as on results—in other words, as much on *how* we get the puzzle together as on *whether* we get it together.

Consider first the following list of words:

hinder	wonder	uncle	aunt	ink
umbrella	chant	ankle	amble	end
humble	impasse	pants	shanty	hand
finger	taunt	anger	slant	into

What do you notice about the sound structure of each of these words (aside from such obvious facts as the presence of both vowels and consonants)? If you start with the smaller words first—since they contain fewer sounds, they will be easier to work with—it may strike you that each contains a stop. Or maybe you notice that each contains a nasal. Or maybe you even notice that each contains both a stop *and* a nasal. Now look at the rest of the words: Does each of them also contain both a stop and a nasal?

Every word in the list does indeed contain a stop and a nasal. But so what? What else can you say about those stops and nasals? Since at this point you should not discard any piece of information as too insignificant, note the obvious, just for the record: In each of these words, the stop and nasal occur next to one another, and the nasal always comes first. Now it would probably be a good idea to transcribe the "nasal + stop" cluster from each word, since doing so will help you to focus on the sounds rather than on the letters spelling them. Those transcriptions are as follows:

/nd/	/nd/	/ŋk/	/nt/	/ŋk/
/mb/	/nt/	/ŋk/	/mb/	/nd/
/mb/	/mp/	/nt/	/nt/	/nd/
/ŋg/	/nt/	/ŋg/	/nt/	/nt/

What do all these "nasal + stop" clusters have in common? Pronounce each. Write each in its corresponding verbal description. What do you notice?

You should be doing the work, thinking about and answering the questions as you read, and not just quickly skimming through the sentences to get to the answer. If you *have* been thinking and working, you have probably discovered that in each "nasal + stop" cluster, the nasal and stop have a common place of articulation: The /n/ and /d/ are both alveolars, the /ŋ/ and /g/ are both velars, the /m/ and /p/ are both bilabials, and so forth. But there is more; you still need to write a rule describing what you have discovered. That rule might look like this: When a nasal is followed immediately by a stop, the two sounds will have the same place of articulation.

✦ *EXERCISE 2-10*

Answer (a), (b), and (c).

(a) Notice that, in the list of words above, most of the spellings correspond to the phonemic transcriptions in ways we would expect—/m/ is spelled *m*, /t/ is spelled *t*, and so on. But in a few of the words (*uncle, ink, ankle, finger,* and *anger*), the phoneme /ŋ/ is spelled *n*. For the sake of argument, assume that, at one time, centuries ago, each of those *n*'s was pronounced as an alveolar rather than a velar nasal and that, over time, under the influence of the following velar stop, the /n/ slowly changed to /ŋ/. What process does this change represent? (You learned this in Chapter 1.)

____

(b) Does the rule noted above in the text hold true for all "nasal + stop" clusters in English, or are there apparent exceptions? How can you modify the rule to account for such exceptions?

____

____

____

____

____

(c) When any two sounds (not just nasals and stops) occur next to one another and share the same place of articulation, they are said to be **homorganic.** (The rule above could therefore be written using fewer words, thus: When a nasal is followed immediately by a stop, the two sounds will be homorganic.) Give several other examples of words containing homorganic sounds in English, focusing on clusters other than "stop + nasal."

____

____

____

✦ ✦ ✦

Now look at the following data, which are subdivided into three categories:

Contractions

His lip is cut./His lip's cut.
Joan is very tall./Joan's very tall.
The bat is heavy./The bat's heavy.
Brad is a bad boy./Brad's a bad boy.
Math is difficult./Math's difficult.
Her back is sore./Her back's sore.

The dove is white./The dove's white.
Life is funny./Life's funny.
The rush is over./The rush's over.
That car is old./That car's old.

Possessives

Frank/Frank's	Peter/Peter's	Madge/Madge's
Ponch/Ponch's	woman/woman's	ship/ship's
judge/judge's	trout/trout's	Buzz/Buzz's
Angus/Angus's	George/George's	fox/fox's
Joan/Joan's	Sam/Sam's	Paul/Paul's

Verbs

sing/sings	bathe/bathes	trim/trims
break/breaks	tone/tones	wag/wags
love/loves	put/puts	live/lives
loaf/loafs	pad/pads	wrap/wraps
scrub/scrubs	curl/curls	score/scores

Your ultimate task is the same as before: Locate a phonological pattern that all these pairs, regardless of their grammatical category, have in common, and write a rule describing it. In the first group, the members of each pair vary just because one contains a contraction and the other does not; in the second group, one member of each pair is possessive and the other is not; and in the third pair, one verb is an infinitive and the other has been conjugated for the third person, singular, present tense. But what does all of this mean, and again, what do all the pairs in all the categories have in common?

Choose one of the three categories—say, verbs. What is the phonological difference between the first and second verbs in each pair? The answer should be clear: The second verb contains a final /s/ whereas the first does not. Now look at the possessives, and ask the same question: How do the nouns in each pair differ? Since you have already noticed the addition of the final /s/ in the second member of all the pairs of verbs, start there when looking at the nouns. In other words, does one noun in each pair contain a final /s/ and the other one not? (Remember, since you are interested in sounds rather than spelling or grammatical function, the apostrophe is irrelevant.) And is the same thing true of the contractions in the first group?

Now you know that the difference between the first and second members of each pair in all three categories is that a final /s/ has been added to the second member. The next important questions are: How does /s/ occur phonetically, and if it does not always occur as [s], what accounts for the variation?

At this point, as in the problem involving homorganic nasals and stops, it would be wise to phonetically transcribe the "word + /s/" combination from each of the pairs. Those transcriptions follow:

Contractions

lip's [lɪps]
bat's [bæts]
Math's [mæθs]
dove's [dəvz]
bush's [bʊšəz]
Joan's [jonz]
Brad's [brædz]
back's [bæks]
Life's [laɪfs]
car's [kɔrz]

Possessives

Frank's [fræŋks]
Ponch's [pančəz]
judge's [jəjəz]
Angus's [æŋgəsəz]
Joan's [ǰonz]
Peter's [pitɚz]
woman's [wʊmənz]
trout's [traʊts]
George's [ǰorǰəz]
Sam's [sæmz]
Madge's [mæjəz]
ship's [šɪps]
Buzz's [bəzəz]
fox's [faksəz]
Paul's [pɔlz]

Verbs

sings [sɪŋz]
breaks [breks]
loves [ləvz]
loafs [lofs]
scrubs [skrəbz]
bathes [beðz]
tones [tonz]
puts [pʊts]
pads [pædz]
curls [kɚlz]
trims [trɪmz]
wags [wægz]
rushes [rəšəz]
wraps [ræps]
scores [skorz]

Now you can return to the questions posed at the end of the previous paragraph and begin searching for answers. First, how does /s/ occur phonetically at the end of each of these words? Second, what accounts for that phonetic variation? Answering the first question should be relatively straightforward: All you have to do is catalog the various allophones of /s/ that appear in the list—[s], [z], and [əz]. But the answer to the second question is not so obvious. What do you know about phonetics that would help you explain why the allophones of a given phoneme occur as they do?

Think back to earlier examples. What caused the various allophones of /l/, /t/, and the three voiceless stops to occur? In each case, it was true that those allophones were linked to the phonetic environments in which they occurred. And it is safe to assume that the same is true of the [s], [z], and [əz] in this problem. Moreover, since those [s]'s, [z]'s and [əz]'s occur only at the ends of words, the phonetic environments that you need to be concerned with must be merely whatever sound precedes /s/ in each example. Below is a list of those sounds for each of the three allophones:

[s]	[p], [t], [k], [f], [θ]
[z]	[b], [d], [g], [v], [ð], [m], [n], [ŋ], [l], [r]
[əz]	[s], [z], [š], [č], [ǰ]

Now the question is this: Do all the sounds in any given list have anything in common? Clearly, they do. All the sounds listed after [s] are voiceless consonants (you would gain nothing by specifying that they are all obstruents, since no voiceless sonorants exist), all the sounds listed after [z] are voiced consonants, and all the sounds listed after [əz] are sibilants.

✦ *EXERCISE 2-11*

Answer (a), (b), and (c).

(a) Write a rule describing the phonological pattern(s) that result(s) from adding /s/ to a word.

____

____

____

____

____

(b) All the words to which /s/ was added in the preceding problem ended in consonant sounds. Think of several words that end in vowel sounds, and add an /s/ to each of them. Which allophone or allophones occur? How can you modify the rule written in part (a) to accommodate these new words?

____

____

____

____

____

____

____

____

____

(c) All vowels are voiced sounds (which is why *voicing* is not one of the criteria used to specify vowel articulation). Knowing this, how can you rewrite the rule from part (b) to make it shorter without sacrificing accuracy?

____

____

____

____

____

✦ ✦ ✦

For your third problem in this section, begin by looking closely at the following pairs of words:

sit/sitting	fat/fattest	hot/hotter	freight/freighter
but/butter	set/setter	bat/batter	great/greatest
white/whiter	late/later	boat/boating	shoot/shooter

Again, your goal is to specify what phonological pattern occurs in these words and then to write a rule describing it.

Since you are not sure exactly what you are looking for and to ensure that you focus on the sounds of these words rather than on their letters, it would be wise to begin by transcribing each of the pairs phonetically, as follows (the transcriptions are of connected conversation pronunciations):

[sɪt]/[sɪdɪŋ]	[fæt]/[/fædəst]	[hat]/[hadɚ]	[fret]/[fredɚ]
[bət]/[bədɚ]	[sɛt]/[sɛdɚ]	[bæt]/[bædɚ]	[gret]/[gredəst]
[waɪt]/[waɪdɚ]	[let]/[ledɚ]	[bot]/[bodɪŋ]	[šut]/[šudɚ]

Now you can notice that the first word in each pair is pronounced with a final [t], which changes to [d] when /ɪŋ/, /ɚ/, or /əst/ is added. The question is this: When does [t] become [d]? In other words, what is the phonetic environment of [d]?

Since [t] occurs at the ends of words and is always preceded by a vowel and [d] occurs medially and is always preceded and followed by a vowel, one way to formulate a rule describing when [d] occurs would be like this: When /t/ occurs medially and is preceded and followed by vowels, the allophone [d] occurs. Or to shorten the rule, we could replace *occurs medially and is preceded and followed by vowels* with *occurs intervocalically.* (*Intervocalically* literally means "between vowels," and whatever occurs between vowels must be in the middle of a word.)

But now consider the following words, all of which contain an intervocalic /t/ that is pronounced [t] and so are exceptions to the rule:

atomic	autonomy	autumnal	atone
attack	attire	attend	O'Toole
eternal	attempt	attendance	attention

How do these words vary from those given earlier? If you pronounce all the words from both groups, you will notice that, whereas the main stress in the earlier words immediately precedes the medial /t/, the main stress in the words in this group immediately follows it. But you should be able to modify the rule to include this new fact. This is one way to do it: When /t/ occurs intervocalically and immediately follows the main stress of the word, [d] occurs.

✦ *EXERCISE 2-12*

Do (a), (b), and (c).

(a) How does the final version of your rule for the voicing of medial /t/ account for the voiceless /t/ in *skeleton?*

___

___

___

(b) Most textbooks present a rule for the voicing of medial /t/ very similar to the one given above, but that rule seems to ignore words such as *rotten, cotton, mitten, bitten, batten,* and *gluten.* Modify the rule to include these and other similar words.

___

___

___

___

(c) Throughout this problem, we have symbolized voiced /t/ as [d]—which, while accurate enough for our purposes, is correct only from the perspective of broad transcription. Transcribed narrowly, voiced /t/ would be [D], the same symbol used to represent /d/ as most people pronounce it in words such as *Adam* and *ladder.* Does the rule that predicts [D] as an allophone of /t/ also suffice to predict [D] as an allophone of /d/? If so, rewrite the rule again (including the data from part (b) earlier) so that it accounts for the medial occurrence of [D] as an allophone of either /t/ or /d/.

___

___

___

___

✦ ✦ ✦

Thus far, you have studied phonological patterns that vary according to the *qualities* of certain sounds (*how* a final /s/ is pronounced and *how* a medial /t/ is pronounced), but in this problem, you must consider a *quantitative* pattern—that is, not *how* but *for how long.* Read each of the following minimal pairs of words out loud, and notice in which word of each pair you hold the vowel longer before pronouncing the following consonant sound (you may wish to underline the words with the longer vowel, since you will soon need that information):

heat/heed	leave/leaf	cease/sees
pig/pick	rack/rag	fuss/fuzz
Madge/match	teeth/teethe	tight/tide
rib/rip	bed/bet	lope/lobe
loot/lewd	cod/cot	late/laid

The phonetic transcription of the vowels in each of these pairs of words is as follows (the diacritical mark *:* indicates that the preceding vowel is long):

[i]/[i:]	[i:]/[i]	[i]/[i:]
[ɪ:]/[ɪ]	[æ]/[æ:]	[ə]/[ə:]
[æ:]/[æ]	[i]/[i:]	[aɪ]/[aɪ:]
[ɪ:]/[ɪ]	[ɛ:]/[ɛ]	[o]/[o:]
[u]/[u:]	[a:]/[a]	[e]/[e:]

Thus, you see that every vowel phoneme (including diphthongs), which you can symbolize /V/, has two allophones, [V] and [V:]. Your task is to specify when /V/ becomes [V:].

From what you already know about phonological patterns, you can guess that [V:] is conditioned by something in its phonetic environment. (Stress cannot be a factor, since all the words contain just one syllable.) But since in each pair of words the sounds preceding the vowel are identical, they can be eliminated from consideration. That leaves the sounds following /V/ and raises this question: For any pair of words, how do the sounds following the vowel differ?

The question should be a fairly easy one to answer. The difference between the /t/ and /d/ in *heat* and *heed,* respectively, is one of voicing: /t/ is voiceless and /d/ is voiced. The same is true of the /s/ and /z/ in *cease* and *seize,* the /p/ and /b/ in *lope* and *lobe,* and so forth. Because [V:] always precedes a voiced sound, you could write a rule such as this: /V/ becomes [V:] when the following sound is voiced. But now consider the following groups of words, again noting the various lengths of the vowels as you pronounce them:

rise/write/ride/rice	less/let/led	bus/buzz/but/bud
wrote/rose/road	hit/his/hiss/hid	lit/Liz/lid
lout/loud/louse	hope/hoed/hose	lathe/laid/late
life/live/light	ruse/roof/root	load/lows/loaf

The rule cannot distinguish between the lengths of these vowels simply because each group contains three or four words—too many to be accounted for by the two options *voiced* and *voiceless*. That being the case, you must be more specific in defining the kind of sound that follows the /V/ in each word: It is voiced or voiceless and what else?

But first we must agree on the lengths of the vowels themselves. Most speakers judge those lengths as follows (the numbers correspond in position to the words above, with *1* indicating shortness and higher numbers indicating progressively greater lengths):

4/1/3/2	2/1/3	2/4/1/3
1/3/2	1/4/2/3	1/3/2
1/3/2	1/2/3	3/2/1
2/3/1	3/2/1	2/3/1

Now you must determine what else (besides voicing) about the consonant following the vowel causes that vowel to be pronounced with greater length.

Simply as a place to begin, examine the first group of words, *rise/write/ride/rice*. If you note all the phonetic characteristics of each of the consonants following /V/, then arrange them according to the numbers they were assigned above, you get this:

1: voiceless, alveolar stop
2: voiceless, alveolar fricative
3: voiced, alveolar stop
4: voiced, alveolar fricative

For this group of consonants, place of articulation is obviously unrelated to the length of /V/, since all are alveolars yet occur in words with vowels of various lengths. In consonants of equal voicing, however, the feature *fricative* consistently produces greater length in /V/ than the feature *stop*. (That is, the vowel followed by the voiceless fricative is longer than the vowel followed by the voiceless stop; and the vowel followed by the voiced fricative is longer than the vowel followed by the voiced stop.) And for consonants having the same manner of articulation, the feature *voiced* consistently produces greater length in /V/ than the feature *voiceless*. (That is, the vowel followed by the voiced sound is longer than the vowel followed by the voiceless sound.)

Is this pattern true of the other four-word groups: *bus/buzz/but/bud* and *hit/his/hiss/hid?* Yes. In each case, the consonant sound following /V/ is an alveolar, rendering that characteristic unimportant; and when the fricative and stop agree in voicing, the fricative produces greater length in the preceding /V/ than the stop; and when the sounds agree in manner of articulation but not in voicing, the voiced sound produces greater length in the preceding /V/ than the stop. Several of the remaining groups, however—*lathe/laid/late, life/live/light, ruse/roof/root,* and *load/lows/loaf*—present a potential problem, for they contain words in which the consonant following the /V/ is an interdental rather than an alveolar. Does this change in place of articulation affect the pattern established above? In fact, does that pattern even hold true for the three-word groups in which the consonants following the /V/'s are consistently alveolars?

Both questions can be addressed simultaneously without much difficulty. For each of the three-word groups, all you must do is determine whether the length of the /V/, from shortest to longest, fits into the following sequence (do not confuse the numbers preceding each of the following verbal descriptions with the numbers assigned to the various words in the three-word groups: the numbers below indicate the *relative order* of four different sounds following progressively longer /V/'s, and one of those sounds will of course be absent when a word group contains only three members):

1. voiceless alveolar stop
2. voiceless alveolar/interdental fricative
3. voiced alveolar stop
4. voiced alveolar/interdental fricative

If you approach each three-word group separately, you will see that its members do indeed fit into this hierarchy. We therefore know what kinds of sounds produce various lengths in the /V/'s they follow for all 12 of the original word groups.

✦ *EXERCISE 2-13*

Do (a), (b), and (c).

(a) From the preceding problem, you know that the length of a vowel is affected by the voicing and manner of articulation of the following consonant and that whether the consonant is an alveolar or an interdental is unimportant. Is it possible to extend this last claim to velars and palatals? In other words, is it true that fricatives and stops other than alveolars and interdentals will also fit into the hierarchy established above? Explain how you arrived at your answer.

(b) Thus far, all the words in the various groups have been only one syllable long. Can the patterns you established be generalized to words of other lengths, as well? Are there any restrictions that must be added for the patterns to be valid?

(c) Write a rule describing what you know about how the relative lengths of /V/'s followed by consonants are determined.

____

____

____

____

____

____

____

✦ ✦ ✦

For the next problem, examine each of the following words and their phonemic transcriptions, paying special attention to the consonant clusters:

kicked /kɪkt/	shaft /šæft/	judged /ǰəǰd/
ribbed /rɪbd/	pushed /pʊšt/	loft /lɔft/
bent /bɛnt/	history /hɪstɚi/	pride /praɪd/
glass /glæs/	raised /rezd/	admire /ædmaɪr/
mostly /mostli/	blade /bled/	won't /wont/
shrimp /šrɪmp/	quick /kwɪk/	cute /kjut/
scrap /skræp/	munched /mənčt/	

This time, you must determine the phonological pattern operating within these clusters of consonant sounds and then write a rule describing it.

The real question here is this: What do the consonants of any given cluster have in common? Since only three criteria are used to describe consonant sounds, you can assume that the answer to this question is *voicing, place of articulation,* and/or *manner of articulation.* If you examine the first row of words, you will see that, while none of the sounds in any given cluster share the same place of articulation and while the sounds in only two of the clusters (those in *kicked* and *ribbed*) share the same manner of articulation, the sounds in *all* the clusters do indeed agree in voicing. It may also be worthwhile to notice that all the clusters thus far occur at the ends of words. A good hypothesis at this point would be that the sounds in any final consonant cluster agree in voicing.

A glance at the second row, however, will tell you that this hypothesis needs to be revised: First, the sounds in the /ft/ and /st/ clusters in *lofty* and *history,* respectively, do not occur finally; second, the sounds in the /nt/ cluster in *bent,* though they do occur finally, do not agree in voicing. The first problem can be dealt with quite easily; all you must do is remove the word *final* from the hypothesis above. But the second problem forces you to reexamine the eight clusters in the words looked at so far. What do the seven consonant clusters in *kicked, shaft, judged, ribbed, pushed, lofty,* and *history* have in common that is not also true of the cluster in *bent?*

One good answer to this question would be that *bent* contains a nasal in its cluster, whereas the sounds in all the other clusters are uniformly stops, fricatives, or affricates. So a revised hypothesis might look like this: The sounds in any given consonant cluster agree in voicing unless the cluster contains a nasal. But now look at row three, where you will notice that, while the consonant sounds in the clusters in *raised* and *admire* conform to the new hypothesis, those in *pride* and *glass* do not. Since the clusters in these latter words contain either an /r/ or an /l/, perhaps the hypothesis could be modified again, namely: The sounds in any given consonant cluster agree in voicing unless the cluster contains a nasal or a liquid.

The words in row four confirm this last hypothesis; the words in row five, however, do not. Notice that the clusters in *quick* and *cute* contain neither a nasal nor a liquid yet contain consonants that do not agree in voicing. The hypothesis will therefore need to be revised once more: The sounds in any given consonant cluster agree in voicing unless the cluster contains a nasal, a liquid, or a glide. Since this hypothesis works for all the consonant clusters in the data, it can serve as the basis for our rule. All you still must do is determine whether there is a more economical way of saying the same thing—that is, saying the same thing in fewer words by capturing generalizations not made explicit in the most recent form of the hypothesis.

For example, the hypothesis now contains the phrase *a nasal, a liquid, or a glide.* Since these are precisely the groups of consonant sounds that comprise the category *sonorants,* the rule could be written like this: The sounds in any given consonant cluster agree in voicing unless the cluster contains a sonorant. Again, this is true enough, but it can still be written using fewer words. What does the rule really say? If the sounds in any given consonant cluster agree in voicing unless the cluster contains a sonorant, then the clustered sounds that *do* agree in voicing must all be obstruents. The rule could therefore be rewritten simply as: Clusters of obstruents agree in voicing (with no mention of sonorants being necessary, since their absence is implied).

✦ *EXERCISE 2-14*

Do both (a) and (b).

(a) How would the rule just written have to be modified to account for the consonant clusters in words such as *obtuse* and *birdhouse?*

____

____

____

____

____

(b) In connected conversation pronunciation, speakers of English sometimes *reduce* certain consonant clusters by deleting one of the sounds. In the sentence *John kicked the ball over the fence,* for example, the cluster in *kicked* (/kɪkt/) would probably be reduced to just /k/. After examining the following words and transcriptions, write a rule specifying what must be true before the italicized sound in each consonant cluster can be deleted. (Actually, whether the deletion occurs also depends on the sound following the cluster—it must be a consonant with a place of articulation close to that of the sound deleted—but for this exercise, you can ignore that fact; just describe what must be true of the cluster itself and the sounds within it.)

canned /kæn*d*/	milk /mɪl*k*/	old /ol*d*/
passed /pæs*t*/	lamp /læm*p*/	and /æn*d*/
bathed /beð*d*/	don't /don*t*/	ant /æn*t*/
parked /pɔrk*t*/	kicked /kɪk*t*/	most /mos*t*/

____

____

____

____

____

____

✦ ✦ ✦

Phonological Processes: Optional versus Obligatory

As you now know, phonological rules specify the mechanisms by which sound changes occur. Those mechanisms are known as **phonological processes** and are either **optional** or **obligatory.** Optional phonological process may or may not occur, depending on who the speaker is and whether he or she is using a reading pronunciation or connected conversation pronunciation. Obligatory processes, however, occur regardless of who the speaker is and what kind of pronunciation he or she is using. Obligatory processes describe the things that all speakers of a language tend to do the same, such as (for English) begin initial C-C-C clusters with /s/ or aspirate word-initial voiceless stops. The use or nonuse of optional processes by speakers of various geographic origins and demographic groups, however, is responsible for the great amount of dialectal variation in English: Some speakers pronounce *creek* as /krɪk/ and others pronounce it as /krik/, some speakers insert an /r/ into words such as *wash* and *Washington,* and so forth.

As other examples of optional phonological processes, consider how the alveolar stops and alveolar nasal become homorganic with immediately following stops but only when a connected conversation pronunciation is used: For example, *good boy* /gʊd bɔɪ/ becomes [gʊb bɔɪ], *good girl* /gʊd gɚl/ becomes [gʊg gɚl], *might be* /maɪt bi/ becomes [maɪp bi], *might go* /maɪt go/ becomes [maɪk go], *ran by* /ræn baɪ/ becomes [ræm baɪ], and so forth. Or consider how initial /h/ is deleted in unstressed syllables but again only with a connected conversation pronunciation: *Who handed him his hat* /hu hændəd hɪm hɪz hæt/ becomes [hu hændəd ɪm ɪz hæt]. On the other hand, all speakers always articulate the alveolar stops and nasal as dental sounds (that is, with the tip of the tongue against the back of the upper teeth) rather than as true alveolars when /θ/ follows immediately, as in the words *eighth, width,* and *tenth.* And vowels are always nasalized when the following sound is a nasal, just as voiceless stops are always aspirated when they occur initially in stressed syllables, both regardless of who is speaking, how fast, or in what context. These three phenomena are examples of obligatory phonological processes.

✦ *EXERCISE 2-15*

Label each of the following phenomena as either an *optional* or an *obligatory* phonological process.

(a) the voicing of medial /t/ in words such as *butter* and *latter:*

____

(b) the velarization of /l/ in words such as *bulge* and *milk:*

____

(c) the "raising" of /aʊ/ and /aɪ/ to /əʊ/ and /əɪ/, respectively, in some dialects, in words such as *house, bite,* and *out:*

____

(d) the pronunciation of syllables with no more than three consonant sounds preceding the vowel sound:

____

(e) the pronunciation of *white house* with different juncture and stress patterns to indicate either the president's place of residence or any house that is painted white:

____

(f) the tendency for some speakers to insert /r/ into words such as *wash, Washington,* and *washer:*

____

(g) the articulation of both liquids with less voicing when they occur immediately following a voiceless sound, as in *ply, trip, clap,* and *free:*

____

(h) the pronunciation of *aunt* as /ant/ by some speakers:

____

(i) the tendency to pronounce unstressed vowels as [ə] when words are spoken quickly and informally:

____

(j) the pronunciation of final voiceless stops as *unreleased* sounds—that is, as sounds articulated with no aspiration:

____

✦ ✦ ✦

FOR FURTHER STUDY

Distinctive Features

The only difference between /b/ and /p/ is that /b/ is voiced and /p/ is voiceless. Since that one feature—*voicing*—is responsible for /b/ and /p/ being perceived as different categories of sound, voicing is said to be a **distinctive feature** of English. On the other hand, although the only difference between the two [k]'s in kicked is that one is aspirated and the other is not, the difference between [kʰ] and [k] is allophonic, not phonemic. That is, aspiration does not serve to distinguish phonemes in English, just allophones of the same phoneme. For that reason, it is an example of a **nondistinctive feature.**

In the "For Further Study" section of Chapter 1 that dealt with natural classes and features, you saw that it is possible to describe the similarities and differences between sounds and to group similar kinds of sounds, using more specific features than those used in phonetic verbal descriptions. Those same features can be used to describe the similarities and differences between phonemes and to group similar kinds of phonemes. (We can say, for example, that /s/ is [+ continuant] and /t/ is [– continuant] or that all fricatives are [+ continuant] and all stops are [– continuant].) Considering the large number of features given in Tables 1-6 and 1-7, using them to represent phonemes may seem unnecessarily difficult and unwieldy. However, they can simplify the writing of linguistic rules so that allophonic variation is represented as merely the addition, deletion, or change of a few features.

You saw one example of this at the end of the "For Further Study" section on linguistic notation and descriptive rules, earlier in this chapter. The following rule:

$$\begin{bmatrix} -\text{ continuant} \\ -\text{ voice} \\ -\text{ delayed release} \end{bmatrix} \rightarrow [+\text{ aspiration}] \;/\; \#\,\underline{\quad}\, \underset{[+\text{ stress}]}{\text{V}}$$

means that voiceless stops become aspirated when they occur immediately preceding a stressed syllable. And to indicate that in a word-final cluster of consonants, a final stop can be deleted (as noted in Exercise 2-14(b)), we could write a rule, thus:

$$([+\text{ consonantal}])\;([+\text{ consonantal}])\;[+\text{ consonantal}]\;\begin{bmatrix} -\text{ continuant} \\ -\text{ voice} \\ -\text{ delayed} \\ \text{release} \end{bmatrix}$$

$$\rightarrow ([+\text{ consonantal}])\;([+\text{ consonantal}])\;[+\text{ consonantal}]\;\text{Ø} \;/\; \underline{\quad}\;\#\#$$

(The symbol Ø indicates the nonoccurrence of a sound.)

✦ *EXERCISE 2-16*

Do (a), (b), (c), and (d).

(a) State the following rule in simple prose:

$$\begin{bmatrix} -\text{ vocalic} \\ +\text{ consonantal} \\ -\text{ sonorant} \end{bmatrix} \rightarrow \text{Ø} \;/\; \underline{\quad}\;\#\#$$

____

____

(b) State the following rule in simple prose:

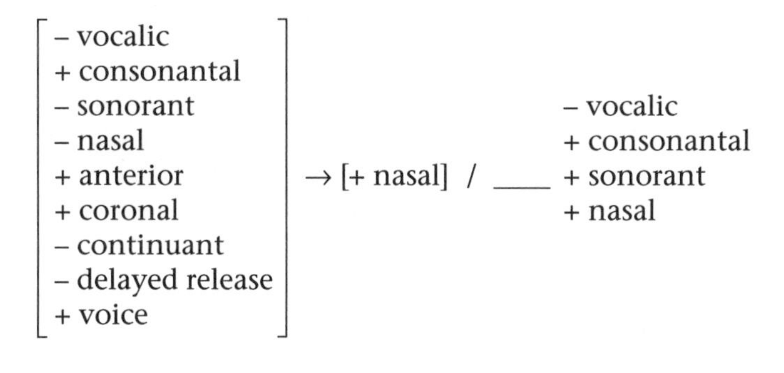

$$\begin{bmatrix} -\text{vocalic} \\ +\text{consonantal} \\ -\text{sonorant} \\ -\text{nasal} \\ +\text{anterior} \\ +\text{coronal} \\ -\text{continuant} \\ -\text{delayed release} \\ +\text{voice} \end{bmatrix} \rightarrow [+\text{nasal}] \;/\; \_\_\_ \begin{matrix} -\text{vocalic} \\ +\text{consonantal} \\ +\text{sonorant} \\ +\text{nasal} \end{matrix}$$

____

____

(c) State the following rule using feature notation: The sequence *word-final /t/ followed by word-initial /j/* becomes /č/.

____

(d) State the following rule using feature notation: /ə/ is inserted after a voiced word-final stop.

____

✦ ✦ ✦

Hints for Solving Phonological Problems

Perhaps the most difficult thing for most students about doing phonology is solving the problems—specifically, locating the important pattern(s). Being confronted with the data and then being told to write a rule describing the phonological process(es) illustrated, many students simply do not know where to begin. As with doing transcription, it is true that the more experience and practice you get at solving such problems, the easier the entire process will be for you. But it is also true that following a logical progression of steps will make the task easier. Following is one such progression:

- Understand what the problem is asking you to do. Must you create your own data, or has it been provided? Have you been told how many parts there are to the pattern or how many patterns there are? Have you been asked merely to verbalize a rule, or must you use the kind of specialized notation discussed in the "For Further Study" section earlier in this chapter? Is the pattern based on segmental or suprasegmental variation? If segmental, is the pattern qualitative (that is, dealing with *how* certain sounds are pronounced) or quantitative (dealing with *how long* certain sounds are pronounced)? And so forth.
- If you have been given a list of words to analyze (which will most frequently be the case), do not try to examine and compare all the words simultaneously; instead, pick two or three of the shortest words (because you will have fewer sounds in each with which to work), and begin with them.
- Make a list of whatever the two or three words you have chosen have in common (beyond such obvious things as containing syllables, consonants, and vowels), remembering to focus on sounds, not letters. Do they begin or end with the same sound or kind of sound (voiced, stop, palatal, sonorant, high, back, tense, diphthong, etc.)? Do they have any sound sequences in common? (Again, the sequences may have the same sounds or merely the same kinds of sounds.) Are there similarities in stress, juncture, or any other suprasegmentals or in syllabification? If you are given pairs of words, does the same sound consistently change between one member of the pair and the other? If so, how, and in what phonetic environments?
- Once you have found something that the words have in common, begin examining the other words—carefully, one by one—to see if they all exhibit the same pattern(s). If they do, you must then merely formulate a rule describing what you have noticed (assuming that is part of the assignment). If they do not, you must decide whether to look for a new pattern (that is, return to the preceding step and look for something else the words have in common) or accept the one you have found and admit that some exceptions exist (in which case, you will pro-

ceed to the next step). In deciding this, you must rely on your own best judgment and common sense; there is no maximum or minimum percent of your words that can be counted as exceptions.

- Examine all the exceptions to discover what they have in common that makes them exceptions. (In other words, repeat the preceding two steps, but this time, focus on the exceptions.) Repeat this step until all of your exceptions are accounted for. (The pattern that you note for your exceptions may itself have exceptions and so on.)
- Formulate a rule that states the process(es) of phonological change and accounts for all the exceptions. In doing this, remember that you should focus on *classes* of sounds rather than on *individual* sounds: For example, /s/, /f/, /θ/, and /h/ are all voiceless fricatives and should be grouped together as such.
- Now test the rule on every word in the list. Should the rule be modified in any way, or does it account for all the data as they are?
- Finally, examine the rule closely to make sure that it is written as economically as possible: Rules that have fewer words are generally preferred over rules that say the same thing but take twice as long to do so.

Summary and Review

You have learned a considerable amount about the phonological structure of English and also how to discuss and account for that structure using phonemes, allophones, rules, and terms such as *complementary distribution* and *free variation*. Below are all the new words and phrases used in this part of the book; if any look unfamiliar, they can be found in the Glossary. (The one marked with an asterisk was introduced in a section marked "For Further Study.")

accidental gap
allophone
complementary distribution
descriptive rule
distinctive feature
free variation
homorganic
minimal pair
minimal set
nondistinctive feature*

obligatory phonological process
optional phonological process
phone
phoneme
phonemic inventory
phonetic environment
phonological process
phonology
phonotactics
prescriptive rule
systematic gap
underlying form
virgules

✦ *EXERCISE 2-17*

A large number of two-syllable words—including *convict, subject, address, object, reject,* and *pervert*—can function as nouns or verbs without any corresponding change in pronunciation other than the placement of main stress: When used as nouns, the first syllable is stressed; when used as verbs, the second syllable is stressed. But the rules governing placement of stress in English are more complex than this pattern suggests. Consider the following words, which are subdivided into verbs, adjectives, and nouns:

Verbs

maintain	carouse	redeem
cajole	exhume	collapse
exist	evict	elect
lament	edit	consider
imagine	promise	follow

Adjectives

supreme	obtuse	complete
foreign	remote	insane
corrupt	immense	intact
inept	baroque	personal
pleasant	older	greenest

Nouns

machine	regime	police
occult	canoe	escrow
houses	drawer	printer
booklet	treetop	veranda
consensus	javelin	venison

Some of these words have their primary stress on the first syllable; the others have their primary stress on the second syllable, regardless of whether a third syllable follows. Now look at the following three rules, one of which accounts for each of the patterns of main stress in the groups of verbs, adjectives, and nouns above (here and for the duration of this exercise, /i/, /e/, /u/, /o/, /ɔ/, /a/, /aɪ/, /aʊ/, and /ɔɪ/ will be counted as tense vowels and /ɪ/, /ɛ/, /æ/, /ʊ/, and /ə/ as lax vowels. A few of these classifications are arguable, but all are necessary to simplify the rules):

(1) *Verbs*—Place the main stress on the last vowel sound in the word if the vowel is tense or is followed by two or more consonant sounds; otherwise, place the stress on the penultimate vowel sound. second from last

(2) *Adjectives*—Use the same rule as for verbs unless the word ends in a suffix having a lax vowel; in that case, follow the rule for nouns below.

(3) *Nouns*—Use the same rule as for verbs, but first, disregard all final syllables containing a lax vowel.

Now respond to all the questions below.

(a) Do the rules not account for the placement of main stress in any of the words? If so, list the words here.

follow - exception

escrow treetop

veranda consensus

(b) Explain why the rules account for the placement of main stress in each of the following words: *maintain, collapse, personal, supreme, cinema, police.*

(c) The rules above will not account for the placement of main stress in any of these words: *insinuate, solidify, extrapolate, hypotenuse, asterisk, formaldehyde, guillotine, pedigree*. Instead of placing the main stress on the correct syllable, where do the various rules place it? Write a rule describing what must be done to the main stress of each word (as predicted by the rules above) to make it "correct." Is such a rule necessary for all multisyllabic words (including ones not in the list above) or only some?

insinuate,
solidify
extrapolate,
hypotenuse,

rule: move main stress two syllables toward front of the word.

(d) You now know that for some multisyllabic words, two rules must apply before the main stress is correctly placed (one from the list of three above and the one written in part (c)). Can those rules apply in any order, or is the order of application important? Why?

✦ ✦ ✦

Exercises for Further Thought and Application

✦ *EXERCISE 2-18*

People occasionally make such phonological "slips of the tongue" in speaking as *stare rake* for *rare steak, skitty school* for *city school, lever come nate* for *never come late, my com the mop* for *my mom the cop,* and *plack ben* for *black pen.* What do such errors imply about how the brain and vocal apparatus work together in producing phonological sequences?

✦ ✦ ✦

✦ EXERCISE 2-19

Following is one possible "Pig Latin" rendition of the sentence *Are you going out tonight?*: "Are-ay ou-yay o-gay ing-ay out-ay o-tay ight-nay?" Using simple prose, describe what must happen phonologically to the original sentence to produce the Pig Latin version.

✦✦✦

✦ EXERCISE 2-20

Do both (a) and (b).

(a) The minimal pairs *low/row, oleo/oreo,* and *pole/pour* illustrate that /l/ and /r/ are phonemic initially, medially, and finally. Construct similar sets of minimal pairs for each of the following pairs:

/s/ and /z/

/p/ and /v/

/m/ and /n/

/l/ and /r/

/g/ and /k/

(b) It is easy to show that /t/, /d/, /č/, /ǰ/, /s/, /z/, /š/, and /ž/ are different phonemes in English; all that must be done is to create minimal pairs similar to those in part (a). Yet /t/, /d/, /s/, and /z/ are frequently palatalized as [č], [ǰ], [š], and [ž] in connected conversation pronunciations, as the following data show:

meet you [mič ju]
made you [meǰ ju]
miss you [mɪš ju]
advise you [ədvaɪž ju]
bit you [bɪč ju]
had you [hæǰ ju]
bus you [bəš ju]
lose you [luž ju]

Using simple prose, write a rule that captures the generalizations of phonological change revealed in these data. (That the second word in each construction is *you* happens to be an accident of the data; that the second word in each construction begins with /j/ is not.) Is such change an optional or an obligatory process?

✦ ✦ ✦

✦ *EXERCISE 2-21*

In Old English (the form of the language that was used from the fifth century until about the twelfth century), the sounds [f], [v], [s], [z], [θ], and [ð] did not each stem from a different phoneme, as they do today. Instead, [f] and [v] were allophones of one phoneme, [s] and [z] were allophones of another phoneme, [θ] and [ð] were allophones of another phoneme, and the two allophones of each of these three phonemes occurred in complementary distribution. Based on the limited data given below and using simple English prose, write a rule describing when each of the six allophones occurred. Be sure to capture as many phonological generalizations as you can in your answer. (Glosses for each of the words are provided but of course are not relevant to your answer.)

folc ("folk") [fɔlk]
sona ("soon") [sona]
bæð ("bath") [bæθ]
fif ("five") [fif]
fifel ("sea monster") [fivɛl]
fifta ("fifth") [fifta]

fæsl ("progeny") [fæzəl]

ofnas ("ovens") [ɔvnas]

hæpse ("hasp") [hæpsə]

maðmas ("treasures") [maðmas]

mase ("titmouse") [mazə]

hus ("house") [hus]

baðu ("baths") [baðu]

___

___

___

✦ ✦ ✦

✦ *EXERCISE 2-22*

The term *phonological cohesion* has been used to describe the linking effect of repeated vowel and/or consonant sounds in a stretch of discourse. Most poetry, for example, displays such phonological cohesion through its rhymes, assonance, and alliteration. And writers of advertisements and political campaign slogans frequently resort to phonological cohesion because the phenomenon causes the words in which it occurs to be remembered more easily. Describe the sound patterns that lend phonological cohesion to each of the following examples.

Veni, vidi, vici. ("I came, I saw, I conquered.")

___

___

___

Sally sold seashells by the seashore.

___

___

___

We will meet or beat any price.

I like Ike.

Tippecanoe and Tyler, too.

✦ ✦ ✦

✦ *EXERCISE 2-23*

The /t/ of words such as *lighter* and *doubter* is narrowly transcribed as [D] (a voiced alveolar flap), a phonological change that can be captured in what is sometimes called the "flapping rule": Medial /t/ becomes [D] when it is preceded and followed by vowels, and main stress does not occur on the following syllable. Similarly, in Canadian English and some dialects of American English, the /aɪ/ and /aʊ/ of words such as *lighter* and *doubter,* respectively, are transcribed as [əɪ] and [əʊ], phonological changes that can be captured in what is usually called the "raising rule" (because the first element of each diphthong has been "raised" from a low, central vowel to a mid, central vowel): /aɪ/ and /aʊ/ become [əɪ] and [əʊ], respectively, when followed by a voiceless consonant. In those dialects in which both rules must apply to produce pronunciations such as [ləɪDɚ] and [dəʊDɚ], must the flapping rule and raising rule occur in a particular order, or can the order in which they occur be random? Explain your response.

✦ ✦ ✦

✦ *EXERCISE 2-24*

Throughout most of the history of the language, English has had both qualitatively long and qualitatively short vowels. At some point between about 1500 and 1800, the seven long vowels underwent phonetic changes now collectively known as the Great Vowel Shift (in the following transcriptions, *:* indicates greater length in the preceding vowel):

[i:] → [aɪ]   [u:] → [aʊ]

[e:] → [i]   [o:] → [u]

[ɛ:] → [e]   [ɔ:] → [o]

[a:] → [e]

Using simple prose, write a rule that describes the vocalic phenomena of the Great Vowel Shift. (For the purposes of your answer, assume that [ɛ:] is pronounced about one place of articulation lower in the mouth than [e:] and that vowel tenseness is not relevant to the answer.) You may, if you wish, write a separate rule for [a:] → [e].

✦ ✦ ✦

✦ *EXERCISE 2-25*

Give several examples of prescriptive and descriptive language rules. What is the key difference between the two kinds of rules?

✦ ✦ ✦

✦ *EXERCISE 2-26*

You have read about various kinds of phonological change in this book but have read very little regarding *why* such changes may occur. Aside from strictly articulatory reasons, why might sound change occur in English (or any other language, for that matter)?

✦ ✦ ✦

✦ *EXERCISE 2-27*

In one of the dialects of English (a dialect called *Black English,* even though its use cannot be correlated dependably with the color of its users' skin), the pronunciations listed below under (a), (b), and (c) occur frequently. Using simple prose, write a rule describing how each of the following phenomena differs from so-called standard English.

(a) bag [bæk] pig [pɪk] led [lɛt]
flood [flət] slowed [slot] tube [tup]
bad [bæt] rug [rək] rib [rɪp]

(b) help [hɛp] door [do] nickel [nɪkə]
farther [fɔðə] killed [kɪd] paper [pepə]
silk [sɪk] poured [pod] serve [səv]

(c) think [tɪŋk] three [fri] both [bof]
math [mæf] thrill [frɪl] thought [tɔt]
ether [ifɚ] moth [mɔf] something [səmfɪn]

(In this last group, the transcription of the final nasal in *something* as an alveolar is not relevant to your answer.)

✦ ✦ ✦

✦ *EXERCISE 2-28*

Discuss the following observation: The phonological structure of English is random, as is which of the many dialectal varieties of that structure is regarded as standard. Yet the American culture consistently punishes people for not speaking standard English.

✦ ✦ ✦

✦ *EXERCISE 2-29*

Discuss the difference between a *phonemic* transcription and a *phonetic* transcription.

✦ ✦ ✦

✦ *EXERCISE 2-30*

If you are a native speaker of English, you knew all the phonological patterns of English long before reading about them in this book. (You must have known them, or you would not have been able to speak English all these years.) Speculate on the nature of that knowledge: How did you acquire it? Did anyone teach it to you? How early in life did you know it? Could you have received it genetically? Has it changed over the years? That is, have you stopped speaking one phonological dialect and begun speaking another? If so, why? Do you have exactly the same knowledge as your parents? How did you come to favor one phonological dialect over the others? And so forth.

✦ ✦ ✦

The Structure of English Morphology 3

In this book, you are working "from the bottom up": First, you learned about the smallest pieces of the English language, its sounds; then, you learned how those sounds fit into categories and into sequential patterns; now you will learn how those categories of sounds combine into meaningful units.

If you thoroughly learned the basic terminology and concepts introduced in Chapter 2—especially phonology, phone, phoneme, allophone, *and* complementary distribution*—then mastering the basic definitions and concepts of Chapter 3 should be no problem. As you will soon see, there are several obvious parallels between phonology and morphology.*

Basic Definitions

Morphology is the study of the smallest meaningful units in a language. The phrase *smallest meaningful units* may seem like mere jargon for *words,* but a little reflection will convince you that is not really the case. Consider the word *cat*. Since there is no way to reduce the size of that word and still have it mean something related to the concept "furry, four-legged feline," it must be a smallest meaningful unit in English. But what of the plural, *cats?* The only structural difference between *cat* and *cats* is the *-s,* and since the two words have meanings that are related but not identical—one is singular, the other plural—it must be true that the difference in meaning is linked to the plural marker. And that means this plural marker, *-s,* is another smallest meaningful unit in English.

Now consider the word *walk.* As the infinitive form of a verb, it has a particular meaning not associated with time. But if *-ed* is added, the meaning changes so that it is associated with just the past; and if *-ing* is added, the meaning changes so that it is associated with progressive or ongoing time. Again, these observations tell us that *-ed* and *-ing* must be smallest meaningful units in English. Similarly, the *un-* in *unhappy,* the *-est* in *longest,* the *pre-* and *-al* in *premedical,* the *-ion* in *fusion,* the *-ness* in *hardness,* the *co-* and *-er* in *coworker,* and the *-ly* in *slowly* are all smallest meaningful units in English.

Just as it is a mistake to equate *smallest meaningful unit* with *word,* so also would it be a mistake to equate *smallest meaningful unit* with *syllable.* All the examples given thus far happen to have just one syllable, but smallest meaningful units are often longer. The word *aqua,* for example, has two syllables but cannot be reduced and still mean something related to "bluish-green color," just as the suffix *-ity* has two syllables but cannot be reduced and still mean something related to "state or quality of." And notice that the word *kangaroo,* though it has three syllables, is still a smallest meaningful unit in English.

In linguistics, actual instances of smallest meaningful units are called **morphs,** and classes or categories of similar morphs are called **morphemes.** (Morphs and morphemes are parallel to phones and phonemes, respectively, in phonology.) If, for example, you say *cat* 50 times, you have articulated 50 morphs, or smallest meaningful units; but because those 50 morphs all have the same meaning, they are members of the same morpheme, or category of smallest units of meaning. As with phonemes, morphemes are not tangible things; they are abstract *types* or *groups* that we assume exist because of how morphs pattern in languages as they are used by speakers. Every morpheme contains an infinite number of morphs, all of which are identical in meaning and similar, though not identical, to one another phonetically. To keep morphs and morphemes distinct in print, morphemes are enclosed in curly brackets ({ }), like this: {cat}.

If two or more morphs of the same morpheme are phonemically distinct—that is, if they vary in ways that native speakers of the language can easily recognize—they are called **allomorphs.** (Allomorphs are to morphemes what allo*phones* are to phonemes.) The 50 instances of *cat* from the preceding paragraph are not phonemically distinct; they are all pronounced with /k/ followed by /æ/ followed by /t/. But whereas the plural *-s* added to *cat* is pronounced /s/, the same plural *-s* is pronounced /z/ when it is added to *hero* and /əz/ when it is added to *judge;* thus, /s/, /z/, and /əz/, being phonemically distinct but having the same meaning ("plural"), must be allomorphs of {plural}, the plural morpheme. (The plural morpheme is symbolized by {*plural*} rather than {*-s*} to keep it distinct from the possessive and third-person, singular morphemes, which also involve adding /s/ to words.) Another way to remember the distinction between morphs and allomorphs is this: Morphs of the same morpheme, because they are phonemically identical, will always have the same broad transcription; but allomorphs, because they are perceived as phonemic variants of one another, will always have different broad transcriptions.

Not all morphs are as easy to distinguish as the examples given so far may suggest. Consider the word *woman.* Because it contains the word *man,* with which it has much in common in terms of meaning, you might guess that it contains two morphs—*man* and *wo.* But every morph must, by definition, contain meaning, and what does *wo* mean? However, after you look at the word *woman* as it was spelled 1,500 years ago—*wifmann*—you can guess that there is a link in meaning between *wif* and the modern English *wife.* That link has been obscured by some 1,500 years of sound and spelling changes in the language, but it still exists. In the same way, you might suspect that the *berry* of *cranberry* is a morph of {berry}, but what does *cran* mean? Again, that meaning has been obscured by history, but it exists nonetheless. (*Cran* was formerly spelled *crane,* and *craneberries* were apparently so named because they grow in marshes and bogs and are a favorite food of the cranes that live there.) Such morphs, because of this latter example, are called **cranberry morphs,** and their morphemes are called **cranberry morphemes.**

✦ *EXERCISE 3-1*

Respond to each of the following questions.

(a) Could *poodle, dalmatian, dachshund,* and *terrier* all be considered allomorphs of the morpheme {dog}? Why or why not?

____

____

____

(b) Is every morph also an allomorph? Is every allomorph also a morph? Justify both of your answers.

(c) Does every morpheme necessarily have allomorphs? Does every morpheme necessarily have morphs? Justify both of your answers.

(d) How many different morphemes are represented in each of the following words? (You may need to consult a dictionary for some of the words.) What are they?

student ______________________________

stupidity ______________________________

unfair ______________________________

excellent ______________________________

sleeping ______________________________

unemployed ______________________________

deforms ______________________________

unreliable ______________________________

trial ______________________________

disinfectant ______________________________

unfairly ______________________________

husbands ______________________________

island ______________________________

classroom ______________________________

paper ______________________________

inversion ______________________________

magazine ______________________________

diploma ______________________________

sandwich ______________________________

crinkly ______________________________

(e) Are the *-er* of *longer* and the *-er* of *worker* morphs of the same morpheme, {er}? Defend your answer.

____

____

____

____

____

____

____

✦ ✦ ✦

Most of the other terminology necessary for the study of morphology consists of words and phrases that you almost certainly have learned before but may have forgotten. A quick review of these terms—all of which have to do with nouns, personal pronouns, verbs, descriptive adjectives, and/or adverbs—and how they can be inflected will make much of the rest of this chapter easier to understand.

The most basic morphological distinction among English nouns is one of **number**, which expresses contrasts that involve countable quantities: **singular**, referring to one, versus **plural**, referring to more than one. The plural inflection, of course, is usually designated by a final *-s*. Another distinction that is made among nouns concerns their **case**—that is, how they function in a particular sentence. The most basic case categories are **nominative**, or subject; **accusative**, or direct object; **dative**, or indirect object; and **genitive**, or possessive. Only the genitive case is explicitly inflected in English (with *-'s*); all other case relationships are expressed through word order and the use of prepositions.

English personal pronouns are also inflected for number (compare singular *I* with plural *me*) and case (compare nominative *I* with accusative/dative *me* and genitive *my*/*mine*), though the changes are holistic rather than inflectional. (That is, the entire word changes rather than a suffix simply being added.) In addition, however, such pronouns are inflected for **person**, which differentiates between **first person** (the speaker, as expressed by *I, me, we, us, my, mine,* and *our*), **second person** (the addressee, as expressed by *you* and *your*), and **third person** (everyone else, as expressed by *he, she, it, they, them, his, her,* and *their*).

For English verbs, three basic morphological distinctions exist. The first two are person (first, second, and third, as with personal pronouns) and number (singular and plural, as with nouns and personal pronouns). The third is **tense:** Infinitives in English can be inflected for the **present** and **present participle**, both of which describe a current state or action, and the **past** and **past participle**, both of which describe a previous state or action. (All other tenses can be achieved only through the use of auxiliary verbs such as *will, have,* and *be*.) When the complete set of inflected forms associated with a particular verb is given, as for *help* and *break* in Table 3-1, the result is a **conjugation.**

Adverbs and descriptive adjectives can be distinguished morphologically only two ways—with the **comparative** and the **superlative** inflections, *-er* and *-est,* respectively. The comparative marks the adjective or adverb with the meaning "more," as in *John is taller* (= "more tall") *than Sam* and *Mary runs faster* (= "more fast") *than Susan.* The superlative, on the other hand, marks the adjective or adverb with the meaning "most," as in *John is the tallest* (= "most tall") *boy in his class* or *Mary runs fastest* (= "most fast") *of all the children in the school.* As you will see later, not all adjectives and adverbs can be inflected with *-er* and *-est;* however, with very few exceptions, such adjectives and adverbs form the comparative and superlative with *more* and *most* (for example, *more/most beautiful* rather than *beautifuler/beautifulest* and *more/most swiftly* rather than *swiftlier/swiftliest*).

✦ *EXERCISE 3-2*

Respond to the following questions.

(a) The English language is more than 1,500 years old, and its morphological structure has changed a great deal over the years. For example, English formerly had three distinctions of number rather than two: Besides singular and plural, it used *dual,* which specified "two." (The meaning associated with *plural* was then "more than two.") And it formerly inflected, besides the genitive case, the accusative, dative, and locative cases. (*Locative* designates the geographic or physical location of something.) The loss of these kinds of distinctions has been compensated for by an increased dependency on word order and the

TABLE 3-1 *Conjugations of the Verbs* help *and* break

Tense	***Number***	***Person***		
		First	**Second**	**Third**
Present	**Singular**	help, break	help, break	helps, breaks
	Plural	help, break	help, break	help, break
Past	**Singular/Plural**	helped, broke	helped, broke	helped, broke
Present Participle	**Singular/Plural**	helping, breaking	helping, breaking	helping, breaking
Past Participle	**Singular/Plural**	helped, broken	helped, broken	helped, broken

use of prepositions. Considering the kind of trade-off that has occurred, do you think English has become an easier or more difficult language to learn?

(b) The present- and past-participle forms of verbs must frequently occur with auxiliary verbs—for the present participle, *be;* for the past participle, either *be* or *have*. Is there a pattern to the occurrence of *be* and *have* with past participles? That is, does one occur in one kind of sentence and the other in a different kind? (*Hint:* Use the sample sentences *John has eaten the cake* and *The cake was eaten by John* as models on which to base your answer.)

(c) The text specifically discussed *descriptive* adjectives, but there are other kinds as well—because they modify nouns, for example, articles are considered adjectives, as are demonstrative words such as *this* and *that*. Such nondescriptive adjectives cannot be inflected with {comparative} and {superlative}, but can they be inflected with any other morphemes discussed so far? Explain your answer.

____

____

____

✦ ✦ ✦

Kinds of Morphemes

All morphemes can be divided into the categories **lexical** and **grammatical.** A lexical morpheme has a meaning that can be understood fully in and of itself—{boy}, for example, as well as {run}, {green}, {quick}, {paper}, {large}, {throw}, and {now}. Nouns, verbs, adjectives, and adverbs are typical kinds of lexical morphemes. Grammatical morphemes, on the other hand—such as {of}, {and}, {the}, {ness}, {to}, {pre}, {a}, {but}, {in}, and {ly}—can be understood completely only when they occur with other words in a sentence. (Just try to understand *to* or *-ly* in isolation, and you will appreciate the difficulty involved.) Typical kinds of grammatical morphemes include prepositions, conjunctions, articles, and all prefixes and suffixes.

Both lexical and grammatical morphemes can be further subdivided into **bound** and **free** morphemes. Bound morphemes are so called because they must be "bound" to other morphemes, whereas free morphemes can occur independently as words. (In *untie,* for example, {tie} is free—*tie* is a word in its own right—and {un} is bound, since it can occur only if it is attached to at least one other morpheme.) Because *dog* is a word that can both occur and be understood apart from other morphemes, {dog} is an example of a morpheme that is free and lexical. But the *-cept* in words such as *exception, concept,* and *intercept* is an example of a morpheme that is bound and lexical because, while it does have its own understandable meaning (it comes from a Latin verb meaning "to take"), it can occur only attached to a variety of prefixes and suffixes. Similarly, {at}, {but}, and {in} are free grammatical morphemes: Each is its own, freely occurring word but cannot be understood clearly except in combination with other words. However, {plural} and {past tense} are both bound and grammatical, since they can neither occur unattached nor be understood except in relation to other words.

The final distinction to be drawn here is between bound grammatical morphemes that are **inflectional** versus those that are **derivational.** Because all the morphemes in both groups are both bound and grammatical, none can occur freely and all have meaning that is easily understandable only in relation to at least one other morpheme. Inflectional morphemes, however, modify the grammatical usage of a word (that is, change a word's tense, plurality, etc., but *not* its part of speech: *cat* and *cats* are both nouns, *walk* and *walked* are both verbs, and so forth), whereas derivational morphemes do not (although derivational morphemes *may* change the part of speech of a word: *hospital* is a noun, but *hospitalize* is a verb). And whereas inflectional morphemes must always occur at the ends of words, derivational morphemes can occur anywhere. (Try pluralizing any noun, regardless of its length, and you will see that the *-s* is always added finally; it never occurs anywhere else.) English has only eight inflectional morphemes, which were reviewed earlier:

- {plural} and {possessive}—for nouns and personal pronouns
- {comparative} and {superlative}—for descriptive adjectives
- {present}, {past}, {present participle}, and {past participle}—for verbs)

All other bound grammatical morphemes in English are derivational. (They are always either prefixes or suffixes, which together are known as **affixes.**) You will see later the patterns that occur when derivational and inflectional morphemes appear in words.

The various categories of morphemes outlined in this section may seem a bit complicated, but they can be summed up easily, as shown in Figure 3-1.

✦ *EXERCISE 3-3*

Respond to each of the following questions.

(a) Identify the following morphemes as *lexical* or *grammatical* and *bound* or *free:*

{count} ________________________________

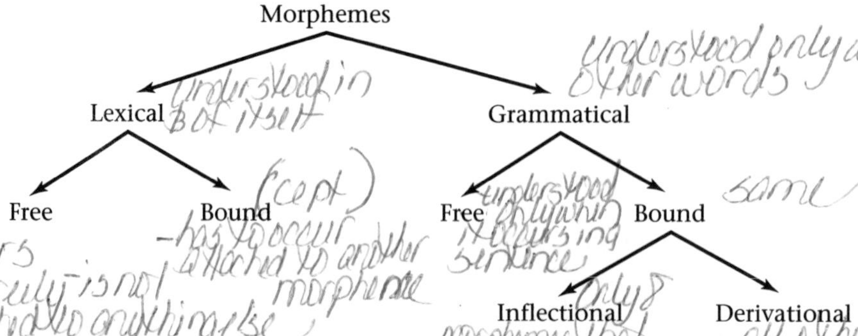

- Morphemes
  - Lexical
    - Free
    - Bound
  - Grammatical
    - Free
    - Bound
      - Inflectional
      - Derivational

FIGURE 3-1 *Relationships Among Categories of Morphemes*

{re-} ______________________________

adjectival {-er} ______________________________

{fast} ______________________________

{the} ______________________________

{house} ______________________________

{-ly} ______________________________

{wood} ______________________________

{five} ______________________________

{swing} ______________________________

(b) Underline the derivational morpheme(s) in each of the following words:

depose	readily	colder	active	beheads
action	repackage	rewriting	unchanged	forcefully

(c) In the discussion of lexical versus grammatical morphemes, pronouns were not classified as members of either category. Some pronouns—such as *I, me, he, she,* and *it*—are obviously lexical morphemes; others, however—*this* and *that,* for example—seem more grammatical. Can pronouns such as *his, we,* and *myself* be classified as either lexical or grammatical? Why or why not?

____

____

____

____

(d) In the text above, it was stated that "the *-cept* in words such as *exception, concept,* and *intercept* is an example of a morpheme that is bound and lexical because, while it does have its own understandable meaning (it comes from a Latin verb meaning "to take"), it can occur only attached to a variety of prefixes and suffixes." If *-cept* has an "understandable meaning," why is it so difficult for most speakers of English to state it?

____

____

✦ ✦ ✦

Inflectional Morphemes

Just as phonemes do not occur randomly in words, neither do morphemes; in fact, morphemes are as patterned and rule governed as phonemes. In this section, you will examine the patterns that occur when lexical morphemes and inflectional morphemes combine; and in the next, you will look at some of the patterns that occur when lexical morphemes and derivational morphemes combine. (Because of the nature of free, grammatical morphemes, they do not combine with other morphemes and so will not concern us here.)

When an inflectional morpheme is applied to a class of words—a process known as **inflection**—the result is often very predictable. Consider, for example, Table 3-2, which illustrates the inflection of some nouns with {plural}. There we see that, when {plural} is added

TABLE 3-2 *The Inflections of Some English Nouns with {plural}*

Singular Noun	***Plural Noun***	***Allomorphic Form of {plural}***
cat	cats	/s/
body	bodies	/z/
bag	bags	/z/
house	houses	/əz/
judge	judges	/əz/
bed	beds	/z/
bush	bushes	/əz/
way	ways	/z/
curl	curls	/z/
ship	ships	/s/
elbow	elbows	/z/
song	songs	/z/
pass	passes	/əz/
back	backs	/s/
shore	shores	/z/
lathe	lathes	/z/
ton	tons	/z/

Singular Noun	*Plural Noun*	*Allomorphic Form of {plural}*
dove	doves	/z/
laugh	laughs	/s/
tub	tubs	/z/
buzz	buzzes	/əz/
shoe	shoes	/z/
show	shows	/z/
tie	ties	/z/
bunch	bunches	/əz/
limb	limbs	/z/

to an English noun, only one of three allomorphs occurs—/s/, /z/, and /əz/. If we wanted to write a rule specifying the conditions under which each allomorph appears, we could do so easily: /əz/ occurs when the final sound of the original noun is a sibilant; /s/ occurs when the final sound of the original noun is any other voiceless phoneme; and /z/ occurs when the final sound of the original noun is any other voiced phoneme. Such rules, because they specify the phonemic details of morphological inflection, are frequently called **morphophonemic rules.**

Morphophonemic rules, unlike the allophonic rules of Chapter 2, have numerous exceptions. If you look again at Table 3-2, for example, you will see that it contains only nouns that form plurals by adding an /s/, /z/, or /əz/. But what happens when nouns such as *ox, goose, tooth, deer, sheep, child, shrimp,* and *fish* are pluralized? According to the morphophonemic rule just formulated, we should expect *oxes* /aksəz/, *gooses* /gusəz/, *tooths* /tuθs/, *deers* /dirz/, *sheeps* /šips/, *childs* /čaɪldz/, *shrimps* /šrɪmps/, and *fishes* /fɪšəz/, but of course, we actually get none of these. Instead, two plurals are formed with an internal vowel change (*geese, teeth*), two are formed with an irregular suffix (*oxen, children*), and four have plurals that are identical to their singular forms (*deer, sheep, shrimp, fish;* these are called **zero plurals**). Such irregular allomorphs are said to be **morphologically conditioned:** Instead of adhering to the prevalent morphophonemic pattern, they follow idiosyncratic morphological patterns that can be explained only by examining the history of the language. By contrast, allomorphs that *do* follow morphophonemic patterns—that is, which are determined by the phonological structure of the words to which they are added—are **phonologically conditioned.**

✦ *EXERCISE 3-4*

Respond to each of the following questions.

(a) Explain why {possessive}, when applied to a group of nouns, should produce the same allomorphs and the same morphophonemic rule as those given in the text for {plural}.

____

____

____

(b) At some point in elementary school, you probably learned a definition for *noun* similar to this: "A noun is any person, place, animal, or thing." Morphologically, however, a different definition could be written: "A noun is any word to which can be applied {plural} and {possessive}." Will this new definition work for all nouns? In other words, are there any nouns that cannot be made plural and/or possessive?

____

____

____

____

____

(c) The history of the English language reveals that many more exceptions formerly existed to the morphophonemic rule for the formation of plurals than currently do. For example, several centuries ago, the plural of *eye* was *eyen,* the plural of *shoe* was *shoon,* and nouns such as *folk, kind,* and *horse* had zero plurals. (Notice that a few of these older plural forms—*brethren,* for example—still exist.) Do you think that *oxen, sheep,* and the other irregular plurals listed in the text will eventually conform to the morphophonemic rule, too? Explain your answer.

____

____

____

____

____

(d) Young children as well as nonnative speakers who are in the initial stages of learning English often produce incorrect plurals such as *womans, mans, shrimps,* and *childs*. Why should that be the case?

____

____

____

____

____

____

(e) Some speakers of English no longer follow the morphophonemic rule for the formation of plural allomorphs as strictly as it was stated earlier. Specifically, such speakers often produce /s/ and /əs/ where the rule predicts /z/ and /əz/, respectively. Such "devoicing" of /z/ is neither right nor wrong, but it does illustrate an important fact about

English (and about language in general). What is that fact? (*Hint:* Read part (c) again.)

____

____

(f) Some English nouns ending in /f/ or /θ/ voice those final sounds before the plural allomorph is added: *Wife* /waɪf/, *thief* /θif/, and *bath* /bæθ/, for example, become *wives* /waɪvz/, *thieves* /θivz/, and *baths* /bæðz/, respectively. If a new word such as *loof* were to enter the language, is it more likely that its plural would be *loofs* /lufs/ or *looves* /luvz/? Why?

____

____

____

____

____

✦ ✦ ✦

Now consider verbs. If we inflect most infinitives by adding the present-tense morpheme, there will be a zero change except in the third-person, singular form, as Table 3-3 illustrates for *kick, wish,* and *run*. And since the only change in the third-person, singular forms of these verbs is the addition of *-s,* the patterns that have already been established for the addition of *-s* to words (both in Chapter 2 and in the preceding examples of {plural} and {possessive}) will be followed: The allomorph /əz/ will occur when the verb ends in a sibilant; the allomorph /s/ will occur when the verb ends in any other voiceless sound; and the phoneme /z/ will occur when the verb ends in any other voiced sound. Thus /əz/, /s/, and /z/ are phonologically conditioned. And when the present-tense forms of verbs are constructed irregularly (that is, in ways other than through the addition of *-s*—such as with *be: am/are/is* in the singular, *are* in the plural), the forms are morphologically conditioned.

TABLE 3-3 *Inflections of* kick, wish, *and* run *with {present tense}*

First Person **(I/we)**	***Second Person*** **(you/you)**	***Third Person*** **(he, she, it/they)**
Singular = *kick, wish, run* Plural = *kick, wish, run*	Singular = *kick, wish, run* Plural = *kick, wish, run*	Singular = *kicks, wishes, runs* Plural = *kick, wish, run*

✦ *EXERCISE 3-5*

The first word in each of the following pairs is the infinitive form of a verb; the second word is the same infinitive with {past tense} added. Examine each pair of words closely; then respond to the questions that follow.

sip/sipped	lob/lobbed	jog/jogged	pick/picked
erode/eroded	shoot/shot	live/lived	laugh/laughed
pass/passed	buzz/buzzed	bathe/bathed	sing/sang
push/pushed	sin/sinned	time/timed	call/called
roar/roared	singe/singed	pit/pitted	quit/quit
flit/flitted	die/died	lay/laid	mend/mended

(a) What are the allomorphs of the past-tense morpheme? Base your answer only on the above pairs of words.

____

____

____

____

(b) Write a rule describing when the most frequently occurring allomorphs of {past tense} occur.

____

____

____

____

(c) Why does the rule you wrote for part (b) not account for all the past-tense forms in the data?

____

____

(d) Are the phonologically conditioned allomorphs of {past tense} in complementary distribution? Explain why or why not.

____

____

____

(e) The past-tense forms of some verbs—*sell/sold, sleep/slept,* and so on—seem to follow the rule you wrote for part (b) but also involve an internal vowel change. Would you say that such past tenses are phonologically or morphologically conditioned? Why?

____

____

____

____

✦✦✦

And what are the allomorphs of {present participle}? Consider the following pairs of words, in which each first member is an infinitive and each second member is the same infinitive with {present participle} added:

eat/eating	sip/sipping	walk/walking
live/living	draw/drawing	use/using
wash/washing	judge/judging	ache/aching
call/calling	roar/roaring	rig/rigging
pan/panning	sing/singing	pass/passing
laugh/laughing	do/doing	row/rowing

It would be tempting to conclude that {present participle} has just one allomorph, /ɪŋ/. But remember the definition of *allomorph*—"alternate phonemic forms of the same morpheme"—and ask yourself whether you ever pronounce the *-ing* of present participle verbs any other way(s) besides /ɪŋ/.

You do. Sometimes you replace the velar nasal with an alveolar nasal: /ɪn/. (This is a universal aspect of English usage: Everyone who speaks the language occasionally pronounces *-ing* as /ɪn/, even if they claim otherwise.) So there are two allomorphs of {present participle}, /ɪŋ/ and /ɪn/, and the question now becomes one of determining when each allomorph occurs. When are you more likely to say, for example, /fɪšɪŋ/, /wɚkɪŋ/, /bekɪŋ/, and /slipɪŋ/, and when are you more likely to say /fɪšɪn/, /wɚkɪn/, /bekɪn/, and /slipɪn/? You will not be able to write a rule predicting exactly when /ɪŋ/ and /ɪn/ are used, but can you write a rule specifying when each variant is *more likely* to be used than the other?

The rule you write must center on the kinds of situations in which you find yourself speaking: In more formal contexts, such as a public speech, you would tend to use /ɪŋ/; in less formal contexts, such as a party with friends, you would tend to use /ɪn/. Since the choice of variants has to do with the particular set of circumstances surrounding their use rather than with the phonology or morphology of the original verb, such allomorphs are said to be **stylistically conditioned** (or sometimes **contextually conditioned**).

The past-participle forms of verbs follow a regular pattern in their formation, as well, though that pattern is morphologically rather than phonologically or stylistically conditioned. So-called *weak verbs*—that is, those that form their past tenses by adding either a *-d, -t,* or *-ed* suffix, with or without a corresponding internal vowel change (such as *wave/waved, deal/dealt,* and *share/shared*)—form their past participles the same way. (Thus, the pasts and past participles of such verbs are identical.) And so-called *strong verbs,* which form their past tenses with an internal vowel change but without any corresponding suffix (such as *sing/sang, find/found,* and *forget/forgot*), form their past participles through an internal vowel change and/or by adding an *-n* or *-en* suffix (thus, for the verbs already given, *sung, found,* and *forgotten*).

✦ *EXERCISE 3-6*

Respond to each of the following questions.

(a) In Exercise 3-4(b), a new definition of *noun* was written based on the kinds of morphemes that can be applied to nouns but not to any other parts of speech: "A noun is any word to which can be applied {plural} and {possessive}." Write a similar definition for *verb.* (*Hint:* What kinds of morphemes can be applied to verbs but not to any other parts of speech?) Does your definition work for all verbs, or are there exceptions?

____

____

____

____

____

(b) The dividing line between weak and strong verbs is not really as clear cut as the discussion in the text makes it seem. In fact, some verbs are both strong and weak—that is, they have two acceptable past participles. List some of these verbs, and provide both past-participle forms.

____

____

____

✦ ✦ ✦

Finally, we come to adverbs and descriptive adjectives. A little reflection will tell you that, when {comparative} and {superlative} are applied to such words, three different results are possible, as follows:

1. The original word may be suffixed with *-er* and *-est,* respectively (occasionally with an accompanying change in spelling), as in *happy/happier/happiest* and *fast/faster/fastest.*
2. The original word may be prefixed with *more* and *most,* respectively, as in *more/most magnanimous* and *more/most interesting.* (This is sometimes known as **periphrasis.**)
3. The original word may change to an entirely different word, as in *good/better/best* and *bad/worse/worst.*

Adjectives that fall into category (3) above are so idiosyncratic that they must be learned individually and so will concern us no further. However, do adjectives that fall into the first two categories occur in any noticeable pattern, or do they simply occur randomly?

Consider the following list of adjectives and their comparative and superlative forms:

old/older/oldest
neat/neater/neatest
thick/thicker/thickest
small/smaller/smallest
fast/faster/fastest
pure/purer/purest
cold/colder/coldest
young/younger/youngest

big/bigger/biggest
green/greener/greenest
low/lower/lowest
short/shorter/shortest
free/freer/freest
warm/warmer/warmest
red/redder/reddest
slim/slimmer/slimmest

Now compare that list to this one:

complicated/more complicated/most complicated
democratic/more democratic/most democratic
inflectional/ more inflectional/ most inflectional
beautiful/ more beautiful/ most beautiful
historical/ more historical/ most historical

Based on data such as these, you can conclude that, in general, monosyllabic adjectives form their comparatives and superlatives by adding *-er* and *-est* whereas adjectives having three or more syllables form their comparatives and superlatives with *more* and *most.* (Notice the phrase *in general,* which is necessary because of such counterexamples as *fun, gold* and all trisyllabic adjectives beginning with the prefix *un-*, as in *unhappy* and *untidy*.)

And what of disyllabic adjectives—that is, adjectives having exactly two syllables? Such adjectives often take the inflections *-er* and *-est,* though they also have the option of using *more* and *most: politer/politest* but also *more polite/most polite*. The kinds of disyllabic adjectives that take the inflections most readily are those ending in unstressed vowels (*early, easy, happy, funny, pretty, mellow, shallow,* and the like) or /ə/ + /l/ (as in *noble, feeble, gentle, simple,* and *able*).

✦ *EXERCISE 3-7*

Respond to each of the following questions.

(a) Present- and past-participle verb forms are frequently used as adjectives in English, as the following sentences attest:

(1) John is an *interesting* man.
(2) Mary has a *wounded* ego.
(3) The dog is *bathed* and ready to go.

When such participles are used as adjectives, regardless of their length, how do they typically form their comparatives and superlatives?

____

____

(b) Most adjectives that are inflected with *-er* and *-est* also typically take the periphrastic *more* and *most—wealthy/wealthier/wealthiest,* for example, but also *wealthy/more wealthy/most wealthy*—but more readily in one kind of sentence than in others. Specify the kind of sentence.

____

____

____

____

(c) Do adverbs follow the same patterns as descriptive adjectives in forming comparatives and superlatives? If not, specify the differences.

____

____

____

____

____

✦ ✦ ✦

Derivational Morphemes

As you have just seen, there are only eight inflectional morphemes in English, and that number is unlikely to change unless something cataclysmic happens to the language (such as when, in 1066, England was conquered by the Normans, and French became the official language of the government, the courts, and the schools). But there is an open-ended number of derivational morphemes, at least in theory: new ones can be added to the language and old ones dropped without affecting the basic grammatical structure of English. Since it would be impossible to try to give an exhaustive list of these derivational morphemes, we therefore have to be content with examining just a few representative examples.

Look closely at Tables 3-4 and 3-5, which catalog some of the most frequently occurring derivational suffixes and prefixes in English and the kinds of words they can attach to. One thing the tables do not make clear is that although derivational morphemes greatly outnumber inflectional morphemes, they have a much narrower range of application. In other words, while the various inflectional morphemes can be added to nearly all the words in a given class (as with {plural} and nouns, for example, or {present participle} and verbs), derivational morphemes can be added to only relatively few words in a given class ({a} and {trans} will combine with only a small number of adjectives and {ful}, with only a small number of nouns). Something else the tables do not make clear is that if more than one derivational suffix or prefix is added to the same word, they must be

TABLE 3-4 *Some Frequently Occurring Derivational Suffixes in English*

Add this suffix . . .	***To this kind of word . . .***	***And get this new part of speech and/or meaning:***	***Examples***
{ize}	noun, adjective	verb	*modern* + {ize} = *modernize* *style* + {ize} = *stylize* *equal* + {ize} = *equalize* *rubber* + {ize} = *rubberize*
{ful}	noun	adjective ("full of")	*help* + {ful} = *helpful* *play* + {ful} = *playful*
{ly}*	adjective	adverb ("in a manner with this quality")	*quick* + {ly} = *quickly* *careful* + {ly} = *carefully*
{ly}*, {y}	noun	adjective ("having this characteristic")	*friend* + {ly} = *friendly* *home* + {ly} = *homely* *blood* + {y} = *bloody* *health* + {y} = *healthy*
{less}	noun	adjective {"without"}	*home* + {less} = *homeless* *tree* + {less} = *treeless*

{ship}, {hood}	**concrete noun**	**abstract noun**	*friend* + {ship} = *friendship* *town* + {ship} = *township* *man* + {hood} = *manhood* *neighbor* + {hood} = *neighborhood*
{ment}	verb	noun	*amaze* + {ment} = *amazement* *establish* + {ment} = *establishment*
{en}	adjective	verb ("make")	*sweet* + {en} = *sweeten* *bright* + {en} = *brighten*
{er}	verb	noun ("one who")	*teach* + {er} = *teacher* *run* + {er} = *runner*
{ion}	verb	noun	*exert* + {ion} = *exertion* *coerce* + {ion} = *coercion*
{like}	noun	adjective ("like")	*child* + {like} = *childlike* *book* + {like} = *booklike*
{al}	noun	adjective ("characterized by," "relating to")	*fiction* + {al} = *fictional* *direction* + {al} = *directional*

*Note that {ly} has two different meanings, depending on whether it's used to form an adverb or adjective.

TABLE 3-5 *Some Frequently Occurring Derivational Prefixes in English*

Add this prefix . . .	***To this kind of word . . .***	***And get this new part of speech and/or meaning:***	***Examples***
{un}, {a}	adjective	adjective ("not")	{un} + *happy* = *unhappy* {un} + *likely* = *unlikely* {a} + *sexual* = *asexual* {a} + *problematic* = *aproblematic*
{dis}	verb	verb ("not")	{dis} + *agree* = *disagree* {dis} + *allow* = *disallow*
{anti}	noun	noun ("not")	{anti} + *aircraft* = *anti-aircraft* {anti} + *American* = *anti-American*
{trans}	adjective	adjective ("across")	{trans} + *continental* = *transcontinental* {trans} + *Atlantic* = *transatlantic*
{de}	verb	verb ("do the opposite of")	{de} + *vitalize* = *devitalize* {de} + *activate* = *deactivate*

{re}	verb	verb ("again")	{re} + *adjust* = *readjust* {re} + *name* = *rename*
{en, em}	noun	verb ("provide with")	{em} + *power* = *empower* {en} + *throne* = *enthrone*
{in, im, il, ir}	adjective	adjective ("not")	{in} + *conclusive* = *inconclusive* {in} + *accurate* = *inaccurate* {im} + *proper* = *improper* {im} + *pure* = *impure* {il} + *legal* = *illegal* {il} + *logical* = *illogical* {ir} + *reconcilable* = *irreconcilable* {ir} + *reducible* = *irreducible*
{iso}	adjective	adjective ("same," "uniform")	{iso} + *genic* = *isogenic* {iso} + *cyclic* = *isocyclic*

added in a certain order: We must say *hopefully,* for example ({hope} + {ful} + {ly}), rather than *hopelyful* and *unempowered* ({un} + {em} + {power} + {ed}) rather than *emunpowered.*

✦ *EXERCISE 3-8*

Respond to each of the following questions.

(a) The text states that "inflectional morphemes must always occur at the ends of words." This statement implies that, if both an inflectional morpheme and a derivational morpheme are attached as suffixes to the same word, the derivational morpheme will always attach first. (For example, if we begin with the verb *sweet* and add both {en} and {pres}, the {en} will always have to be attached first so that we finally arrive at *sweetens* and not *sweetsen;* or if we begin with the noun *friend* and add both {ly} and {superlative}, the {ly} will always have to be attached first so that we finally get *friendliest* and not *friendestly.*) Are there any exceptions to this general rule? That is, are there instances in which it is not clear whether the derivational or inflectional morpheme should attach to a particular word first? If so, how can such discrepancies be resolved?

___

___

___

___

___

___

___

___

___

___

___

(b) Is there a limit to the number of inflectional or derivational morphemes that can be attached to a given word? Give some examples to support your answer.

____

____

____

____

____

____

(c) Are the specific words to which a particular derivational morpheme can be attached predictable by rule? In other words, is the possible appearance of a given derivational morpheme governed by phonological or stylistic conditioning? Explain your answer.

____

____

____

____

____

(d) In the text, examples illustrate that if more than one derivational suffix or prefix is added to the same word, they must be added in a particular order. Can the same argument be made if exactly one derivational prefix *and* suffix are added to the same word, as in *unhappiness?* That is, can you argue for either {*un*} + *happiness* or *unhappy* + {*ness*}? Explain your answer.

____

____

(e) Explain how your implicit knowledge of inflectional and derivational morphology can help you decode the meanings of words you have not seen or heard before. What can you say about the meanings of such creations as *unfligged, transbotulizing,* and *blegs,* for example?

(f) In Table 3-4, {un} is listed as attachable to verbs and adjectives but not to nouns. (We cannot say *undesk,* for example, or *undog.*) How, then, do you explain the occurrence of *Uncola* in the world of advertising?

✦ ✦ ✦

Methods of Making Words

Since morphology is the study of the smallest meaningful units in a language, it includes the study of how those units come together to form words. You have already studied two of those methods—inflection and derivation—but there are many others, the most important of which we will discuss in this section. First, however, you must learn some more new terminology having to do with words, their classes, and their parts.

All the words in any language can be broadly divided into two categories, **open** and **closed.** The closed category is so called because it does not easily accept new words. Its members are fixed and do not usually change unless the language undergoes the kind of cataclysm mentioned at the beginning of the preceding section. (Another good example of such cataclysm is the three centuries of Scandinavian raids that the English people and their language had to endure from the ninth to the eleventh centuries. One result of those raids was a change in the personal pronoun system: *They, them,* and *their* are not native to English; they were introduced by the Scandinavians.) The closed category of words (also known as **function words**) includes nondescriptive adjectives, pronouns, conjunctions, prepositions, and determiners (*the, a, an, this, those, that,* and so forth). The open category, on the other hand, contains nouns, verbs, adverbs, and descriptive adjectives—exactly those parts of speech that remain open to new additions and which we will focus on in this section.

Words in the open category are usually further divided into **simple** and **complex** words. Simple words contain just one morpheme (*house,* for example, or *walk, slow,* or *green*), whereas complex words contain more than one (*houses, walking, slowly,* or *greenest*). And besides specifying the various affixes in complex words, we can identify their **roots** and **stems.** The root of a word is the morpheme that remains when all the affixes have been stripped away: In *friendliest,* for example, the root is *friend,* just as in *nationality,* the root is *nation.* (Notice that not all roots are free: *-cept* is the root of *concept,* *accept, intercept,* and other similar words, but it cannot stand alone. Also notice that some words, such as *redbird* and *trustworthy,* contain more than one root.) But a stem is any morpheme or combination of morphemes to which an affix is added—*friendly* is the stem of *friendliest, nation* is the stem of *national,* and *national* is the stem of *nationality.* All words must have at least one root, but only affixed words contain stems.

✦ *EXERCISE 3-9*

Respond to each of the following questions.

(a) Identify each of the following as a member of either the open or closed category of words, and for those words in the open category, further specify whether each is simple or complex:

mice ____________________

of ____________________

and ____________________

show ____________________

paperclip ____________________

her ____________________

three ____________________

this ____________________

food ____________________

round ____________________

(b) Identify all the roots and stems in each of the following words:

dragged ____________________

deactivate ____________________

impossible ___________________________

thumbtack ___________________________

hopefully ___________________________

unassuming ___________________________

redness ___________________________

racketeers ___________________________

cloudiness ___________________________

exceptionally ___________________________

(c) Write a definition of *word,* focusing on what a word must contain morphologically to be considered a word.

____

____

____

____

____

✦ ✦ ✦

New words can enter English in only two general ways: Either they are borrowed from another language, or they are created from elements that already exist in English. Borrowed words are usually not the subject of morphology (they are typically dealt with in courses focusing on language development and history), but, of course, created words are. Such creations, if they are neither the product of inflection nor derivation, can usually be accounted for by one of the processes discussed in the remainder of this section.

If two or more existing roots or stems combine to make a new word, **compounding** has occurred. Examples of English compounds are numerous, since compounding is one of the most prolific processes of word formation in the language: *cornflake* (*corn* + *flake*), *blackbird* (*black* + *bird*), *fastbreak* (*fast* + *break*), *busybody* (*busy* + *body*), *egghead* (*egg* + *head*), and *two-by-four* (*two* + *by* + *four*) are all compounds. Notice that compounding is not restricted to only certain parts of speech in the open category, either; compound nouns exist (*handbook, greenhouse*), as do compound verbs (*firebomb, overturn*), compound adjectives (*store-bought, red-hot*), and compound adverbs (*moreover, indeed*). English even contains a few compound prepositions (*alongside, notwithstanding*), conjunctions (*whenever, whereas*), and pronouns (*myself, you-all*). (Prepositions, conjunctions, and pronouns are still considered to be in the closed category, however, since the addition of *new* words in these groups is very unlikely.)

A special instance of compounding known as **reduplication** occurs when a single root or stem repeats itself or nearly so, as in *boogie-woogie, tick-tock, hanky-panky, do-do, tiptop, dilly-dally, pooh-pooh, super-duper, lovey-dovey, nitwit, pitter-patter,* and *wiggle-waggle*. Notice that very few reduplications involve a morpheme that is repeated exactly; more often, either a vowel (*wishy-washy, flip-flop, ding-dong*) or a consonant (*razzle-dazzle, teeny-weeny, roly-poly*) changes.

Not all new words result from adding roots and/or stems together; in fact, many are formed when multisyllabic words are shortened, a process known as **clipping.** Clipped words seem especially numerous on college campuses—*exam* (from *examination*), *dorm* (from *dormitory*), *lab* (from *laboratory*), *prof* (from *professor*), *math* (from *mathematics*), *ed* (from *education*), and *psych* (from *psychology*) are all clippings—though of course they also occur elsewhere (compare *phone, auto, mike, memo, deli, porno, plane, burger, bike,* and *condo*). Clipping also occurs whenever a personal name is shortened, as when *Steven* becomes *Steve, Thomas* becomes *Tom,* or *Angela* becomes *Angie.*

Occasionally, a word is shortened to form a new word that looks as if it should have been the originator of the word it was shortened from. For example, the verb *peddle* looks like the origin of *peddler*, but, in fact, the opposite is true: *Peddler* can be traced as far back as the fourteenth century but *peddle* only to 1532. The first users of *peddler* must have assumed that *peddle* existed (what else would describe what a peddler does?) and so created it through the process of **back-formation.** The same phenomenon occurred in the creation of *edit* (back-formed from *editor*), *hedgehop* (from *hedgehopper*), *donate* (from *donation*), *resurrect* (from *resurrection*), and *orient* and *orientate* (from *orientation*). Notice that back-formation always involves deaffixation and most frequently results in a verb being formed from a noun.

If two or more words are combined after at least one of them has been shortened, the result is a **blend.** *Gasohol,* for example, is a blend of *gasoline* and *alcohol, smog* is a blend of *smoke* and *fog,* and *brunch* is a blend of *breakfast* and *lunch.* Other common blends include *motel* (from *motor* and *hotel*), *transistor* (from *transfer* and *resistor*), *telecast* (from *televised* and *broadcast*), *permapress* (from *permanent* and *press*), and *escalator* (from *escalade* and *elevator*). When *all* the words that are combining have been shortened and to such an extent that only the initials or first few letters of each remain, an **acronym** has been formed. Thus, *Nabisco* is the result of the shortening and subsequent combining of *National Biscuit Company, NATO* abbreviates *North Atlantic Treaty Organization,* and *WASP* is the acronymic form of *White Anglo-Saxon Protestant.* Notice that, while most acronyms are pronounced as words (*NOW* for *National Organization for Women, AIDS* for *acquired immune deficiency syndrome,* and *NASA* for *National Aeronautics and Space Administration*), occasionally, each letter is sounded out separately (as in *RV* for *recreation vehicle, PMS* for *premenstrual syndrome, ICBM* for *intercontinental ballistics missile, NFL* for *National Football League,* and *IUD* for *intrauterine device*).

Sometimes new words are simply the by-products of creative imaginations—that is, they are **inventions.** Most inventions come as the result of advertisers searching for catchy names for their products, as in *Kodak, Kleenex, Jell-o,* and *nylon* (and notice that sometimes these brand names eventually become the generic term for all similar items: if you sneeze, for example, you are more likely to ask for a *Kleenex* than a *facial tissue*). But non–brand name inventions certainly exist as well, as *goof, dingbat,* and *blurb* attest. And if the sounds of the new word are suggested by the meaning it describes—*hiss* both sounds like and means "hiss" /hɪs/—then the result is an **echoism** (also known as an **onomatopoetic word**). *Click, quack, moan, boom, sizzle, buzz,* and *cuckoo* are common examples of echoisms.

If a personal name or place-name is adapted to a new meaning, the result is **antonomasia**. Probably the best known example of antonomasia in modern times is *Frisbee,* which ultimately derives from the name of the Frisbee Bakery in Bridgewater, Connecticut. The bakery's piepans (with *Frisbee* printed on the side in large letters) are said to have been sailed through the air by college students at a neighboring university in the same way that millions of Americans sail the plastic counterparts to the piepans today. And when someone who has damaged another's personal property is called a *vandal,* the allusion is to the warmongering Vandals of Europe, who looted and destroyed Rome in the fifth century. Other examples of common words with name-related histories include *sandwich* (named for the Earl of Sandwich, who supposedly loved to gamble so much that he would not leave the gaming tables even for lunch and so created the now familiar meat-between-two-slices-of-bread concoction), *hamburger* and *frankfurter* (named for German cities), and *fahrenheit* (named for the scientist).

If the pronunciation of a root or a stem is reinterpreted by its users so that its corresponding meaning makes more sense, the result is a **folk etymology.** If you play tennis, for example, you may have heard someone refer to a serve that touches the top of the net as a *net ball,* which, although it makes very good sense, is actually a corruption of *let ball* (350 years ago, *let* meant "to interfere with"). Or perhaps you have been in a restaurant that listed *cold slaw* on the menu rather than *coleslaw*. Not many Americans know that *coleslaw* comes from the dutch term *koolsla,* which literally means "cabbage salad," and since coleslaw is always served cold, of course *cold slaw* makes more sense and so is preferred to *coleslaw*. Or, again, perhaps you have used the word *bridegroom,* which is now the standard English way to refer to a soon-to-be or recently married man. But *bridegroom* is actually the folk-etymologized corruption of *bridegome,* which was the standard English term 600 years ago, when everyone knew than *gome* meant "man."

Finally, sometimes a root or stem is merely adapted to a new part of speech, as when the nouns *father* and *butter* began to be used as verbs. This process is called **shifting** or **zero-conversion** or **zero-derivation.** Some of the most common shifts from recent history include *rip-off* and *edit* (as nouns, adopted from their corresponding verbs), *cameo* (as an adjective, adopted from the noun), *zap* (as a verb, adopted from the interjection), and *no way* (as an interjection, adopted from the noun phrase).

The various kinds of word formation discussed above are not always as clear cut as they may seem. In fact, many gray areas exist, and it is often difficult or even impossible to classify a new word as belonging strictly in one category or another. When Ronald Reagan was president, for example, someone coined *Reaganomics* to describe his economic policies and philosophies. Should *Reaganomics* be classed as antonomasia or as blending? Is *poli-sci* really a clipping, as some textbooks label it, or is it actually a blend of *political* and *science?* Are the generic terms *Band-Aid* and *Kleenex* examples of invention, as listed above, or antonomasia (since they derive from brand names)? Answers to such questions amount to nothing more than opinions; the important point is that the various categories of word formation are really only approximations.

✦ *EXERCISE 3-10*

Respond to each of the following questions.

(a) Look again at the various compounds listed in the text as examples (and think of as many others as you can). What pattern do you notice regarding the relationship between the meanings of the two halves of the various compounds?

____

____

____

____

(b) In the text, the various blends given as examples highlight the fact that such words are *phonological* blends of their components, but are they *semantic* blends, as well? That is, do blends combine the meanings as well as the sounds of the words they join? Defend your answer.

____

____

____

____

____

____

____

(c) Indicate the method of formation of each of the following words (a desktop dictionary may be necessary in some cases):

airstrip ____________________

deplane ____________________

quark ____________________

disco ____________________

growl ____________________

van ____________________

blurt ____________________

greed ____________________

hangnail ____________________

jeans ____________________

zigzag ____________________

carryall ____________________

Mike ____________________

curio ____________________

floozy ____________________

shutout ____________________

OK ____________________

televise ____________________

leotard ____________________

redo ____________________

✦ ✦ ✦

Summary and Review

You have had two basic tasks in Chapter 3: first, to learn the general terminology necessary to study morphology; and second, to examine the morphological structure of English, including inflections, derivations, and methods of creating new words. Below are all the new words and phrases used in this chapter; if any are unfamiliar, consult the Glossary at the back of the book.

abstract noun
accusative case
acronym
affix
allomorph
antonomasia
back-formation
blending
bound morpheme
case
clipping
closed class of words
comparative
complex word
compounding
concrete noun
conjugation
contextually conditioned
count noun
cranberry morph
cranberry morpheme
dative case
derivational morpheme
echoism
first person
folk etymology
free morpheme
function word
genitive case
grammatical morpheme
inflection
inflectional morpheme
invention
lexical morpheme
morph
morpheme
morphologically conditioned
morphology
morphophonemic rule
nominative case
number
onomatopoetic word
open class of words
past participle
past tense
periphrasis
person
phonologically conditioned
plural
present participle
present tense
reduplication
root
second person
shifting
simple word
singular
stem
stylistically conditioned
superlative
tense
third person
zero-conversion
zero-derivation
zero plural

affix ~~affixe~~ suffix or prefix

✦ *EXERCISE 3-11*

For each word in the following list, specify (a) all the morphemes it contains, (b) whether its morphemes are bound or free, (c) whether it is simple or complex, (d) what its root(s) and stem(s) are, and, if the word is complex, (e) how it was formed.

uglier ______________________________

bush ______________________________

chairs ______________________________

erasers ______________________________

potted ______________________________

mist ______________________________

Band-Aid ______________________________

reforest ______________________________

sawdust ______________________________

____

escalator ______________________________

____

✦ ✦ ✦

Exercises for Further Thought and Application

✦ EXERCISE 3-12

Focusing on the word *unloadable,* use morphology to explain the ambiguity in the sentence *That truck is unloadable.*

2 meanings: not able to be loaded
able to be unloaded
unloadable
un load-able un-loadable
the meaning depends upon the order
of prefix & suffix

✦ ✦ ✦

✦ EXERCISE 3-13

Phrases such as *kick the bucket* and *beat around the bush* are called *idioms,* while phrases such as *peanut butter and jelly* and *macaroni and cheese* are called *collocations.* Using what you know of morphology, write definitions for *idiom* and *collocation* based on the examples given. (*Hint:* Your definitions will need to deal with such questions as (a) Do idioms and collocations literally mean what the words say? and (b) Can idioms and collocations be expanded with the addition of other words, such as *kick the wooden bucket* and *peanut butter and grape jelly*?)

✦ ✦ ✦

✦ *EXERCISE 3-14*

Specify what morphological process each of the following lists of word pairs exemplifies.

house/houses; walk/walking; red/redder inflection

do/undo; happy/happily; work/workable derivation

vibrations/vibes; Joseph/Joe; delicatessen/deli Clipping

typewriter/typewrite; hang glider/hang glide; lazy/laze back-form.

áddress/addréss; cónvict/convíct; ímport/impórt shifting

✦ ✦ ✦

✦ *EXERCISE 3-15*

No one can say precisely how many words and phrases have been formed through invention, simply because most pass into disuse before they can be recorded. (This is especially true of slang creations.) On the other hand, some new coinages are written down immediately, since they are created as parts of literary works. Of the words in this latter group, a few become so familiar and so often used outside the literature in which they originated that their literary roots are eventually forgotten. Determine the literary origin of each of the following (for some, you may need to consult a historical dictionary such as the *Oxford English Dictionary*):

blatant ____________________

malapropism The Rivals - Richard Sheridan

sensuous ____________________

yahoo ____________________

serendipity ____________________

✦ ✦ ✦

✦ *EXERCISE 3-16*

Do both (a) and (b).

(a) When {plural} is added to most nouns, the result is definite and predictable; however, {plural} added to a few words produces two plural forms instead of one. Consult the following examples of such dual-plural nouns, and then explain why such plural forms exist: *index* (*indexes* or *indices*), *cherub* (*cherubs* or *cherubim*), *stratum* (*stratums* or *strata*), *matrix* (*matrixes* or *matrices*).

index → indixes | indices
cherub → cherubs | cherubim
stratum → stratums | strata
matrix → matrices | matrices

follow normal rules for pluralization in English

Latin pluralization (folk etymology)

(b) When {past} is added to most verbs, the result is definite and predictable; however, {past} added to a few words produces two past-tense forms instead of one. Consult the following examples of such dual-past-tense nouns, and then explain why both plural forms exist: *dive* (*dived* or *dove*), *hang* (*hanged* or *hung*), *shine* (*shined* or *shone*).

✦ ✦ ✦

✦ *EXERCISE 3-17*

Folk etymology is especially common among people just learning English—whether they are children learning their primary language or adults learning a second language. Examine each of the following folk-etymological errors, and explain how the learner of English made the mistake. In other words, what does each error reveal about the language learner's knowledge of the morphology of English?

polyglot to mean "more than one glot" ______

"poly" means many

stalemate to mean "the spouse is no longer interested" ______

meaning of two roots

meteorology to mean "the study of meteors" ______

"study of" -ology

finesse to mean "a female fish" ______

suffix "esse" denotes female

diatribe to mean "food for the whole tribe" ______

know what "diet" means but does not know how to spell it.

✦ ✦ ✦

✦ EXERCISE 3-18

The English language provides many ways of describing a person from a particular place, all of which involve adding a derivational suffix to the place name—a person from Missouri is a *Missourian,* for example, one from Japan is a *Japanese,* and so forth. Consider the following place names: *New York, Denver, Illinois, Oakland, New Haven, Nebraska, Riverside, South Bend, Arkansas, Virginia.* Using only these names as data, state what phonological constraint(s) exist on when the morpheme {er} cannot be added to a place name to denote someone from that place.

any word that does not end w/ a vowel sound or [ər] can take on {er}

✦ ✦ ✦

✦ *EXERCISE 3-19*

For each of the following series of words, state whether the words are related by inflection or derivation.

(a) do, doing, does inflection

(b) appreciate, appreciable, appreciation derivation

(c) strong, stronger, strongest inflection

(d) boat, boats, boat's inflection

(e) preach, preacher, preachy derivation

(f) cut, uncut, cutter derivation

(g) good, better, best inflection morphologically cond.

(h) be, were, is inflection

(i) geography, geographic, geographer derivation

(j) mouse, mouse's, mice inflection

✦ ✦ ✦

✦ *EXERCISE 3-20*

The suffix *-able* can be added to many verbs to create corresponding adjectives that have meanings that can usually be expressed as "able to be X'd"—*break* + *-able* yields *breakable,* for example, just as *wash* + *-able* produces *washable.* But other verbs, such as *sit, go,* and *rest,* clearly do not accept *-able*. Having noted this, do (a), (b), and (c) below.

(a) Write a rule describing when *-able* can be added to verbs. (*Hint:* Think of *kinds* of verbs. What feature do *break* and *wash* share that *sit, go,* and *rest* do not?) take D.O.

transitive verbs can have the suffix "able" added to them

(b) Does your rule have any exceptions? If not, consider verbs such as *walk* and *run*. Are such verbs *real* exceptions or only *apparent* exceptions? Explain your answer.

In some instances, verbs can take objects.
They can either be trans or intrans
- take objects or not

(c) When *-able* is added to any verb, is its pronunciation predictable or unpredictable? Explain your answer.

predictable always /əbəl/

✦ ✦ ✦

✦ ***EXERCISE 3-21***

For each of the following sets of words, state how the second word has been formed from the first word(s).

back-formation/back-form ____________________

beef, buffalo/beefalo ____________________

fast, ball/fastball ____________________

short, stop/shortstop ____________________

typographical/typo ____________________

influenza/flu ____________________

énvelope/envélop ____________________

action/actionable ____________________

suburb/burb ____________________

rough, neck/roughneck ____________________

✦ ✦ ✦

✦ *EXERCISE 3-22*

American television shows and movies that feature time settings markedly different from the present usually depict a form of English morphologically identical to that used in late-twentieth-century American English. Do you believe such depictions to be accurate? Why or why not? If not (and assuming that producers strive for authenticity whenever possible), explain the decisions underlying the lack of variability in English morphology. If this question had been asked in Chapter 2, would your answer regarding a similarly invariable phonology be the same as your answer here? Why or why not?

____

____

____

____

____

____

____

✦ ✦ ✦

✦ *EXERCISE 3-23*

Imagine that you have volunteered to spend the afternoon with a group of first-generation Americans who have not yet mastered English. These people's mistakes in the use of the language fall into three broad categories—phonological (they mispronounce some of their words), morphological (they misconjugate some of their verbs), and lexical (they mix up the names of some things, such as *couch* and *chair*). At the end of the afternoon (assuming you are like most Americans), which of these three kinds of mistakes do you think will probably begin to irritate you most? Explain your response.

____

____

____

____

____

____

____

____

✦ ✦ ✦

✦ *EXERCISE 3-24*

In each of the following sentences, underline all the affixes that are derivational morphemes, and circle all the affixes that are inflectional morphemes.

The ballerina's toes cramped into knots as she attempted the dance.

John's new car was very inexpensive.

Mary's bike is the newest on the block.

Salt had totally corroded the car's front fenders.

Fred's cough means that he still smokes.

✦ ✦ ✦

✦ *EXERCISE 3-25*

Lewis Carroll's "Jabberwocky" is famous for being a poem that seems, at first glance, to be morphological nonsense but which, after further analysis, yields certain kinds of information to its readers. In the phrase *slithy toves,* for example, we can tell that *slithy* is an adjective modifying *toves* and that *toves* is plural; thus, a *tove* must be a **count noun,** and *slithy,* which could be a blend of *slimy* and *lithe,* must be capable of describing it. While such an analysis tells us little or nothing of the *lexical meanings* of the morphemes *slithy* and *toves,* it does tell us a great deal about their *grammatical meanings*—that is, the senses that words acquire when they are put together into a sentence. Explain the kinds of grammatical meaning that can be derived from the following sentence:

By mimsling the prefexed blostos and orepping all klegs, a pliffer can slis a vorg in dolkorizm with smah.

✦ ✦ ✦

✦ *EXERCISE 3-26*

Create new words for each of the following things by using the method of word formation specified in parentheses.

a town on the border of Kansas and Colorado (blend) Kanorado

able to be contacted (derivation) contactable

Cat Lovers Anonymous of Wyoming (acronym) CLAW

a lawnmower to be used only for trimming (compound) trimming-lawnmower

using bubblewrap to pad a package (shift) bubblewrap - verb

a new dance, invented by Gertrude (antonomasia) The Gertrude

a course in morphology (clipping) Morph

do clipperization (back-formation) clipperize

✦ ✦ ✦

✦ *EXERCISE 3-27*

Some proponents of gender equality have claimed that English is a very sexist language and not least in its morphology. They suggest, for example, that words containing *man* (*mailman, businessman, manhole,* etc.) ought to be replaced with more gender-neutral terms (such as, for the examples cited, *letter carrier, member of the business community,* and *utility access hole*). Discuss the necessity for such reform as well as the pros and cons associated with it. Is it likely to occur? Why or why not?

✦ ✦ ✦

✦ *EXERCISE 3-28*

After studying the examples that follow, state the allomorphs of the definite article {the}, and write a rule describing when each occurs. How are the allomorphs conditioned? Is the use of any similar morpheme(s) conditioned in the same way?

(a) John wants to hire the best person for the job.

(b) The opener is in the top drawer.

(c) He plays ball for the Angels.

(d) The eagles next out by the lake.

(e) The money in the account was withdrawn.

✦ ✦ ✦

✦ *EXERCISE 3-29*

Look up the words *perihelion* and *aphelion* in a desktop dictionary, noting their pronunciations as well as their meanings. What problems arise in determining the words' morphological structures? Explain your response.

____

____

____

____

____

____

____

____

____

____

✦ ✦ ✦

✦ *EXERCISE 3-30 (for discussion only)*

New events, technology, illnesses, foods—indeed, almost anything new—can cause words to be created in English. Read a recently published newspaper or magazine, and note all the words that have been coined within the last 25 years. What methods of word formation seem most prodigious?

✦ ✦ ✦

Answers to Exercises

✦ *EXERCISE 1-1, page 3*

If you are disappointed in your performance, keep in mind that most students can think of no more than 6 or 7 different spellings in the first minute and that, even when given several minutes, the vast majority of students never come up with more than about 10. As far as I know, no trick will suddenly reveal all the various spellings; you must simply allow your mind to wander and hope you get lucky. Consider the italicized letters in each of the following words:

1. b*e*
2. rec*ei*ve
3. b*ea*t
4. bod*y*
5. gu*i*llotine
6. m*ee*t
7. p*eo*ple
8. *ae*gis
9. ouij*a*
10. q*uay*
11. bel*ie*ve
12. am*oe*ba
13. p*i*ano
14. k*ey*
15. g*uy*ot

(Some speakers pronounce *ouija* with a final "uh" sound, but the "long *e*" is just as common.) The instructions for this exercise say that there are at least these 15 spellings; there may also be others. (Several students, for example, have offered *-uee* in *marquee, -uis* in *marquis,* and *-ix* in *prix,* but the final *-e, -s,* and *-x* may simply be silent.) Can you think of any others?

✦ *EXERCISE 1-2, page 6*

English consonant sounds that involve the tip of the tongue being on or very near the alveolar ridge include the sounds represented by:

1. the *s-* in *soup*
2. the *z-* in *zoo*
3. the *n-* in *no*
4. the *l-* in *low*
5. the *r-* in *rough*

You should have been able to get the first four without much difficulty, just by experimenting. The last one, however, may have given you some trouble, since the body of the tongue is closer to the rear of the mouth for English *r* sounds and the tip does not make direct contact with the alveolar ridge.

✦ *EXERCISE 1-3, page 7*

(a) The sounds you are producing are probably closest to those typically represented by the letters *b* (for *m*), *d* (for *n*), and *g* (for *ng*).

(b) The words that result are *boat, dear, tubby, rudder, rigging, robe, side* (or *sighed*), and *log.*

(c) The phonetic relationship between the pairs of sounds represented by *m* and *b*, *n* and *d*, and *ng* and *g*, respectively, must be a very close one if the first sound in each pair can so easily turn into the second. Specifically, the only difference between the sounds in each pair lies in where the airstream exits the head: For *m, n,* and *ng,* the airstream exits the nose; for *b, d,* and *g,* the airstream exits the mouth. (Notice that when you pronounce the *m* and *b,* the part of your head primarily responsible for the sounds is your two lips; *n* and *d* primarily involve the tip of the tongue being on the alveolar ridge; and *ng* and *g* primarily involve the body of the tongue retracting to the velum.)

✦ *EXERCISE 1-4, page 15*

(a)
"p" voiceless bilabial stop
"k" voiceless velar stop
"v" voiced labiodental fricative
"s" voiceless alveolar fricative
"č" voiceless affricate
"š" voiceless palatal fricative
"g" voiced velar stop
"f" voiceless labiodental fricative
"r" retroflex
"ǰ" voiced affricate
"b" voiced bilabial stop
"l" lateral
"j" palatal glide
"t" voiceless alveolar stop
"h" glottal fricative
"w" bilabial glide
"d" voiced alveolar stop
"θ" voiceless interdental fricative
"ð" voiced interdental fricative
"ž" voiced palatal fricative
"z" voiced alveolar fricative
"m" bilabial nasal
"n" alveolar nasal
"ŋ" velar nasal

(b)

voiceless bilabial stop	"p"
bilabial nasal	"m"
voiceless interdental fricative	"θ"
retroflex	"r"
voiced palatal fricative	"ž"
voiceless affricate	"č"
voiced alveolar fricative	"z"
voiced velar stop	"g"
voiced labiodental fricative	"v"
voiced bilabial stop	"b"
alveolar nasal	"n"
velar nasal	"ŋ"
voiceless alveolar stop	"t"
bilabial glide	"w"
voiceless palatal fricative	"š"
palatal glide	"j"
voiceless alveolar fricative	"s"
voiceless velar stop	"k"
voiceless labiodental fricative	"f"
glottal fricative	"h"
voiced interdental fricative	"ð"
lateral	"l"
voiced alveolar stop	"d"
voiced affricate	"ǰ"

If any of your answers were wrong, be sure to look again at the consonant chart, Table 1-1. It is important that you be able to read that chart easily and correctly.

✦ *EXERCISE 1-5, page 21*

*sh*rink	[š]	voiceless palatal fricative
cou*gh*	[f]	voiceless labiodental fricative
*j*udge	[ǰ]	voiced affricate
si*ng*er	[ŋ]	velar nasal
fi*ng*er	[ŋg]	velar nasal followed by voiced velar stop
wal*ked*	[kt]	voiceless velar stop followed by voiceless alveolar stop
rou*g*e	[ž]	voiced palatal fricative
*th*ere	[ð]	voiced interdental fricative
u*n*til	[n]	alveolar nasal
bu*tch*er	[č]	voiceless affricate
*y*early	[j]	palatal glide
o*v*er	[v]	voiced labiodental fricative
hea*r*t	[r]	retroflex

shu*cks*	[ks]	voiceless velar stop followed by voiceless alveolar fricative
mo*th*	[θ]	voiceless interdental fricative
i*mp*erial	[mp]	bilabial nasal followed by voiceless bilabial stop
e*lb*ow	[lb]	lateral followed by voiced bilabial stop
hot*d*og	[d]	voiced alveolar stop
cra*z*y	[z]	voiced alveolar fricative
*wh*oa	[w]	bilabial glide
*h*earing	[h]	glottal fricative
thoug*h*	no symbol, no verbal description (the *-gh-* is silent)	

If you missed any of these, it is probably because you confused the sound(s) you heard with the letter(s) you saw. That problem can be overcome only through lots of practice listening and transcribing.

✦ *EXERCISE 1-6, page 27*

(a)

[i]	high, front, tense vowel
[ʊ]	high, back, lax vowel
[o]	mid, back vowel
[ɔ]	low, back vowel
[u]	high, back, tense vowel
[æ]	low, front vowel
[e]	mid, front, tense vowel
[ɛ]	mid, front, lax vowel
[a]	low, central vowel
[ɪ]	high, front, lax vowel
[ə]	mid, central vowel
[aɪ]	low, central to high, front, lax diphthong
[ɔɪ]	low, back to high, front, lax diphthong
[aʊ]	low, central to high, back, lax diphthong

If you forgot the word *vowel* or *diphthong* in any of your answers, you cannot count those answers as being correct. Remember: *high, front, lax* and *low, central to high, back, lax* are nothing but strings of modifiers; the nouns *vowel* and *diphthong* must be included for the answers to be complete.

(b)

low, back vowel	[ɔ]
low, central vowel	[a]
high, front, tense vowel	[i]
high, back, lax vowel	[ʊ]
low, front vowel	[æ]

mid, front, lax vowel	[ɛ]
mid, central vowel	[ə]
high, back, tense vowel	[u]
high, front, lax vowel	[ɪ]
mid, front, tense vowel	[e]
mid, back vowel	[o]
low, central to high, front, lax diphthong	[aɪ]
low, back to high, front, lax diphthong	[ɔɪ]
low, central to high, back, lax diphthong	[aʊ]

As with Exercise 1-4, make sure you understand how to read the vowel chart (Table 1-4) and thoroughly learn all the information it contains. Not understanding something thoroughly now could well affect your progress through the rest of this book.

✦ *EXERCISE 1-7, page 30*

j*a*b	[æ]	low, front vowel
r*o*t	[a]	low, central vowel
wr*o*te	[o]	mid, back vowel
wr*o*ng	[ɔ]	low, back vowel
curi*ou*s	[ə]	mid, central vowel
b*e*d	[ɛ]	mid, front, lax vowel
b*ea*d	[i]	high, front, tense vowel
ab*i*de	[aɪ]	low, central to high, front lax diphthong
b*i*d	[ɪ]	high, front, lax vowel
j*ui*ce	[u]	high, back, tense vowel
m*ai*d	[e]	mid, front, tense vowel
b*oi*l	[ɔɪ]	low, back to high, front, lax diphthong
*a*round	[ə]	mid, central vowel
b*ou*nd	[aʊ]	low, central to high, back, lax diphthong
j*ury*	[ɚ]	r-colored schwa
bl*ou*se	[aʊ]	low, central to high, back, lax diphthong
sh*u*t	[ə]	mid, central vowel

Allow me to remind you of two things that are especially important when you transcribe vowels: First, try to forget how the word is spelled—just *listen* to how it is pronounced. Second, if you speak a different dialect than the one I speak, some of your answers will be different from the ones above. Ask your teacher to arbitrate any inconsistencies you think exist (and keep in mind that your teacher may speak yet another dialect).

✦ *EXERCISE 1-8, page 34*

The pitch of the stressed sound(s) is usually higher than that of the surrounding sound(s).

✦ *EXERCISE 1-9, page 35*

(a) (1) The vowels in *all so* are held for a longer period of time than the vowels in *also*.

(2) In *bluebird,* the first syllable contains the primary stress, and the second syllable contains only secondary stress; but in *blue bird,* the stress on both words is equal.

(b) (3) A fast rate of speech would probably indicate extreme excitement, and a very slow rate of speech—perhaps accompanied by a definite juncture between each of the words—would probably convey shock (as though the speaker had just learned that he or she had won the money and the news still had not fully sunk in). But a normal rate of speech would probably indicate that the speaker really did not care about winning the money, as though it were an everyday occurrence.

(4) A fast rate of articulation seems to convey just anger, but a slow rate of articulation conveys even *more* anger, as though the speaker can hardly container himself or herself.

(5) If "getting out of here fast" is important to the speaker, he or she certainly would not waste time saying it slowly.

(c) Greater volume is usually used to convey excitement or anger or to call attention to oneself; conversely, lower volume may convey secrecy or intimacy.

(d) (6) The pitch begins high for *oh,* then dips noticeably for *I don't know*—though it rises sharply again for during the pronunciation of the vowel in *know*.

(7) The intonation rises from *search* to *me* but then falls off sharply as the vowel of *me* concludes.

(8) The intonation falls from *yeah* to *right*.

(e) Pitch can and does convey meaning but usually in conjunction with intonation and/or stress. Sentences conveying anger or excitement, for example, tend to be spoken in a higher pitch than sentences conveying depression, intimacy, or secrecy.

✦ *EXERCISE 1-10, page 41*

Word	***Reading Pronunciation***	***Connected Conversation Pronunciation***
working	[wɚkɪŋ]	[wɚkɪn]
you	[ju]	[jə]
probably	[prabəbli]	[prabli]
can	[kæn]	[kɪn], [kɛn], [kən]
Sunday	[sənde]	[səndi]
sandwich	[sændwɪč]	[sænwɪč]
go to	[gotu]	[godə], [gotə]
give me	[gɪvmi]	[gɪmi]
don't know	[dontno]	[dono], [dəno]
should have	[šʊdhæv]	[šʊdəv], [šʊdə]
his and hers	[hɪzændhɚz]	[hɪzənhɚz]
five or six	[faɪvorsɪks]	[faɪvɚsɪks]

By this time, you have probably done enough transcription to begin noticing a pattern to your mistakes—you may be mixing up certain sounds and their symbols, you may have a hard time hearing the difference between certain sounds, and so forth. Extra practice transcribing words containing those sounds will probably clear up your problems.

✦ *EXERCISE 1-11, page 43*

(a) cupboard	[kəbɚd]	deletion (the [p] is not pronounced, as it is in *cup*)
relevant	[rɛvələnt]	metathesis (the [l] and [v] have been transposed)
incomplete	[ɪŋkəmplit]	assimilation (the nasal has velarized to agree with the [k])
pronounce	[pɚnaʊnts]	metathesis (the [r] and following vowel have been transposed) and epenthesis (a [t] has been inserted between the [n] and [s])

parade [pred]	deletion (the [ə] has been omitted)
warmth [wɔrmpθ]	epenthesis (a [p] has been inserted between the [m] and [θ])
length [lenθ]	assimilation (the [ŋ] has become [n]—that is, has become more like the following [θ] by moving toward the front of the mouth)
once [wəntst]	epenthesis (a [t] has been added between the [n] and [s]) and epithesis (a final [t] has been added)
athlete [æθəlit]	epenthesis (a [ə] has been added between the [θ] and [l])
used to [justə]	deletion (the [d] has been omitted)
dreamt [drɛmpt]	epenthesis (a [p] has been added between the [p] and [t])
suppose [spoz]	deletion (the vowel between the [s] and [p] has been omitted)
horseshoe [horšu]	deletion (the [s] has been omitted)

(b)

Reading	*Connected Conversation*	*Coarticulation Process(es)*
[ɪn maɪ]	[ɪm maɪ]	assimilation
[bɛst we]	[bɛs we]	deletion
[kʊkiz]	[kʊgiz]	assimilation (both [g] and vowels are voiced)
[sɪt daʊn]	[sɪdaʊn]	deletion
[no hɪm]	[nowɪm]	deletion, epenthesis
[nem ɪz]	[nemz]	deletion
[maɪ ædvaɪs]	[maɪjəvaɪs]	deletion, epenthesis
[old mæn]	[olmæn]	deletion
[ɔl raɪt]	[ɔraɪt]	deletion
[ɪnkohɛrənt]	[ɪŋkohɛrənt]	assimilation

✦ *EXERCISE 1-12, page 49*

(a)

[f]:[v]	[voice]
[i]:[ɪ]	[tense]
[i]:[e]	[high]
[w]:[j]	[back]
[l]:[r]	[lateral]
[ʊ]:[ɪ]	[back]

(b) [f], [s], [z], [č]	[+ consonantal], [+ strident]
[l], [n], [w]	[+ sonorant], [+ voice]
[a], [æ]	[+ low]
[t], [θ]	[+ consonantal], [+ anterior], [+ coronal]
[m], [g], [p]	[+ consonantal]
[s], [š]	[+ consonantal], [+ coronal], [+ continuant], [+ strident]

Again, getting the correct answers in this exercise merely requires that you be able to read the feature matrixes. If you made any mistakes, be sure to look at the matrixes again.

✦ *EXERCISE 1-13, page 54*

something	[səmθɪŋ]
history	[hɪstɚi]
French	[frɛnč]
examination	[ɛgzæmɪnešən]
sprightly	[spraɪtli]
arrange	[ərenǰ]
wherever	[wɛrɛvɚ], [hwɛrɛvɚ]
Illinois	[ɪlɪnɔɪ]
Kleenex	[klinɛks]
manual	[mænjuwəl]
alabaster	[æləbæstɚ]
binding	[baɪndɪŋ]
jovial	[jovijəl]
bathroom	[bæθrum]
absolutely*	[æbsəlutli]
desktop	[dɛsktap]
billiards	[bɪljɚdz]
verify*	[vɛrəfaɪ]
midwestern	[mɪdwɛstɚn]
coastal	[kostəl]
revolution*	[rɛvəlušən]
regional	[riǰənəl]
disgusting	[dɪsgəstɪŋ]
tithe	[taɪð]
extensive*	[ɛkstɛnsəv]
bulletin	[bʊlətɪn]
blustery	[bləstɚi]
blanket	[blæŋkɪt]
Wisconsin	[wɪskansɪn]
Indiana	[Indijænə]

hue	[hju]
hounds	[haʊndz]
sideways	[saɪdwez]
conflict	[kanflɪkt]
steering	[stirɪŋ]
mediate	[midijet]
woodpile	[wʊdpaɪl]
opinion	[əpɪnjən]
shoveling	[šəvəlɪŋ]
toiling	[tɔɪlɪŋ]

If you are still having problems remembering which sounds go with which symbols, you simply need to spend more time feeling the sounds as you articulate them and memorizing the consonant and vowel charts given earlier. If, however, you are having trouble hearing the difference between two or more sounds, be sure to ask your teacher for help. Clearing up the problem now will make Chapters 2 and 3 that much easier for you.

✦ *EXERCISE 1-14, page 58*

[supɚkæləfræjəlɪstɪkɛkspijæladošəs]

If you got this one correct, congratulations!

✦ *EXERCISE 1-15, page 58*

If you combine the *-gh* of *rough* ([f]) with the *-o-* of *women* ([ɪ]), and the *-ti-* of *nation* ([š]), the result is *ghoti* ([fɪš]).

✦ *EXERCISE 1-16, page 59*

People who have resisted spelling reform in English have offered several reasons for that resistance. First, such reform would only "correct" the spelling/pronunciation problems of the present day; it would do nothing to change the spelling of the millions of items that have already been published in the current "flawed" system. (This means that users of English would essentially have to learn two spelling systems, which would be burdensome, or that everything already in print would have to be reprinted using the new spelling system, which would be very expensive.) Second, since the pronunciation of English continues to change slowly from generation to generation and since foreign words continue to be added to the language, any new spelling system would probably be outdated relatively quickly. Finally, many people simply believe that tinkering with English spelling would be the wrong thing to do: Such people tend to have strong feelings about "rightness" and "wrongness" in language and bristle at change of any kind.

✦ *EXERCISE 1-17, page 60*

(a) *awry:* instead of being read *a-* + *-wry* ([ə] + [raɪ]), it might be read *aw-* ([ɔ], as in *awful*) + *-ry* ([ri], as in *canary, tawdry,* and lots of other words).

misled: instead of being read *mis-* + *-led* ([mɪs] + [lɛd]), the *-ed* might be read as the past-tense suffix, thus giving [mɪsəld].

democracy: it might be read with the main stress on the first syllable instead of the second (parallel, for example, to *democrat*).

soften: it might be read phonetically rather than as having a "silent *t.*"

Worcester: it might be read phonetically rather than as having only two syllables (with a "silent" medial *-e-*: [wʊstɚ]), especially since the word may be unfamiliar to many Americans and the two-syllable pronunciation tends to be primarily British.

(b) *theater:* the initial *th-* was formerly pronounced as [t].

forehead: it was formerly pronounced [fɔrəd] (which is still used in England) rather than [forhɛd]. Note that the older pronunciation must occur in the once-popular children's rhyme (or the rhyme is broken): "There once was a girl / Who had a little curl / Right in the middle of her forehead. / And when she was good, / She was very, very good. / And when she was bad, / she was horrid."

author: the medial *-th-* was formerly pronounced [t].

habit: the initial *h-* was formerly "silent."

hospital: the initial *h-* was formerly "silent."

✦ *EXERCISE 1-18, page 62*

The speech sounds most affected by a cold, inflexible tongue are naturally those in which the tongue plays a major role in articulation: among the consonants, the alveolars and interdentals, especially, but also the palatals and velars; and among the vowels, nearly all but the central [ə] and [a].

✦ *EXERCISE 1-19, page 62*

(a)

any two nasals	some combination of [m], [n], [ŋ]
any three voiceless fricatives	some combination of [f], [s], [θ], [š], [h]
any two palatals	some combination of [ž], [š], [ǰ], [č], [j]
any two voiceless stops	some combination of [p], [t], [k]
any four nonvocalic sonorants	some combination of [m], [n], [ŋ], [l], [r], [w], [j]
all the sibilants	[z], [s], [ž], [š], [ǰ], [č]
all the bilabials	[b], [p], [m], [w]
all voiced velar sounds	[g], [ŋ]; you may also have listed [r] and [w]
any two nonfricative obstruents	some combination of [b], [p], [d], [t], [g], [k], [ǰ], [č]
all the liquids and glides	[l], [r], [w], [j]
any three front vowels	some combination of [i], [ɪ], [e], [ɛ], [æ]
all the high, back vowels	[u], [ʊ]
all the low vowels	[æ], [a], [ɔ]
all the central vowels	[ə], [a]
any two diphthongs	some combination of [aɪ], [aʊ], [ɔɪ]
all the back vowels	[u], [ʊ], [o], [ɔ]
any three lax vowels	some combination of [ɪ], [ɛ], [æ], [ə], [a], [ʊ], [ɔ]
any two tense vowels	some combination of [i], [e], [u], [o]
all the mid vowels	[e], [ɛ], [ə], [o]
all the diphthongs ending in the high, front portion of the mouth	[aɪ], [ɔɪ]

(b)

[b], [m]	both are voiced bilabials
[t], [f], [s]	all are voiceless
[g], [v], [l]	all are voiced

[l], [n], [t]	all are alveolars
[š], [č]	both are voiceless palatals
[p], [w]	both are bilabials
[θ], [f]	both are voiceless fricatives
[g], [ŋ]	both are voiced velars
[z], [n], [d]	all are voiced alveolars
[r], [s]	both are alveolars
[i], [u]	both are high, tense vowels
[o], [u]	both are back, tense vowels
[e], [i], [u]	all are tense vowels
[a], [æ]	both are low, lax vowels
[ɛ], [ə]	both are mid, lax vowels
[æ], [e], [ɪ]	all are front vowels
[ɛ], [o], [ə]	all are mid vowels
[ə], [a]	both are central, lax vowels
[ɛ], [ɪ]	both are front, lax vowels
[aʊ], [aɪ]	both are diphthongs beginning with the low, central vowel and ending in a high, lax vowel

✦ *EXERCISE 1-20, page 64*

(a)

ambidextrous	12	[æmbədɛkstrəs]
calamity	8	[kəlæmədi]
federated	8	[fɛdɚedɪd]
gargantuan	11	[gɔrgænčuwən]
jambalaya	9	[ǰambəlaja]
kalamazoo	8	[kæləməzu]
monstrous	8	[manstrəs]
perceptibly	10	[pɚsɛptəbli]
sagaciously	9	[səgešɪsli]
victimized	10	[vɪktəmaɪzd]

(b) Students typically take courses in linguistics for one of three reasons: Sometimes such courses fulfill requirements established by the state for teacher certification; other times the courses fulfill a particular English department requirement; and still other times students take the courses just out of curiosity.

✦ *EXERCISE 1-21, page 66*

(a) For the woman to misunderstand the man, she would have to ignore the stress, juncture, and intonation of his statement. In "You look like Helen Brown," there is no juncture between the two syllables of *Helen;* but a definite juncture exists between *hell* and *in* in "You look like hell in Brown." And the *hell* of the second sentence would be stressed, unlike the first syllable of *Helen* in the first sentence. Finally, the extra stress on *hell* would cause the sentence intonation to rise at that point, so that *hell in* would be pronounced with a high-to-low pattern; but in *Helen,* the pattern would be low-to-high.

(b) For the second man to misunderstand the first, he would have to mistake the stress pattern of *misery* (emphasis on the first syllable) with that of *Missouri* (emphasis on the second syllable). Both men, of course, would also have to pronounce *Missouri* with a final [i] rather than a final [ə] (both pronunciations are common).

(c) The primary difference between *ATLASTA MOTEL* and "At last! A Motel!" (which a weary driver might well proclaim) is in juncture: The name of the motel would be spoken with no juncture; the weary driver's proclamation would be spoken with a large juncture between *last* and *a*.

✦ *EXERCISE 1-22, page 67*

(a) The transcription probably more nearly reflects a connected conversation pronunciation.

(b) Most of the changes would come in the representation of the vowels. Vowels in connected conversation pronunciations tend to move toward the center of the mouth.

✦ *EXERCISE 1-23, page 67*

would of (*instead of* would have): The student is probably hearing not *would have* ([wʊd hæv]) but the contraction *would've* (with the *h*- deleted and the vowel changed from [æ] to [ə]). The resulting broad phonetic representation is identical to that for *would of* ([wʊd əv]).

pitcher (*instead of* picture): The student is probably deleting the medial [k] of *picture* ([pɪkčɚ]), and the result is identical to the broad phonetic transcription of *pitcher* ([pɪčɚ]).

alot (*instead of* a lot): The student is probably just misanalyzing the two-word construction *a lot* as a single word, *alot.* The broad phonetic representations of the two constructions are identical (there is no juncture between spoken *a* and *lot* that corresponds to the space between written *a* and *lot*), as is the adverbial function of each in sentences.

good riddens (*instead of* good riddance): The student is probably deleting the [t] from *riddance* ([rɪdənts]), and the [s] then assimilates to the [d] in voicing (that is, the voiceless [s] is becoming a voiced [z]). The resulting transcription ([rɪdənz]) is then spelled *riddens.*

coulda (*instead of* could have): As with *would of,* discussed earlier in this exercise, the student is probably hearing not *could have* ([kʊd hæv]) but the contraction *could've* (with the *h-* deleted and the vowel changed from [æ] to [ə]). The resulting broad phonetic representation is ([kʊd əv]). But then, as frequently happens in connected conversation pronunciation, the final [v] is deleted, and the student writes *coulda* instead of *could have* or *could've.*

somethin (*instead of* something): in connected conversation pronunciation, the final velar nasal is frequently replaced with the alveolar nasal (especially if the initial sound in the following word is pronounced nearer the front than the back of the mouth); thus, the student hears [səmθɪn] and writes *somethin.*

complain to (*instead of* complained to): Because *complained* ends in an alveolar stop and *to* begins with an alveolar stop, the two are coarticulated (which means that the first one is deleted: [kəmplentu]). Since the student does not hear the *-ed* on *complained,* he or she does not spell it, either.

drownded (*instead of* drowned): If the student's pronunciation of *drown* includes a final *-d* ([draʊnd], which is an example of epithesis) and that pronunciation is made past tense with the addition of *-ed,* then the resulting *drownded* ([draʊndəd], in which the medial [d] is now an example of epenthesis) is unavoidable.

✦ *EXERCISE 1-24, page 69*

(a) In general, babies learning to speak English tend to acquire their consonant sounds "from the front of the mouth to the back" (that is, bilabials first, labiodentals next, and velars only later); and they acquire their vowels "from the bottom of the mouth to the top" (that is, low vowels first and high vowels last).

(b) You would have to explain that, rather than pronouncing the sounds with the top teeth against the outside of the bottom lip, the tip of the tongue must be placed between the front teeth. In both pronunciations, the airstream tends to exit the mouth from the corners rather than the middle.

✦ *EXERCISE 1-25, page 70*

(a) [i] most often tends to be associated with lightness, airiness, and perhaps happiness and [ə], with heaviness, darkness, and perhaps clumsiness. As to why this is the case, no one knows for sure; but maybe the reason has to do with [i] being pronounced on a generally higher (and thus "lighter"?) pitch than [ə].

(b) Many people associate the initial [sl] with feelings of sleaziness, sliminess, wetness, and the like—probably because words such as *slease* and *slime* begin with [sl].

(c) Many people associate the final [əmp] with feelings of clumsiness, heaviness, and the like—perhaps because words such as *bump, dump, lump,* and others end in [əmp].

(d) People almost uniformly associate *loomalah* with the rounded figure and *kratchak* with the squared off-figure, explaining that the sonorants of *loomalah* sound "more flowing and rounded" than the "harsh, angular" obstruents of *kratchak.*

✦ *EXERCISE 1-26, page 72*

England has one standard spoken dialect, which the royal family, the upper class, the BBC, and all members of parliament are expected to use in formal, public contexts. But the United States (in spite of having a standard *written* dialect) does *not* have just one standard spoken dialect; rather, it has several standard spoken dialects, depending on the speaker's geographic origins, socioeconomic class, and so forth. For this reason, no U.S. president would probably ever have to take speech lessons before he or she were inaugurated. (However, the United States *does* have a dialect that is typically accorded more prestige than other dialects. It is sometimes referred to as "newscaster English"—since most television journalists use it—and can be heard throughout a large part of the Midwest.) In fact, many presidents have used their diverse dialects to their advantage: Kennedy's New England accent was often perceived as charismatic; Johnson's Texan accent was regarded as sincere and heartfelt; Gerald Ford's accent was thought of as straightforward and businesslike (which were necessary attributes for a Republican following the Watergate scandal); Carter's southern accent was heard as hospitable and friendly; and Clinton's Arkansan accent is regarded as "down-home."

✦ *EXERCISE 1-27, page 72*

Several separate but related forces may be at work here. First, such eye-dialect spellings violate what we expect to see on the printed page and so are perceived as nonstandard or wrong. Second, eye-dialect spellings usually reflect connected conversation pronunciations, which, when spelled out, violate the rules of standard written English. Third, many if not most people are unaware of what they sound like when they speak and so regard pronunciations such as [fɚ] for *for* as somehow deviant (and therefore wrong). And finally, linguistic research of the past 40 years has shown that, while nearly all speakers use words such as *gonna* and *workin',* members of the lower classes do tend to use them more often than members of the upper classes. (In other words, the association in readers' minds is not entirely wrong, especially if it is based on tendencies rather than absolutes.)

✦ *EXERCISE 1-28, page 73*

It is difficult to say *any* long sequence of words very quickly—the brain gets ahead of the mouth, the vocal apparatus wants to coarticulate consecutive sounds, and so on—and that difficulty is magnified when one or two sounds keep repeating themselves. Tongue-twisters are even more difficult when two similar sounds alternate, as with the [s] and [š] in the famous "Sally sold seashells at the seashore . . ."

✦ *EXERCISE 1-29, page 74*

Of course it would be possible for a language to convey meaning with no reliance on phonetics. The most obvious example would be when deaf people use American Sign Language to communicate. But much of what we all communicate on a daily basis is done not with sounds but with kinesics (body language, including eye and hand movements), proxemics (how close in distance you are to the person you are communicating with), haptics (how and whether you touch the person you are communicating with), and so forth.

✦ *EXERCISE 1-30, page 74*

No answer is given here because students' selections of poems will be individualistic. Answers should be evaluated according to how well they address the author's purposeful use of phonetics to enhance meaning.

✦ *EXERCISE 2-1, page 79*

(a) A distinctly different [t] occurs in each of the five words. In *time,* the [t] is pronounced with a great deal of aspiration; in *cat,* the [t] tends to be pronounced with no aspiration at all (it is *unreleased*); in *mitten,* the articulation of the [t] is achieved without the tip of the tongue touching the alveolar ridge (thus making it more of a glottal than an alveolar sound); in *butter,* the [t] becomes voiced as the tip of the tongue flaps up against the alveolar ridge; and in *stop,* the [t] is pronounced with the tip of the tongue on the alveolar ridge and a quantity of aspiration approximately midway between that necessary for *time* and *cat.*

(b) The [t] in *time* occurs at the beginning of a syllable (or one-syllable word), and the next sound is the diphthong /aɪ/. The [t] in *cat* occurs at the end of a syllable (or one-syllable word), and the preceding sound is a vowel, /æ/. The [t] in *mitten* occurs in the middle of a two-syllable word and is preceded by a stressed vowel, /ɪ/, and followed by an unstressed vowel, /ə/, and /n/ (or, in narrow transcription, a *syllabic* /n/). The [t] in *butter* occurs in the middle of a two-syllable word and is preceded by a stressed vowel, /ə/ and followed by an unstressed r-colored schwa, /ɚ/. And the [t] in *stop* occurs in the middle of a syllable (or one-syllable word) and is preceded by /s/ and followed by a vowel, /a/.

(c) Figure 2-1 *is* a good representation of the relationship between /t/ and its various phones, since it shows that the phoneme branches into each of the five phones when it occurs in different phonetic environments. In other words, /t/ is the category from which the five [t]'s are derived.

(d) These linguists must be assuming that the phone [D] is a member of /t/ as well as /d/.

✦ *EXERCISE 2-2, page 82*

(a) [b] and [p] are both bilabial stops; they vary only in voicing.

(b) [s], [θ], [z], and [ð] are all fricatives—the first two voiceless, the second two voiced; the sounds in each pair vary only in place of articulation ([s] and [z] are alveolars; [θ] and [ð] are interdentals).

(c) [l] and [r] are both voiced, alveolar liquids.

(d) [b] and [β] are both voiced and bilabial; they vary only in manner of articulation.

✦ *EXERCISE 2-3, page 83*

(a) Yes, the same pattern of greater aspiration with initial [k] and lesser aspiration with medial [k] holds for the [k]'s in each of these words. And yes, the same pattern holds for the initial and medial allophones of /p/ and /t/. One single descriptive statement that captures the various patterns is this: When a voiceless stop occurs initially, it will have more aspiration than when it occurs medially. (If you wrote a statement like that one for each of the phonemes /p/, /t/, and /k/ or if you listed /p/, /t/, and /k/ separately rather than referring to them as *voiceless stops,* you did not capture the fact that they all are members of the same class of sounds—an important generalization.)

(b) Yes, all these words contradict the statement written for (a) above, since each word in the list contains a medial voiceless stop that is as heavily aspirated as initial voiceless stops. Additionally, *compute* contains a final (as opposed to medial) voiceless stop that also has less aspiration than initial voiceless stops. But the original statement can be modified to include both of these facts, as follows: When a voiceless stop occurs at the beginning of a syllable, it will have more aspiration than when it occurs elsewhere.

(c) The difference between these words and those listed in part (b) is where the primary stress of the word falls: In those from (b), the primary stress follows the voiceless stop; in these, primary stress precedes the voiceless stop. So the descriptive statement from (b) would have to be further modified as follows: When a voiceless stop occurs at the beginning of a syllable that contains a stressed vowel, it will have more aspiration than when it occurs elsewhere.

✦ *EXERCISE 2-4, page 85*

(a) The allophones of /l/ are [l] and [ɫ], and they are in complementary distribution, since each occurs in a phonetic environment different from the other (which would not be the case if they were in free variation). The allophones' phonetic environments are as follows: [ɫ] occurs following a vowel unless the /l/ begins a syllable; [l] occurs elsewhere (that is, initially, following a consonant, and following a vowel if the /l/ begins a syllable).

(b) The two pronunciations must stem from /u/ and /ju/. If there were one just phoneme, /u/, with the two allophones [u] and [ju], then the difference between [u] and [ju] would be simply phonetic (that is, would be one merely of pronunciation and not meaning). But the difference between the two variants is phonemic, since /j/ is a phoneme in its own right, and, in fact, there is a difference in meaning between /ju/ and /u/ (not in *due, news,* or *Tuesday* but in the minimal pair *ooh* /u/ and *you* /ju/). The phonetic environment in which both /u/ and /ju/ occur is immediately following a nonliquid alveolar sound.

(c) The phonetic environment is immediately preceding a nasal sound. Nasalization and nonnasalization occur in complementary distribution, since nasalization occurs only if the vowel precedes a nasal and nonnasalization occurs everywhere else. (In other words, the two phenomena occur in patterned, mutually exclusive environments.)

(d) [əɪ] and [əʊ] occur only immediately before voiceless sounds; [aɪ] and [aʊ] occur elsewhere (that is, finally and immediately before voiced sounds). Since the two sets of diphthongs do not occur in the same phonetic environments, they must be in complementary distribution.

(e) It is impossible for phonemes to occur in complementary distribution, since, by definition, they must be contrastable in minimal pairs. Consider the two phonemes /t/ and /k/, for example. If they were in complementary distribution and occurred only in nonoverlapping phonetic environments, then minimal pairs such as *cot* and *tot* could not be formed.

✦ *EXERCISE 2-5, page 89*

Yes, the suprasegmentals stress, juncture, intonation, and tone are phonemic, since their various uses are responsible for changes of meaning in the segmental sounds with which they occur.

✦ *EXERCISE 2-6, page 92*

(a) See the table on page 217.

Syllable	***Phonemic Transcription***	***Consonant/Vowel Sequence***
weird	/wird/	C V C C
lumps	/ləmps/	C V C C C
-ry	/ri/	C V
-tion	/šən/	C V C
pre-	/pri/	C C V
frame	/frem/	C C V C
stride	/straɪd	C C C V C
elves	/ɛlvz/	V C C C
side	/saɪd/	C V C
cloud	/klaʊd/	C C V C
oh	/o/	V
bulk	/bəlk/	C V C C
streaks	/striks/	C C C V C C
craft	/kræft/	C C V C C
them	/ðɛm/	C V C
quartz	/kwɔrts/	C C V C C C
twelfth	/twɛlfθ/	C C V C C C
time	/taɪm/	C V C
bold	/bold/	C V C C
search	/sɚč/	C V C C

(b) The word I gave you the hint for is *strengths* (/strɛŋkθs/; C C C V C C C C). If you can think of any others, please let me know.

(c) To allow for the option of a second vowel phoneme following immediately after the first, the formula would have had to look like this:

(C)(C)(C)V(V)(C)(C)(C)(C)

If you enclosed the first rather than the second *V* in parentheses, your answer is still correct; it does not matter which vowel phoneme is considered mandatory and which is considered optional.

(d) Every phoneme in English can begin an English syllable except one—/ŋ/. In fact, the reason that the made-up word from several pages ago, *ngobngoboo,* sounded so odd is that /ŋ/ is initial in the first two syllables. (This constraint does not exist in all languages, however. In Italian, for example, words beginning with /ŋ/ are fairly common.)

✦ *EXERCISE 2-7, page 94*

(a) Some of the C-C clusters that I have listed occur in words that were either borrowed (*shtick,* 1959) or created (*vroom,* 1965) after Hill's book was published. One other (*sferics*) is largely a scientific term and still does not occur in many standard desktop dictionaries. Or perhaps the author of the other book was not taking into account obvious borrowings from other languages at all (*shlep, bwana, mridanga*). These reasons could account for all the discrepancies except the omission from the other book of /vj/, /mj/, and /nj/, which begin words (*view, mew, news*) that are neither new to the language nor recently borrowed. I cannot explain why /vj/, /mj/, and /nj/ were left out. (If the other author discounted clusters that occur only in certain English dialects—/nj/, for example—then why did he not also exclude /tj/, /dj/, /sj/, and /hw/?)

(b) /sh/ systematic gap
/pt/ systematic gap
/gj/ accidental gap
/kk/ systematic gap
/fw/ accidental gap
/ds/ systematic gap
/θl/ accidental gap
/zg/ systematic gap

/ps/ systematic gap
/df/ systematic gap

(c) /ps/ violates the phonotactic constraints of English and so could never be pronounced initially in a word; instead, the /p/ became silent, leaving just the /s/.

(d) Yes, the phonotactic constraints of a language can change. They are, after all, part of the language, and languages change constantly. Whether initial /ts/ will ever be viewed as *accounted for* rather than *an exception* in English remains to be seen, but it may be worth noting that at least two other terms with initial /ts/ have entered the language since *tsetse* in 1849—*tsunami* (1907) and *tsutsugamushi* (1917).

(e) I could not think of any others. If you can, please let me know.

(f) The eight C-C-C clusters that occur initially in English are /str/ (*strike*), /spr/ (*spray*), /skr/ /*scrape*), /spl/ (*splash*), /skl/ (*sclerosis*), /spj/ (*spew*), /skj/ (*skew*), and /skw/ (*square*). One way to write the descriptive statement is like this: In C-C-C clusters occurring initially in English, the first phoneme is always /s/ (or the voiceless alveolar fricative), the second is always a voiceless stop, and the third is always a liquid or a glide. (If you tried to count among the eight consonant clusters the initial sequences in words such as *school, three,* and *shrink,* you were paying attention to the spellings of the words rather than to the sounds they represent: *school, three,* and *shrink* each begin with three letters but only two sounds.) We know that it is impossible for C-C-C-C clusters to occur initially in English because the description of syllable structure discussed earlier stated that the maximum number of consonant sounds beginning any syllable (and therefore any word) is three.

✦ *EXERCISE 2-8, page 99*

The nine final C-C-C-C clusters in English that I know of are /ksts/ (*texts*), /rldz/ (*worlds*), /ŋkθs/ (*lengths*), /rsts/ (*bursts*), /ksθs/ (*sixths*), /lkts/ (*mulcts*), /mpts/ (*prompts*), /ŋkst/ (*angst*), and /ntst/ (*fenced*). If you can think of any others, please let me know. One descriptive statement of what kinds of phonemes occur in each of the four positions is: In C-C-C-C clusters occurring finally in English, the first consonant is always either a liquid, a nasal, or /k/; the second consonant is a voiceless stop, /s/, or /l/; the third consonant is an alveolar stop, /s/, or /θ/; and the fourth consonant is an alveolar fricative or /t/.

✦ *EXERCISE 2-9, page 102*

(a) Using the first method of linguistic notation would produce:

/l/ → [ɫ] / V ___ unless # /l/

(b) Using the first method of linguistic notation would produce:

V → Ṽ / ___ nasal

(It is not necessary to specify *bilabial, alveolar,* or *velar* in front of *nasal,* since the occurrence of all three nasals—the only three in English—cause the preceding vowel to become nasalized.)

✦ *EXERCISE 2-10, page 104*

(a) This change represents the process of assimilation, in which one sound is influenced in pronunciation by another sound or sounds near it.

(b) Considering all the words that exist in the English language, it would never be safe to generalize from a list of only 20. In words such as *incoherent,* for example, the nasal is alveolar (for most speakers) unless a connected conversation pronunciation is used; and in words such as *empty,* a connected conversation pronunciation may eliminate the /p/, which leaves a bilabial nasal followed by an alveolar stop. But the rule can be modified to handle all such exceptions in at least two ways: We can either restrict the rule to the 20 words in the list or modify the end of the rule so that it reads: . . . the two sounds will *tend to* have the same place of articulation. The second alternative would be better, since it allows the rule to remain useful for the entire language rather than just a small portion of it.

(c) Literally thousands of examples exist; the clusters in the following words represent just a few: *fast, old, trip, belt, drain, cars, mats, card.*

✦ *EXERCISE 2-11, page 108*

(a) One way to write the rule is like this: When /s/ is added to a word, the allophone [əz] occurs if the sound immediately preceding /s/ is a sibilant; the allophone [s] occurs if that sound is any other voiceless consonant; and the allophone [z] occurs if that sound is any other voiced consonant.

(b) The words I chose are *Jimmy, way, shoe, flow, saw, sofa, cow, toy,* and *sigh;* the allophone that occurs after each is [z]. To accommodate these words, the rule from part (a) could be changed as follows: . . . and the allophone [z] occurs if that sound is any other voiced consonant or a vowel.

(c) The rule can now be rewritten like this: . . . and the allophone [z] occurs if that sound is any other voiced sound.

✦ *EXERCISE 2-12, page 110*

(a) The /t/ in skeleton does not *immediately* follow the main stress of the word.

(b) Words like *rotten, cotton, mitten, bitten, batten,* and *gluten* uniformly end in [ən]. (In narrow transcription, this would be symbolized [n] and called *syllabic /n̩/.*) The rule could be modified to account for such words like this: When /t/ occurs intervocalically and immediately follows the main stress of the word, [d] occurs unless the following syllable is [ən].

(c) Yes, the same rule that predicts [D] as an allophone of /t/ also suffices to predict [D] as an allophone of /d/. The final version of the rule—the one that accounts for the medial occurrence of [D] as an allophone of either /t/ or /d/—would therefore look like this: When /t/ or /d/ occurs intervocalically and immediately follows the main stress of the word, [D] occurs unless the following syllable is [ən]. (You could also substitute *alveolar stops* for */t/ or /d/.*) You should know, however, that traditional phonemics usually prohibits the same allophone from being assigned to two different phonemes (which is, and rightly so, more of a problem for traditional phonemics than for students trying to learn the structure of English).

✦ *EXERCISE 2-13, page 114*

(a) Yes, it is possible to extend the last claim to velars and palatals. All you have to do is substitute new words into the appropriate places in the word groups given earlier (or, alternatively, create new word groups) and then note that the relative lengths of the vowels have gone unchanged. Of course these new words will have to have "/V/ + consonant" sequences, and the consonants will have to vary from the consonants in the words they are replacing only in place of articulation. For example, you could replace *hit* with *hick* in *hit/his/hiss/hid,* since the /k/ and /t/ are both voiceless stops, but one is an alveolar and the other a velar. Similarly, you could replace *led* in *less/let/led* with *leg,* since the /d/ and /g/ are both voiced stops, but one is an alveolar and the other a velar. Or again, you could create a new word group, such as *wish/wit/wig/whiz,* and note that the relative vowel lengths are 2/1/3/4—just what would be expected, given the pattern you established.

(b) Essentially, the patterns established can be generalized to words of any length, as long as the /V/ and following consonant are in the same syllable. Notice, for example, the relative lengths of the boldfaced /V/'s in groups of words such as *er**a**se/ber**a**te/sash**ay**s/repl**ay**ed* (2/1/4/3) and *repr**i**sal/pr**i**de/l**i**ghtning/sh**y**ster* (4/3/1/2).

(c) This would be one way to do it: /V/ becomes longer when followed immediately by a voiced and/or fricative consonant in the same syllable (though voicing promotes greater length than frication) than when followed by a voiceless and/or stop consonant.

✦ *EXERCISE 2-14, page 118*

(a) The consonant clusters in *obtuse* and *birdhouse* are both split by syllable boundaries (/ab#tus/ and /bɚd#haʊs/); thus, to account for them, the rule would have to read: Clusters of obstruents *in the same syllable* agree in voicing.

(b) To arrive at this answer, you first have to notice what the various clusters have in common: (1) they occur finally; (2) the last sound in each is a stop; and (3) it is always the last sound in the cluster—the stop—that is deleted. (The fact that each is preceded by a vowel is unimportant, since a vowel must precede *every* final consonant cluster.) It then becomes a matter of incorporating these facts into a rule, thus: When a consonant cluster occurs finally and ends with a stop, that stop may be deleted. (If we added the other information given in the problem, the rule would end: . . . if the following word begins with a consonant close in place of articulation to the stop.)

✦ *EXERCISE 2-15, page 120*

The key here is realizing which of these phonological processes *sometimes* occur and which *always* or *must* occur. The former are optional; the latter, obligatory.

(a) Optional (because the /t/ *can* be voiceless and frequently is when the words are read)

(b) Optional (again, the /l/ *can* be articulated as a true alveolar sound)

(c) Optional (if such raising were obligatory, it would occur in all dialects)

(d) Obligatory (syllables pronounced otherwise simply are not English)

(e) Obligatory (or the meaning changes to "presidential mansion")

(f) Optional (*all* speakers do not do this, and those who do usually do it only some of the time)

(g) Obligatory (it is nearly impossible *not* to do this when we speak)

(h) Optional (only some speakers do it this way)

(i) Optional (this usually occurs only in connected conversation pronunciation)

(j) Optional (because they are sometimes pronounced with various amounts of aspiration)

✦ *EXERCISE 2-16, page 122*

(a) An obstruent is deleted when it occurs at the end of a word.

(b) /d/ becomes nasalized when it occurs immediately preceding a nasal.

(c)

$$\begin{bmatrix} -\text{vocalic} \\ +\text{consonantal} \\ -\text{sonorant} \\ -\text{nasal} \\ +\text{anterior} \\ +\text{coronal} \\ -\text{continuant} \\ -\text{delayed release} \\ -\text{voice} \end{bmatrix} \;\#\# + \#\#\; \begin{bmatrix} -\text{syllabic} \\ -\text{consonantal} \\ +\text{sonorant} \\ -\text{vocalic} \\ -\text{back} \end{bmatrix} \rightarrow \begin{bmatrix} +\text{delayed release} \\ -\text{voice} \end{bmatrix}$$

(The /_____ notation cannot be used here since / ____ ## ## ____ would stipulate that the sequence /t/ + /j/ would occur twice—once at the beginning of the word and once at the end of the word.)

(d)

$$\emptyset \rightarrow \begin{bmatrix} -\text{vocalic} \\ +\text{reduced} \end{bmatrix} \; / \; \begin{bmatrix} +\text{consonantal} \\ -\text{sonorant} \\ -\text{nasal} \\ -\text{continuant} \\ +\text{voice} \end{bmatrix} \; \underline{\quad\quad} \; \#\#$$

(In this instance, Ø is necessary to indicate the absence of something that is later inserted.)

✦ *EXERCISE 2-17, page 126*

(a) To answer this question, you must simply work through the rules for each of the words. Having done that, you will see that the rules do not work for *follow, escrow, treetop, veranda,* and *consensus.*

(b) Again, you must work through and understand the rules to be able to do this.

maintain (verb)—The final vowel sound is tense, so it receives the main stress.

collapse (verb)—The final vowel sound is followed by two consonant sounds, so it receives the main stress.

personal (adjective)—The suffix contains a lax vowel, so the rule for nouns is followed. The final syllable is disregarded before following the rule for verbs; then, since the remainder of the word, *person,* neither ends in a tense vowel sound nor two or more consonant sounds, the main stress goes on the penultimate syllable, *per-*.

supreme (adjective)—The word does not end in a suffix having a lax vowel, so the rule for verbs is followed. Since the final vowel sound is tense, it receives the main stress.

cinema (noun)—The final syllable contains a lax vowel and therefore is disregarded before the rule for verbs is followed. After the final syllable is disregarded, the remainder of the word, *cine-*, neither ends in a tense vowel sound nor two or more consonant sounds; thus, the main stress goes on the penultimate syllable, *ci-*.

police (noun)—The final syllable does not contain a lax vowel, so the rule for verbs is followed with the entire word intact; and since the final vowel sound is tense, it receives the main stress. (Notice, however, that in some dialects of English speakers stress *po-* rather than *-lice*.)

(c) In each of these words, the various rules place the stress exactly two syllables to the right of where it should be, as follows: *insinuáte, solidifý, extrapoláte, hypotenúse, asterísk, formaldehýde, guillotíne, pedigrée.* One way to write a rule describing what must be done to the main stress of each word to make it "correct" is this: In any sequence of three syllables (regardless of what precedes and/or follows the sequence) in which the main stress of the word falls on the third syllable, shift the stress to the first syllable of the sequence. This rule is necessary for only some multisyllabic words, since it is fairly easy to think of examples—*vigilante, halitosis, hippocratic,* and so forth—where the rule should not apply. Rules such as this one are called *optional rules* (because they describe optional phonological processes) and contrast with the three *obligatory rules* (because they describe obligatory phonological processes) given earlier.

(d) The order in which the two rules apply *is* important. The first, obligatory set of rules produces a main stress that the second, optional rule needs before it can apply. (In other words, the optional rule *could not* operate before the mandatory rule in this problem.) In situations where more than one rule must apply to achieve a desired result, the rules are almost always ordered in some way; random ordering is very rare.

✦ *EXERCISE 2-18, page 129*

Since the initial sounds or sound sequences of two of the words in each phrase have been transposed, the implication is that the brain plans phonological sequences well before the vocal apparatus actually articulates them. In *my com the mop,* for example, the brain must be planning the /k/ of *cop* when the vocal apparatus is still in the process of articulating *mom.*

✦ *EXERCISE 2-19, page 130*

There are many ways of describing what must happen to the original to produce the "Pig Latin" version. Here is one: The initial sound of each syllable, if that sound is a consonant, is moved to the end of the syllable and followed with *-ay*. If the initial sound of the syllable is a vowel, however, it remains syllable initial and the syllable is merely followed with *-ay*.

✦ *EXERCISE 2-20, page 130*

(a) Many possible answers exist for each pair of sounds; following are just the ones I happened to think of. The important things to look for in your answers are (1) that the sounds in question actually occur initially, medially, or finally and (2) that the words you chose are actually minimal pairs—that is, that they vary only by the sounds in question. (This will vary from dialect to dialect.)

/s/ and /z/	*sue/zoo; fussy/fuzzy; Bruce/bruise*
/p/ and /v/	*pile/vile; leaping/leaving; rope/rove*
/m/ and /n/	*moon/noon; simmer/sinner; dumb/done*
/l/ and /r/	*low/row; bowled/bored; pole/pour*
/g/ and /k/	*gold/cold; boogie/bookie; rig/Rick*

(b) /t/, /d/, /s/, and /z/ are frequently palatalized as /č/, /j/, /š/, and /ž/ in connected conversation pronunciations when they occur at the end of a word and the following word begins with a palatal glide.

✦ *EXERCISE 2-21, page 131*

The three voiced allophones occurred only when their respective phonemes were in voiced phonetic environments (between some combination of vowels and voiced consonants); the three voiceless allophones occurred elsewhere (initially, finally, and when at least either the preceding or following sound was voiceless).

✦ *EXERCISE 2-22, page 132*

Veni, vidi, vici ("I came, I saw, I conquered")—The initial sound in each word is /v/; the second sound in each word is a front, tense vowel; the third sound in each word is an alveolar; and the final sound in each word is /i/. (Notice that most of the phonological cohesion is lost in the translation.)

Sally sold seashells by the seashore—Of the six initial sounds, four are /s/; in those /s/-initial words, /š/ occurs medially twice, /l/ occurs medially three times (and the other liquid, /r/, occurs finally once), and /i/ repeats three times (once finally and twice following /s/); and the three two-syllable words all have the main stress on their first syllables. (If you mentioned nothing about stress in your answer, you may have forgotten that phonology includes suprasegmentals as well as segmentals.)

We will meet or beat any price—Of the six vowels, five are front (and the diphthong has a front component); the sound /w/ occurs twice in succession; all of the words that begin with consonant sounds (five of the seven) are bilabial-initial; in the sequence *meet or beat,* the first and last words constitute a minimal pair; and the fact that six of the seven words are short and monosyllabic causes the stress pattern of the phrase to be somewhat choppy.

I like Ike—The diphthong /aɪ/ occurs once in each word (to the exclusion of any other vowel or diphthong); *like* and *Ike* constitute a minimal pair; and all the words are brief and monosyllabic, which (especially with the final /k/'s of *like* and *Ike*) causes the stress pattern of the phrase to appear very staccato.

Tippecanoe and Tyler, too—Three of the four words begin with /t/ (and of 10 consonant sounds, 6 are stops); the final /u/'s of *Tippecanoe* and *too* cause a rhyme; and the final six syllables of the phrase have an iambic stress pattern. (That is, unstressed and stressed syllables alternate, with an unstressed syllable beginning the sequence.)

✦ *EXERCISE 2-23, page 133*

The rules must be ordered, with the "raising rule" occurring first. If the "flapping rule" were to occur first, the /t/ following the diphthong would become [D], a voiced sound, and the raising rule would then be blocked. (It can operate only when the diphthong is followed by a voiceless sound.)

✦ *EXERCISE 2-24, page 134*

You could write the rule many ways, one of which is: In the Great Vowel Shift, long vowels were raised one place of articulation in the mouth (and /a:/ was also fronted), and vowels that could not be raised (that is, vowels that were pronounced as high in the mouth as possible) became diphthongs.

✦ *EXERCISE 2-25, page 135*

The possible answers to this question are numerous. All of the rules formulated in this book are *descriptive,* and probably most of the rules you learned in elementary and secondary English classes were *prescriptive.* The important difference between the two kinds of rules is that descriptive rules merely give an objective account of linguistic behavior, and prescriptive rules attempt to (subjectively) legislate linguistic behavior.

✦ *EXERCISE 2-26, page 136*

Three kinds of nonarticulatory reasons are frequently offered for phonological change (or any kind of change) in a language:

1. If one language comes into contact with another (as through invasions, migrations, wars, and the like) and the speakers of the two languages mix sufficiently (as through marriage), the two languages will almost always influence one another. Some sounds will be poorly copied, others may be borrowed outright, and still others may cease to be used. Some of the best examples of such influence on English phonology resulted from the Scandinavian raids of the ninth, tenth, and eleventh centuries (when the sound sequence /sk/, as in *skirt,* was adopted) and the Norman Conquest in 1066 (when numerous sound changes occurred, among them the addition of /f/, /s/, and /θ/ to the phonemic inventory).
2. Succeeding generations of children are known to have an impact on phonological change, usually because each generation perceives which sounds are prestigious or stigmatized differently from earlier generations. (In the late twentieth century, for example, many young speakers who were upwardly mobile attached some prestige to the use of /æ/ as the first element of the diphthong [aʊ] in words such as *round* and *house.*)
3. The socioeconomic class structure of societies is known to be responsible for phonological change, simply because different classes of people speak different dialects. The following progression of events has been shown to occur:

   Stage 1—People are stratified into socioeconomic classes, and each class uses a distinct variety of English.

   Stage 2—Each class's linguistic variants are accorded a level of prestige consistent with the social class of their users, resulting in both prestige and stigmatized variants.

   Stage 3—The younger members, especially, of the lower-middle class, because of their great linguistic insecurity and their desire to be associated with the prestige variety rather than the stigmatized variety of the language, begin to imitate and eventually adapt to the upper-class's speech forms.

Stage 4—The upper class, over time, perceives the linguistic shifts of the lower-middle class, and because the upper class wishes to maintain the present system of social stratification—a part of which is the corollary linguistic stratification—its speakers gradually adopt a new series of speech variants, which quickly become labeled *prestige*.

Stage 5—People are still stratified into socioeconomic classes, and each class still uses a distinct variety of English (as in Stage 1), but those speech varieties have changed.

When the number of allowable variants associated with a particular speech variable is very few, the result of several generational cycles of these five stages can produce interesting results. For example, postvocalic /r/ has only two variants—it is either pronounced or not—and the last 350 years of linguistic history in England show that each variant has alternately been accorded great prestige and great stigma. The cycle is vicious and probably perpetual.

✦ *EXERCISE 2-27, page 136*

Each of these rules could be written in a number of ways. Check your answers for both correctness and conciseness.

(a) Final, voiced stops are devoiced in stressed syllables. (From the data given, you may have specified that the devoicing occurs in one-syllable words.)

(b) Postvocalic liquids are deleted if they are followed immediately by a consonant sound or occur finally. (Notice that the phrase *postvocalic liquids* automatically implies that the liquids occur medially or finally.)

(c) /θ/ occurs as [f] unless the /θ/ is initial and the next sound is anything but /r/, in which case it occurs as [t].

✦ *EXERCISE 2-28, page 138*

The statements are, unfortunately, true. Phonological structure *must* be random, since language is, by definition, randomly symbolic. That being the case, it makes no sense to claim that one variety of the language is inherently better or worse than any other. (For example, *am not* may be held in higher regard than *ain't,* but it certainly is not objectively better than *ain't.*) In fact, the levels of prestige that are attached to the various dialects of English occur as they do purely through accidents of sociocultural history. (For example, if, in American culture, the group of people who speak the dialect known as Black English were generally held in higher regard, so would their dialect be held in higher regard.) It may not be fair, but it is true: Speaking certain ways in the United States (and many other countries) will get some people the job, the promotion, the pay raise, or whatever; and speaking certain different ways will hold other people back.

✦ *EXERCISE 2-29, page 139*

A *phonemic transcription* records only the broad categories of sound that occur sequentially in a word, whereas a *phonetic transcription* records the actual sounds themselves. Since phonetic transcriptions can range from very broad to very narrow, varying levels of phonetic detail can be recorded, from only the basic segmental sounds to every articulatory feature of speech. (While the broadest of phonetic transcriptions may look very similar to phonemic transcriptions—except for the use of square brackets or virgules, the same segmental IPA characters are used—they convey different sorts of information nonetheless.)

✦ *EXERCISE 2-30, page 139*

The acquisition of a language by a newborn child represents one of the great mysteries of human maturation. Seemingly without effort or formal instruction, the child acquires language by a very early age. (Most five-year-olds can carry on fairly complex conversations.) The only requirements that must be met are that he or she be of at least minimally average intelligence (children with Down syndrome typically have some problems with language acquisition) and be raised in a verbal environment (that is, the child must hear language spoken; children raised in isolation will acquire no language as long as they are isolated). Even more mysteriously, most of the available evidence suggests that this ability to acquire language diminishes markedly following the onset of puberty, almost as though a switch in the brain has been thrown to the "off" position. (This is why most high school and college students have such difficulty learning a foreign language in school. One of the ironies of American culture is that nearly all of its formal foreign language instruction occurs too late in students' lives.)

As to whether linguistic ability is genetic, the jury is not yet in. Certainly, *something* linguistic seems to be encoded in our DNA—how and why else could humans (and only humans) acquire the creative use of language so easily with no instruction? But what exactly it might be is not at all well understood. Clearly, what is *not* encoded is specific language ability: You were not born with English ability any more than a Parisian baby would be born with French ability. We learn whatever language(s) we are exposed to in the early years of our development, regardless of our genetic ethnicity.

Sometimes, however, the way a person *uses* his or her language changes over the years. A child will usually begin to acquire whatever dialect his or her parents or siblings speak, but then, on maturing to school age, will usually (under the effect of peer pressure) begin to acquire whatever dialect the other school-age children use. If the child then grows up and moves to a region of the country where a different dialect is spoken, the child as an adult will usually acquire that dialect in direct proportion to how well he or she fits in (or wishes to fit in) with the other people in the area. Such adults can therefore choose whether to *accommodate to* or *dissociate from* the people with whom they share their community. (And, of course, as adults, we all have the ability to shift or not shift the formality of our speech based on who we are speaking to, what we are speaking about, where we are speaking, and so forth.)

Finally, when adults perpetuate the species, they pass on the *tendency* to acquire language to the new generation (as noted above), but the actual language that the new generation acquires must be at least a little different from the language the preceding generations used, or language would never change. (And if anything about language is certain, it is that it changes constantly.)

✦ *EXERCISE 3-1, page 143*

(a) No, *poodle, dalmatian, dachshund,* and *terrier* are not allomorphs of the same morpheme, {dog}. They are phonemically distinct, but they also have very different meanings: A poodle is one kind of dog, a dalmatian is another kind of dog, and so forth. To be allomorphs, variants must share precisely the same meaning.

(b) Every morph is not also an allomorph, simply because not every morpheme has variant phonemic forms. No matter how many different ways you pronounce *cat,* for example, they would all be transcribed /kæt/. On the other hand, every allomorph must also be a morph: Every alternate phonemic form of a morpheme is also, by definition, a form of that morpheme.

(c) Not every morpheme necessarily has allomorphs, since not every morpheme has variant phonetic forms. (Look again at the example of *cat* in part (b).) But of course, every morpheme *must* have morphs: A category of something cannot exist without the things that define it.

(d)

student	1: {student}
stupidity	2: {stupid} + {ity}
unfair	2: {un} + {fair}
excellent	3: {ex} + {cell} + {ent}
sleeping	2: {sleep} + {ing}
unemployed	4: {un} + {em} + {ploy} + {ed}
deforms	3: {de} + {form} + {s}
unreliable	4: {un} + {re} + {li} + {able}
trial	2: {tri} + {al}
disinfectant	4: {dis} + {in} + {fect} + {ant}
unfairly	3: {un} + {fair} + {ly}
husbands	3: {hus} + {band} + {s}
island	2: {is} + {land}
classroom	2: {class} + {room}
paper	1: {paper}
inversion	3: {in} + {ver} + {sion}
magazine	2: {maga} + {zine}
diploma	2: {di} + {ploma}
sandwich	2: {sand} + {wich}
crinkly	2: {crink} + {ly}

(e) It must be true that the *-er* in *longer* and the *-er* in *worker* come from two different morphemes, not the same one (even though in both cases, it is spelled and pronounced the same). In *longer,* the *-er* means something like "more than," whereas in *worker* it means "one who"; and if the two instances of *-er* were morphs of the same morpheme, they would have the same meaning.

✦ *EXERCISE 3-2, page 147*

(a) From your perspective, English has probably become a much easier language to learn. After all, we no longer have all to memorize all the extra inflections that marked the dual number and the nominative, accusative, dative, and locative cases. And if you have ever studied a foreign language that has such distinctions (such as Latin, Greek, or German), you know that all the memorizing involved is no easy task. But look at it from another point of view: What if your native language were one that had all these inflectional distinctions but also had a much freer word order than English does? Then, in learning English, you would have to remember which words must follow which other words to achieve a desired meaning. The point is this: *Easier* and *more difficult* are relative terms, and one method of conveying meaning is only easier or more difficult than another depending on which you are used to. The fact is, *both* methods are easy and difficult but to people coming from different linguistic backgrounds.

(b) Yes, there is a pattern: Some form of the auxiliary *have* always occurs with the past-participle form of the verb if the sentence is in the **active voice**—that is, if the subject of the sentence denotes the actor or agent (as in *John has eaten the cake*)—and some form of the auxiliary *be* always occurs with the past participle if the sentence is in the **passive voice**—that is, if the subject denotes the recipient of the action (as in *The cake was eaten by John*).

(c) Yes, *this* and *that,* when pluralized, become *these* and *those.*

✦ *EXERCISE 3-3, page 151*

(a)

{count}	lexical and free
{re-}	grammatical and bound
{-er}	grammatical and bound
{fast}	lexical and free
{the}	grammatical and free
{house}	lexical and free
{-ly}	grammatical and bound
{wood}	lexical and free
{five}	lexical and free
{swing}	lexical and free

(b) The derivational morpheme(s) is italicized in each of the following words:

*de*pose	readi*ly*	cold*er*	act*ive*	*be*heads
act*ion*	*re*pack*age*	*re*writing	*un*changed	force*fully*

Some important notes: First, the *-fully* in *forcefully* is two morphemes, *-ful-* and *-ly*. Second, the *-i-* in *readily* is not part of the suffix; it is merely the *-y* from {ready}, which has changed to *i* to allow the addition of the suffix. Finally, if you underlined the *-s* of *beheads,* the *-ing* of *rewriting,* or the *-ed* of *unchanged,* you mistook inflectional morphemes for derivational morphemes (the *-s* is {present}; the *-ing* is {present participle}; and the *-ed* is {past participle}).

(c) No, the pronouns listed here—*his, we,* and *myself*—are not morphemes but combinations of morphemes. *His* is the possessive form of *he* ({he} + {possessive}), *we* is the plural of *I* ({I} + {plural}), and *myself* is reflexive ({me} + {possessive} + {self}). In fact, pronouns in general are problematic when it comes to morphology. Some linguists do not classify *me* as a single morpheme, for example, but as two—{I} + {dative case}; and others might say that *I* is actually {me} + {nominative case}; and still others might say that we start with some hypothetical nonword morpheme, {X}, and then add {first person}, {singular}, and {nominative case} to get *I* and {first person}, {singular}, and {dative case} to get *me.* Most textbooks sidestep such difficulties by not discussing the morphology of pronouns at all; but you should realize that, like most disciplines, linguistics still has not had all its theoretical kinks worked out. The truth is that many gray areas still demand attention, and the morphological analysis of pronouns happens to be one of them.

(d) *cept* happens to be a cranberry morph, like the *wo* of *woman.* And, as noted in the text, it derives from Latin, which not many speakers of English know.

✦ *EXERCISE 3-4, page 156*

(a) The application of the possessive morpheme to a group of nouns will produce the same morphophonemic rule as the one written for the plural morpheme because both involve the addition of an *-s* to a word—and as you saw in Chapter 2, *-s* added to a word always produces the same three endings, regardless of the grammatical purpose the *-s* serves.

(b) No, this new definition will not work for all nouns. What about *dirt, salt, coffee,* and other nouns that must be understood as masses of things? (Yes, a sentence such as *John ordered two coffees* could conceivably occur but only with the understanding that *coffees* refers to "kinds of coffee" or "quantities of coffee.") Or, again, what about nouns such as *happiness* or *infinity,* which name abstract concepts that are difficult if not impossible to conceptualize as plurals? Exceptions of the first sort are called **mass nouns** (as opposed to **count**

nouns, which name countable things, such as chairs, pencils, floors, and trees); exceptions of the second sort are **abstract nouns** (as opposed to **concrete nouns,** which name things that are physically real and perceptible with the senses).

(c) For the immediate future, these kinds of irregular plurals will probably stay in the language; they have already occurred in print thousands if not millions of times, and linguistic changes that also involve changes in spelling happen only very rarely once that spelling has been mass produced. (Such mass production of written documents in English began in 1476, when William Caxton introduced the printing press to England. Before that time, English spelling changed a great deal; subsequently, however, it has changed relatively little.) On the other hand, language *does* tend to regularize itself and do away with exceptions, so a few thousand (or perhaps hundred) years from now, speakers of English may well be using *oxes* and *sheeps* rather than *oxen* and *sheep.*

(d) Young children as well as nonnative speakers who are in the initial stages of learning English learn the "easy" morphology of the language first—that is, the morphophonemic rules that govern hundreds and thousands of formations in the language. During this stage of learning, these speakers will often produce plurals such as *womans, mans, shrimps,* and *childs.* Then they have to learn all the exceptions, which, because of the lack of a single pattern, is a much more difficult task.

(e) The devoicing of the allomorphs /z/ and /əz/, like the examples in part (c), illustrates that English, as a language, is not static but is constantly changing.

(f) If a new word such as *loof* were to enter the language, its plural probably would be *loofs* /lufs/, not *looves* /luvz/. The reason is that *wives, thieves,* and *baths* /bæðz/ constitute exceptions to the general morphophonemic pattern for plurals in English, and it is much more likely that a new word would follow this general pattern rather than the relatively minor pattern noted here.

✦ *EXERCISE 3-5, page 159*

(a) The allomorphs of the past-tense morpheme are /t/, /d/, and /əd/ (each of which recurs frequently) and *shot, sang,* and *quit* (each of which occurs just once). If you missed any of the first three in your answer, you probably were not listening carefully enough as you transcribed the past-tense forms: If you say *sipped, lobbed,* and *eroded,* you should be able to hear that *sipped* ends in /t/, *lobbed* ends in /d/, and *eroded* ends in /əd/.

(b) One way to write the rule is like this: The past-tense allomorph /əd/ occurs if the final phoneme of the original verb is an alveolar stop; /t/ occurs following any other voiceless sound; and /d/ occurs following any other voiced sound. If you merely listed the sounds after which each allomorph occurs, you did not capture the important generalizations that /t/ and /d/ are both alveolars and that all the other sounds are either voiced or voiceless.

(c) The rule in part (b) does not account for all the past-tense forms in the data because *shot, sang,* and *quit* are morphologically conditioned.

(d) Yes, they are in complementary distribution, since they occur in a predictable pattern that is defined by mutually exclusive phonetic environments. In fact, *all* phonologically conditioned forms, whether they are allophones or allomorphs, occur in complementary distribution for exactly that same reason.

(e) Actually, the past-tense forms of these verbs are phonologically *and* morphologically conditioned, for just the reasons pointed out in the question: They follow the rule for the phonologically conditioned allomorphs but also exhibit an unpredictable internal vowel change that must be learned separate from the rule.

✦ *EXERCISE 3-6, page 162*

(a) Since the morphemes that can be applied to verbs but not to any other parts of speech are {present}, {past}, {present participle}, and {past participle}, one such definition would be this: "A verb is any word to which can be applied {present}, {past}, {present participle}, and {past participle}." The definition *does* have some exceptions, however. Auxiliary modal verbs such as *ought, must, can, may, will,* and *shall* cannot have all these morphemes applied to them. (*Could, might, would,* and *should* have been excluded only because many linguists consider them the past tenses, respectively, of *can, may, will,* and *shall.*)

(b) This list certainly is not comprehensive, but such verbs include the following: *thrived/thriven, swelled/swollen, showed/shown,* and *hanged/*

hung. (Notice that, for this last pair, the two past participles each serve a different purpose: *Hanged* is used when what is being hung is a person—*They hanged the criminal at dawn*—and *hung* is used when what is being hung is anything other than a person—*They hung the picture over the fireplace.*)

✦ *EXERCISE 3-7, page 164*

(a) Participles used as adjectives typically form their comparatives and superlatives with *more* and *most.* (The words *interesting, wounded,* and *bathed* would not sound like English if *-er* or *-est* were added to them, nor would most other participles-turned-adjectives.)

(b) The kind of sentence is one in which the main verb is some form of *be,* and a clause beginning with *than* follows the adjective: *John is more wealthy than I thought.*

(c) The patterns for adverbs and descriptive adjectives are the same, with one exception: Not all adverbs can be made comparative and superlative. (Neither can all adjectives, which is why we have been discussing only *descriptive* adjectives, as opposed, for example, to *number* adjectives such as *three* and *seven;* but adverbs cannot be divided quite so neatly, as you will soon see.) In general, adverbs of *manner* (which answer the question *How?*) *can* be made comparative and superlative: *fast/faster/fastest, distinctly/more distinctly/most distinctly,* and so forth. But adverbs of *place* (such as *here, home,* etc.) usually cannot and neither can most adverbs of *time* (such as *today* and *soon;* but notice that some, such as *frequently,* can take *more* and *most*) or *degree* (such as *very* and *most;* but again, notice that some, such as *completely,* take *more* and *most*).

✦ *EXERCISE 3-8, page 170*

(a) As a general rule, inflectional morphemes do always occur last in a word (so that the entire word is made plural, past tense, comparative, and so forth). But there are some apparent exceptions to this: Some people say *cupsful* rather than *cupfuls,* for example; *spoonsful* rather than *spoonfuls;* and *sisters-in-law* rather than *sister-in-laws.* The easiest way to resolve such discrepancies is to declare that such words are exceptions to the rule. Historically, however, these exceptions can be explained by noting that words such as *cup, spoon, full, sister, in,* and *law* were all at one time separate lexical morphemes, even when they occurred together—thus, *a cup full of coffee, a spoon full of sugar,* and *a sister in law*—so that {plural} naturally attached to *cup, spoon,* and *sister* (*two cups full of coffee, two spoons full of sugar,* and *two sisters in law*). But over time, *full, in,* and *law* came to be perceived as derivational rather than lexical in such phrases, producing *cupful, spoonful,* and *sister-in-law* (notice that there is no change in pronunciation between *cup full* and *cupful, spoon full* and *spoonful,* and *sister in law* and *sister-in-law*), so the more recent tendency is to add {plural} to the end of the entire construction. Neither method of pluralizing such words is more correct than the other.

(b) In theory, at least, there is no limit to the number of derivational morphemes that can be attached to a given word (consider *organizationally,* for example, which has four suffixes, or *disempower,* which has two prefixes), though, in practice, it is difficult to think of words that have more than five or six. But usually, only one inflectional morpheme can be added to any given word, since verbs can contain just one tense, adjectives can be only comparative or superlative (not both), and so forth. (The word *usually* was included in the last sentence because some nouns can be both plural and possessive, as in *the books' covers* and *the women's purses.*)

(c) No, there are no rules that predict exactly which words can receive which derivational morphemes. Such morphological patterns must be learned individually. (There *are* patterns concerning which derivational morphemes can be added to which parts of speech, however, as reflected in Table 3-4.)

(d) Yes, the same argument can often be made if exactly one derivational prefix and suffix are added to the same word. In *unhappiness,* for example, it must be true that {un} and *happy* combined first and that {ness} was added last, since {un} can be added only to adjectives (such as *happy*) and not to nouns (such as *happiness*).

(e) When we encounter a word we have not seen before, it is natural for us to begin breaking up the word into parts that we *do* understand, and those parts are frequently inflectional and/or derivational morphemes. In *unfligged,* for example, we can recognize {un}, meaning "not" and the *-ed* as an example of either {past tense} or {past participle}; all we lack a meaning for is *flig.* The meaning of *transbotulizing,* on the other hand, has something to do with "across" ({trans}) and must be ongoing ({present participle}). And *blegs* must be either the plural or third-person, present tense of *bleg.*

(f) Advertisers frequently break the rules of pronunciation, word formation, syntax, and language in general just to draw attention to their products. And the gimmicks usually work: Notice, for example, that *Uncola* describes one of the most successful products in history.

✦ *EXERCISE 3-9, page 174*

(a)

mice	open; complex
of	closed
and	closed
show	open; simple
paperclip	open; complex
her	closed
three	closed
this	closed
food	open; simple
round	open; simple

(If you listed *mice* as simple, remember that it contains two morphemes, {mouse} and {plural}. And *three,* though an adjective, is closed because it is nondescriptive.)

(b) *dragged—drag* is both the root and the stem.

deactivate—active is the root; *active* is the stem of *activate; activate* is the stem of *deactivate.*

impossible—-poss- is the root (it is a cranberry morpheme); *-poss-* is the stem of *possible; possible* is the stem of *impossible.*

thumbtack—thumb and *tack* are both roots (since both are words in their own right); but there is no stem here, since *thumbtack* contains no affixes.

hopefully—hope is the root; *hope* is the stem of *hopeful; hopeful* is the stem of *hopefully.*

unassuming—assume is the root; *assume* is the stem of *assuming; assuming* is the root of *unassuming.*

redness—red is both the root and the stem.

racketeers—racket is the root; *racket* is the stem of *racketeer; racketeer* is the stem of *racketeers.*

cloudiness—cloud is the root; *cloud* is the stem of *cloudy; cloudy* is the stem of *cloudiness.*

exceptionally—*-cept-* is the root (it is a cranberry morpheme); *-cept-* is the stem of *except; except* is the stem of *exception; exception* is the stem of *exceptional; exceptional* is the stem of *exceptionally.*

(c) One way to do it would be like this: A word is any free-root morpheme. (Omitting the word *free* would leave an incorrect result, since some roots, such as the *-cept* from the last word in part (b), are bound.)

✦ *EXERCISE 3-10, page 179*

(a) The first half of the compound frequently modifies the second half. For example, the *air* in *airstrip* tells what kind of strip, the *corn* in *cornflake* tells what kind of flake, and so on.

(b) Yes, blends combine the meanings as well as the pronunciations of words. Notice, for example, that *gasohol* does not just sound like parts of *gasoline* and *alcohol;* it actually *is* gasoline and alcohol.

(c)

airstrip	compound (*air* + *strip*)
deplane	derivation (prefix *de-* + *plane*)
quark	invention
disco	clipping (from *discotheque*)
growl	echoism
van	clipping (from *caravan*)
blurt	blending (*blare* + *spurt*)
greed	back-formation (from *greedy*)
hangnail	folk etymology (from *agnail*)
jeans	antonomasia (ultimately from the name of the Italian city *Genoa*)
zigzag	reduplication
carryall	folk etymology (from *carriole*)
Mike	clipping (from *Michael*)
curio	clipping (from *curiosity*)
floozy	invention
shutout	compound (*shut* + *out*)
OK	acronym (from *okay*)
televise	back-formation (from *television*)
leotard	antonomasia
redo	derivation (prefix *re-* + *do*)

✦ *EXERCISE 3-11, page 182*

uglier (complex)—The morphemes are {ugly} (free, root, stem) and comparative {er} (bound); the word was formed through derivation.

bush (simple)—{bush} is the only morpheme here.

chairs (complex)—The morphemes are {chair} (free, root, stem) and {plural} (bound); the word was formed through inflection.

erasers (complex)—The morphemes are {erase} (free, root, stem), agentive {er} (bound; *eraser* is also a stem), and {plural} (bound); *eraser* was formed through derivation and *erasers* through inflection.

potted (complex)—The morphemes are {pot} (free, root, stem) and {ed} (bound).

mist (simple)—{mist} is the only morpheme here.

Band-Aid (complex)—The morphemes are {band} (free, root) and {aid} (free, root); the word was formed through compounding, but because it was originally only a brand name (and technically still is) and not also used as a generic term, invention also played a role.

reforest (complex)—The morphemes are {re} (bound) and {forest} (free, root, stem); the word was formed through derivation.

sawdust (complex)—The morphemes are {saw} (free, root) and {dust} (free, root); the word was formed through compounding.

escalator (simple)—The only morpheme here is {escalator}, which was originally just a brand name rather than a generic term. (*Escalate* was later created through back-formation.)

✦ *EXERCISE 3-12, page 183*

If {un} is attached to *loadable,* then the meaning of *unloadable* is "not able to be loaded"; but if {able} is attached to *unload,* then the meaning of *unloadable* is "able to be unloaded." The resulting sentences, of course, mean two very different things.

✦ *EXERCISE 3-13, page 183*

You might define *idiom* this way: "An idiom is a nonexpandable phrase in which the meaning of the whole does not equal the sum of the meanings of the individual morphemes." (*Nonexpandable* means that words cannot be added to idioms without the meanings changing.) For *collocation,* this would work: "A collocation is an expandable phrase in which the meaning of the whole does equal the sum of the meanings of the individual morphemes but in which the morphemes are habitually placed in a particular order." (Notice that one of the major producers of macaroni and cheese, by the way, has capitalized on the fact that *macaroni and cheese* is a collocation: By advertising its product as *cheese and macaroni,* the company catches the public's ear and makes the point that its product is "cheesier" than the others.)

✦ *EXERCISE 3-14, page 184*

house/houses; walk/walking; red/redder	inflection
do/undo; happy/happily; work/workable	derivation
vibrations/vibes; Joseph/Joe; delicatessen/deli	clipping
typewriter/typewrite; hang glider/hang glide; lazy/laze	back-formation
áddress/addréss; cónvict/convíct; ímport/impórt	shifting

✦ *EXERCISE 3-15, page 185*

blatant—from Edmund Spenser's *The Faerie Queene*

malapropism—from the character Mrs. Malaprop in Richard Sheridan's play *The Rivals*

sensuous—from John Milton's essay titled "Of Reformation Touching Church Discipline in England" (Apparently, Milton wanted to avoid the connotations of *sensual.*)

yahoo—from Jonathan Swift's *Gulliver's Travels*

serendipity—from Horace Walpole's fairy tale *The Three Princes of Serendip*

✦ *EXERCISE 3-16, page 185*

(a) Put simply, two plural forms exist for each of these words because of the words' Latin origins. When the words were "borrowed" into English, of course their Latin plurals were borrowed, too (*indices, cherubim, strata, matrices*); but because the tendency for all borrowed words is to become more like the borrowing language—in this case, English—English plurals were formed, as well (*indexes, cherubs, stratums, matrixes*), by users who either did not know or did not appreciate Latin.

(b) Two past-tense forms exist for each of these verbs because of the many changes the English language has endured over the past 1,500 years. Historically, many more verbs formed their past tenses through an internal vowel change than do now (these are known as *strong verbs*). But since the majority of *all* verbs have always formed their past tenses merely by adding an alveolar suffix (these are known as *weak verbs*) and since the powers of analogy and conformity are very strong forces in language change, the tendency over time has been for strong verbs to become weak. Of course, just because a strong verb acquires a weak past tense does not mean that the strong past tense disappears. (It may, over time, or it may not: Language change tends not to be all that neat and tidy.) The verbs listed in this exercise just happen to have co-existing past-tense forms, one strong and one weak. In two of the three cases, the strong form of the verb is older; with *dive,* however, *dove* is the older form. (This is the only instance in English of a weak verb acquiring a strong past tense.) Interestingly, *hanged* and *hung* have managed to "justify" their co-existence by acquiring slightly different meanings. (*Hanged* is used with people: *They hanged the bank robber at dawn; hung* is used with objects: *They hung the picture on the wall.*)

✦ *EXERCISE 3-17, page 186*

polyglot to mean "more than one glot"—The user knows that *poly-* means "many" and believes that *-glot* is a count noun.

stalemate to mean "the spouse is no longer interested"—The user knows at least one meaning of *stale* ("tedious from familiarity") and one meaning of *mate* ("spouse") but is unaware that *stalemate* is not a combination of the two.

meteorology to mean "the study of meteors"—The user knows that *-ology* means "the study of" but is interpreting *meteor-* as the word *meteor.*

finesse to mean "a female fish"—The user knows that *fin* goes with *fish* (at least, it does in some contexts) and that the suffix *-ess(e),* like *-ett(e),* frequently means "female" (as in, for example, *countess* and *duchess*).

diatribe to mean "food for the whole tribe"—The user has interpreted *diat-* as *diet* (which he or she obviously knows the meaning of) and *-tribe* as *tribe* (which, again, he or she must know the meaning of).

✦ *EXERCISE 3-18, page 187*

The morpheme {er} cannot be added to a placename to denote someone from that place if the placename ends in a vowel sound (including diphthongs) or in /ɚ/. (This answer assumes that in *Illinois,* the final sound is a diphthong rather than /s/ or /z/.)

✦ *EXERCISE 3-19, page 188*

(a) do, doing, does   inflection

(b) appreciate, appreciable, appreciation   derivation

(c) strong, stronger, strongest   inflection

(d) boat, boats, boat's   inflection

(e) preach, preacher, preachy   derivation

(f) cut, uncut, cutter   derivation

(g) good, better, best   inflection

(h) be, were, is   inflection

(i) geography, geographic, geographer   derivation

(j) mouse, mouse's, mice   inflection

(Notice that inflectional morphemes never change the part of speech of the words they are applied to, and derivational morphemes frequently do.)

✦ *EXERCISE 3-20, page 188*

(a) The suffix *-able* can be added to transitive verbs (those that require an object) but not to intransitive verbs (those that do not require an object).

(b) The verbs *walk* and *run* seem to be exceptions to the rule written in part (a)—that is, they are intransitive. (*After dinner, John walked and Mary ran while Fred sat on the couch* is a grammatical sentence, though neither *walk* nor *run* has an object.) But *walk* and *run* can still have

-able suffixed to them. (*That dog isn't walkable* and *That obstacle course isn't runnable* are also both grammatical sentences.) But they are only *apparent* exceptions. To continue with the examples just cited, for a dog to be *walkable* and an obstacle course to be *runnable,* someone has to be able to *walk the dog* and *run the obstacle course*—in other words, the verbs *walk* and *run* must be capable of having objects (as *the dog* and *the obstacle course* are in the phrases just highlighted). The real solution here is in realizing that a small number of English verbs, including *walk* and *run,* can be either transitive or intransitive—that is, they can be used in sentences either with or without objects, depending on the intended meaning.

(c) When *-able* is added to any verb, its pronunciation is predictable: In every instance, the initial vowel will centralize to /ə/, yielding /əbəl/.

✦ *EXERCISE 3-21, page 189*

back-formation → back-form back-formation
beef, buffalo → beefalo blending
fast, ball → fastball compounding
short, stop → shortstop compounding
typographical → typo clipping
influenza → flu clipping
énvelope → envélop shifting
action → actionable derivation
suburb → burb clipping
rough, neck → roughneck compounding

✦ *EXERCISE 3-22, page 190*

Such depictions cannot be completely accurate simply because they do not reflect language change: The morphology of late-twentieth-century American English bears little resemblance to the morphology of English as it was spoken 15 centuries ago and may bear little resemblance to the morphology of English as it will be used 15 centuries hence. Still, producers—even those striving for authenticity whenever possible—are wise to opt for morphological invariability (assuming that producers are even aware that the morphology of English has changed over the years): How many viewers, after all, would pay to listen to a language that they could not understand?

Had this question been asked in Chapter 2, with the focus on phonology rather than morphology, your answer probably would have been about the same. Producers do vary the pronunciations (somewhat, though not a great deal) of characters set in different time periods and are able to do so because variations in phonology are much easier for viewers to follow than are variations in morphology. Once again, the decision is influenced mostly by the pragmatics (read: *economics*) of consumer supply and demand.

✦ *EXERCISE 3-23, page 191*

If you are like most Americans, research indicates that the grammatical mistakes will irritate you the most. We have all been trained to be much more forgiving of phonological and lexical mistakes than those involving grammar. Such training is the result of more than two centuries of grammatical prescriptivism, still occurs in the public and private school systems of the United States, and probably will not subside any time soon.

✦ *EXERCISE 3-24, page 192*

The ballerina's toes cramped into knots as she attempted the dance—You should have underlined *-ina* in *ballerina* and circled *-'s* in *ballerina's* (possessive), *-s* in *toes* and *knots* (plural), and *-ed* in *cramped* and *attempted* (past tense). Neither the *in-* nor the *-to* of *into* is an affix, since *into* is a compound.

John's new car was very inexpensive—You should have underlined *-in* and *-ive* in *inexpensive* and circled *-'s* in *John's* (possessive).

Mary's bike is the newest on the block—You should have underlined nothing and circled *-'s* in *Mary's* (possessive) and *-est* in *newest* (superlative). The word *is* does contain the present-tense morpheme but has no affix.

Salt had totally corroded the car's front fenders—You should have underlined *-ly* in *totally* and circled *-ed* in *corroded* (past tense), *-'s* in *car's* (possessive), and *-s* in *fenders* (plural).

Fred's cough means that he still smokes—You should have underlined nothing and circled *-'s* in *Fred's* (possessive) and *-s* in *means* and *smokes* (present tense).

✦ *EXERCISE 3-25, page 192*

At least the following information can be gleaned from the sentence *By mimsling the prefexed blostos and orepping all klegs, a pliffer can slis a vorg in dolkorizm with smah*:

(1) *Mimsling* and *orepping* are the present participles of two verbs, probably *mimsl(e)* and *orep,* and they describe things that can be done to, respectively, *prefexed blostos* and *klegs.* (We know these things can be "done to" *prefexed blostos* and *klegs* because of the initial word *by.*)

(2) *Prefexed* is an adjective that can modify the count noun *blosto,* which here occurs as the plural *blostos.*

(3) *Kleg* is also a count noun that here appears as the plural *klegs.*

(4) *Pliffer* must be a count noun capable of *slissing a vorg; slis* must be a transitive verb (the count noun *vorg* is its object), the action of which can be done by a *pliffer* and to a *vorg;* and *vorg,* as already noted, must be capable of being *slissed* by a *pliffer.*

(5) *In dolkorizm* is a phrase that either describes how or where a *pliffer* can *slis* a *vorg* or gives more information about what kind of *vorg* is capable of being *slissed. Dolkorizm* is a mass noun.

(6) *With smah* is another phrase and describes how, why, or with what a *pliffer* can *slis* a *vorg* in *dolkorizm. Smah* is another mass noun.

Notice that (quite by accident, of course) the entire sentence could be "translated" into *By doing the assigned exercises and reading all examples, a student can pass a course in linguistics with ease.*

✦ *EXERCISE 3-26, page 193*

a town on the border of Kansas and Colorado (blend)—The most natural-sounding choice here is probably *Kanorado* (which, by the way, really is the name of a town located near the border of Kansas and Colorado).

able to be contacted (derivation)—*Contactable.*

Cat Lovers Anonymous of Wyoming (acronym)—*CLAW.* (As far as I know, no such organization actually exists.)

a lawnmower to be used only for trimming (compound)—*Trimming lawnmower.* (If you suggested something like *trim mower,* you created a blend instead of a compound.)

using bubblewrap to pad a package (shift)—*Bubblewrap* (as a verb: *Margaret bubblewrapped the package before taking it to the post office*).

a new dance, invented by Gertrude (antonomasia)—*The Gertrude.*

a course in morphology (clipping)—Probably either *Morpho* or *Morph.*

do clipperization (back-formation)—Probably *clipperize.* (*Clipperizate* would be another possibility but sounds much less natural, at least to my ears.)

✦ *EXERCISE 3-27, page 194*

The English language really *does* reflect the sexism of the people who used it in its earlier stages of development, and if a majority (or even a significant minority) of the people who use it now are less sexist than their forebears (notice that I avoided *forefathers*), the language should reflect that fact. Historically, men carried all the mail, did all the important business, and entered the bowels of neighborhoods to work on sewers and such; thus, *mailman, businessman,* and *manhole* were quite logical. But times have changed, and the language should reflect those changes. Of course, language change of any kind is viewed negatively by some people and all the moreso when it is done consciously, even legislated, and in the name of equality. Thus, people continue to scoff at attempts to create gender-neutral language, a cause that originated with the women's movement in the 1970s. Likewise, some people are uncomfortable with current efforts to use accurate terms in describing ethnic groups (such as *African American* and *Native American*) and to use less stigmatizing language in describing people with exceptionalities (for instance, using terms such as *disabled* and even *challenged* instead of *handicapped*).

The pros of such change are fairly obvious: The language would more nearly reflect the culture of the people that use it, and more people would feel good about their place in society and as users of English. As for the cons associated with such change, they, too, are obvious: First, a lot of people would be unhappy (or at least profess to be unhappy) about the then current state of the language; second, thousands and thousands of occurrences of sexist and otherwise biased morphology would still exist in print. Personally, I believe the pros far outweigh the cons, but that is a matter of opinion. As to whether such reforms are likely to occur, I offer a cautious "yes."

Admittedly, legislated changes do not often mix well with users' ideas concerning the direction the future of the language should take. (A thorough look at the histories of France, Italy, and the former USSR proves that: All have had their version of a so-called language academy, and all such academies have been quite unsuccessful. In the 1960s, for example, the USSR proscribed the use of two "capitalistic" terms, *bluejeans* and *hotdog*—and a generation later, those two words were among the most frequently heard English borrowings in Moscow's Red Square.) But in the present case, it is a large number of the users of English (larger with each passing year, it seems) who are attempting the desired changes and who are having some success. For example, dictionaries of nonsexist alternatives are being published with increasing frequency, and most style manuals now address issues of gender and ethnicity. Also take a look at your textbooks and other educational materials. The elimination of sexist language and images (as well as other kinds of bias) is currently a significant issue in educational publishing at all levels—from preschool through college. Complete change may not occur for another generation or more, but it *will* probably occur.

Equally important, of course, is what people *think* when they use language: The term *letter carrier* may be the dictionary entry, but if it connotes maleness in the person it defines (as many words do that are technically gender neutral; compare *doctor* and *nurse,* for example), then any gains will have been marginal.

(*Note:* Facts are facts, but a large part of the above answer is personal opinion. If yours does not agree with mine—if, in short, you see no reason for users of English to stop using terms such as *mailman* and *businessman*—that certainly is your prerogative.)

✦ *EXERCISE 3-28, page 195*

The allomorphs of the definite article {the} are /ði/ and /ðə/. Since /ði/ occurs when the following noun begins with a vowel sound (or diphthong) and /ðə/ occurs when the following noun begins with a consonant sound, these allomorphs are phonologically conditioned. And yes, the use of the two indefinite articles is conditioned exactly the same way: *a* occurs with nouns beginning with a consonant and *an* with nouns beginning with a vowel.

✦ *EXERCISE 3-29, page 196*

The problem lies with *aphelion.* Put simply, its phonological structure and morphological structure seem to clash. The morpheme {helion}, which also occurs in *perihelion,* clearly begins with /h/; but in the pronunciation of the word, *-p-* and *-h-* come together as /f/, and there is nothing left to represent the /h/ of {helion}.

✦ *EXERCISE 3-30, page 196*

No answer is given here because the selection of newspaper or magazine will vary from class to class, student to student. The purpose of the exercise is to note contemporary creations of new words and what methods of word formation seem most prodigious.

Glossary

In the following definitions, all cross-references are indicated by boldface type, and an asterisk following a headword indicates that the term was introduced in a section labeled "For Further Study." Please note that the explanations given below are not formal definitions but merely general guidelines for use in review.

Abstract noun A noun denoting a quality or characteristic in general, or anything not physically real and perceptible by the senses, such as *faith, charity,* or *happiness* (compare **concrete noun**).

Accidental gap A gap in a language's inventory of forms that corresponds to a possible but nonoccurring sequence of **phonemes;** for example, neither *plam* nor *crund* violates the **phonotactics** of English and so could be English words, but they do not actually occur (compare **systematic gap**).

Acoustic phonetics The study of the physical properties of speech sound in terms of how they behave as sound waves and how they are heard (compare **articulatory phonetics**).

Accusative case The **case** specifying the direct object in a sentence, as in *John ate the* ***cheesecake*** (compare **dative case, genitive case,** and **nominative case**).

Acronym A word formed by combining the initial letter(s) of all or most of the words in a phrase, as in *NFL* (for *National Football League*), *NATO* (for *North Atlantic Treaty Organization*), and *WASP* (for *White Anglo-Saxon Protestant*).

Active voice The form of sentence in which the grammatical subject is performing the action expressed by the verb, as in *John baked a pie* and *Angela stole $4,000 in cash from the bank* (compare **passive voice**).

Affix A prefix or suffix, as the *un-* and *-able* in *unbearable.*

Affricate A **manner of articulation** that combines the sound of a **stop** with that of a **fricative,** as in the pronunciation of /č/ and /ǰ/.

Allomorph An alternate or variant phonemic form of a **morpheme;** for example, /s/, /z/, and /əz/ are all allomorphs of {plural}.

Allophone An alternate or variant phonetic form of a **phoneme;** for example, [t] and [tʰ] are allophones of /t/.

Alveolar A **place of articulation** in which the tip of the tongue touches or comes close to the **alveolar ridge**, as in the pronunciation of /d/ and /s/.

Alveolar ridge The small, hard ridge that protrudes from the roof of the mouth just behind the top, front teeth.

Alveopalatal A **place of articulation** in which the tongue touches or comes close to the roof of the mouth between the **alveolar ridge** and the **hard palate**; certain palatal sounds, such as /š/ and /ž/, are sometimes classed as alveopalatals.

Anterior* A **distinctive feature** of speech sounds characterized by articulation in front of the **alveopalatal** region, as in the pronunciation of /m/ and /p/.

Antonomasia A method of word-formation in which a name is adapted to stand for something closely associated with it; for example, *sandwich* derives from *Earl of Sandwich; frankfurter* derives from *Frankfurt, Germany;* and *leotard* derives from *Jules Léotard.*

Articulatory phonetics The study of the physical production of speech sounds (compare **acoustic phonetics**).

Aspirated Produced with an accompanying small burst of air, as the initial sounds in *two, kind,* and *pin.*

Aspiration The small burst of air that escapes the mouth when certain sounds are spoken, as with the initial sounds in *time, can,* and *pour.* Aspiration is a **distinctive feature** of speech sounds.

Assimilation An articulatory process in which the pronunciation of one sound is influenced by the pronunciation of the sound(s) next to it, usually resulting in a combination of sounds that is easier to pronounce; for example, using a **connected conversation pronunciation**, many speakers pronounce the first /n/ of *inconsistent* as [ŋ] because of the influence of the following velar /k/.

Back A position of **tongue advancement** used in the pronunciation of some vowels in which the tongue is retracted to the back of the mouth, as in the articulation of /u/ and /o/.

Back* A **distinctive feature** of speech sounds in which the tongue is retracted to the back of the mouth, as in the pronunciation of /g/ and /k/.

Back-formation A method of word formation in which the end of a word is shortened to create a new word that appears to be the source of the original word; for example, *babysit* is back-formed from *babysitter,* even though *babysitter* appears to be the product of *babysit* plus *-er.*

Bilabial A **place of articulation** primarily involving both lips, as in the pronunciation of /b/, /p/, and /m/.

Binary property* Characteristic of **distinctive features** in which each is categorized as either entirely present ([+]) or entirely absent ([–]).

Blade* The body of the tongue just behind the **tip.**

Blending A method of word formation in which the reduced forms of two or more words are combined into a new word; for example, *gasohol* blends *gasoline* and *alcohol* and *slurb* blends *slum* and *suburb.*

Bound morpheme A **morpheme** that cannot occur by itself but must be attached to at least one other morpheme, as the {un} of *unkind* and the {ly} of *happily* (compare **free morpheme**).

Broad transcription A method of representing speech sounds using a phonetic alphabet in such a way that only the major characteristics of the sounds are accounted for (compare **narrow transcription**).

Bronchi* The tubes connecting the **trachea** to the **lungs.**

Case An inflectional category that denotes the grammatical function of nouns and pronouns in sentences; for example, the *-'s* marks *cat's* as possessive.

Central A position of **tongue advancement** used in the pronunciation of some vowels in which the tongue is retracted to the central part of the mouth, as in the articulation of /a/.

Clipping A method of word formation in which an existing word is shortened to form a new word; for example, *exam* is the clipped form of *examination* and *phone* is the clipped form of *telephone.*

Closed class of words The category of words to which new members are added only very rarely, as with pronouns, prepositions, conjunctions, and determiners (compare **open class of words**).

Coarticulation The process (used especially in **connected conversation pronunciation**) of articulating consecutive sounds so that they overlap to some extent, as in /dono/ for *don't know.*

Comparative The inflectional morpheme that, when added to adverbs and adjectives, conveys the meaning "more than"; for example, *happier* and *more beautiful* are both inflected with {comparative} (compare **superlative**).

Complementary distribution The occurrence of forms such as **allophones** and **allomorphs** throughout a language in predictable, mutually exclusive phonetic environments; for example, the plural allomorph [əz] occurs only following sibilants, the plural allomorph [z] occurs only following all other voiced sounds, and the plural allomorph [s] occurs only following all other voiceless sounds, so those three allomorphs are in complementary distribution (compare **free variation**).

Complex word A word that consists of two or more morphemes, such as *unpacked* ({un} + {pack} + {ed}) (compare **simple word**).

Compounding A method of word formation in which two **roots** or **stems** are combined into a new word; for example, *gentleman* is a compound of *gentle* and *man,* and *something* is a compound of *some* and *thing.*

Concrete noun A noun denoting a person or an animate or inanimate being or anything physically real and perceptible by the senses, such as *tree, fire, dog,* or *hunger* (compare **abstract noun).**

Conjugation The complete list of inflected forms associated with a particular verb, such as, for the verb *run, run/runs/ran/running.*

Connected conversation pronunciation The natural process of adding, deleting, substituting, and permutating speech sounds in the production of language, especially in informal contexts, to make one's articulation easier and smoother (compare **reading pronunciation**).

Consonantal* A **distinctive feature** of speech sounds characterized by obstruction occurring in the mouth and/or throat, as in the pronunciation of /z/, /k/, and /b/.

Contextually conditioned When the formality of one's speech is influenced by the context in which one is speaking (also **stylistically conditioned**).

Continuant* A **distinctive feature** of speech sounds characterized by continuous airflow being maintained through the mouth, as in the pronunciation of /u/, /w/, and /h/.

Coronal* A **distinctive feature** of speech sounds characterized by the tongue **tip** or **blade** being raised, as in the pronunciation of /t/ and /s/.

Count noun Any noun capable of being understood in numerical terms; for example, *chair* (two chairs), *boy* (five boys), and *lamp* (a lamp) are all count nouns, but *sand* and *air* are not (compare **mass noun**).

Cranberry morph A **morph** that is neither an **affix** nor capable of occurring alone and that usually has had its meaning obscured by historical changes in the language; for example, the *cran-* of *cranberry* and the *wo-* of *woman* are both cranberry morphs.

Cranberry morpheme A **morpheme** that is neither an **affix** nor a **free morpheme** and that usually has had its meaning obscured by historical changes in the language; for example, the {cran} of *cranberry* and the {wo} of *woman* are both cranberry morphemes.

Dative case The **case** specifying the indirect object in a sentence, as in *John gave **Jane** the book* (compare **accusative case**, **genitive case**, and **nominative case**).

Delayed release* A **distinctive feature** of speech sounds characterized by the flow of air from the mouth being delayed slightly, as in the pronunciation of /č/ and /ǰ/.

Deletion An articulatory process in which a sound is removed from certain phonetic contexts, usually resulting in an easier combination of sounds to pronounce; for example, in **connected conversation pronunciation,** many speakers delete the first vowel in *parade,* leaving [pred].

Dental* 1: Describes the articulation of a speech sound that has been altered so that the tip of the tongue touches the back of the upper teeth rather than the alveolar ridge, as with the /t/ in *width.* 2: A **distinctive feature** of speech sounds characterized by the tongue being placed between, against, or near the front teeth, as in the pronunciation of /ð/ and /θ/.

Derivational morpheme An **affix** that, when added to a word, may change the word's part of speech but does not affect such grammatical features as **tense** or **plurality**, as in the *-ize* of *hospitalize* and the *un-* of *unhappy* (compare **inflectional morpheme**).

Descriptive rule A statement that objectively describes a particular recurring process in language use, as in: Most English words are pluralized by adding /s/ (compare **prescriptive rule**).

Diacritical mark A notation (usually a subscript or superscript) that gives added phonetic information in **narrow transcriptions;** for example, the [ʰ] in [tʰen] indicates that the /t/ is accompanied by **aspiration.**

Diaphragm* The large wall of muscle separating the chest from the abdomen; its expansion and contraction aid in breathing and speaking.

Diphthong The articulation of two consecutive vowels in a single syllable, as in *house, kite,* and *toy* (compare **monophthong**).

Distinctive feature An articulatory characteristic used to contrast speech sounds that could otherwise be identical; for example, [voice] is distinctive in English because it distinguishes between **voiced** and **voiceless** sounds such as /g/ and /k/ or /v/ and /f/ (compare **nondistinctive feature**).

Dorsum* The body and back of the tongue.

Ease of articulation An articulatory process in which easier pronunciations are favored over more difficult ones, as when, for example, /n/ replaces /ŋ/ finally in words ending with *-ing;* in **connected conversation pronunciation**, especially, ease of articulation often leads to such other articulatory processes as **assimilation**, **deletion**, **epenthesis**, **metathesis**, and **epithesis.**

Echoism A method of word formation in which a word mimics the sound for which it stands, as with *meow, quack, boom,* and *splash.* (Such words are also known as **onomatopoeic words.**)

Epenthesis An articulatory process in which a sound is added to the middle of a word in certain phonetic contexts, usually resulting in an easier combination of sounds to pronounce; for example, many people pronounce *athlete* [æθəlit].

Epiglottis* A thin slab of flexible cartilage that folds back over the **glottis** to protect it during swallowing; the epiglottis is also involved in the production of some non-English speech sounds.

Epithesis An articulatory process in which a sound is added to the end of a word in certain phonetic contexts, usually resulting in an easier combination of sounds to pronounce; for example, many people pronounce *across* as [əkrɔst].

First person The speaker(s)—as opposed to the listener(s) and outsider(s)—in the delineation of verbs and pronouns; for example, *I sleep* and *we travel* are both first person (compare **second person** and **third person**).

Flap* A **voiced**, **alveolar** speech sound articulated by the tongue flapping quickly against the front roof of the mouth, as in the medial consonant sound of *ladder.*

Folk etymology A process of word formation in which an existing word is reanalyzed to make more phonological and/or semantic sense; for example, *cold slaw* is a folk-etymologized form of *cole slaw,* and *net ball* is a folk-etymologized form of *let ball.*

Free morpheme A **morpheme** that is a word in its own right and so can occur freely, as in {cat} and {tree} (compare **bound morpheme**).

Free variation The unpatterned, unpredictable occurrence of allophones and/or phonemes in a given phonetic environment; for example, *economics* can be pronounced with either an initial /i/ or an initial /ɛ/ (compare **complementary distribution**).

Fricative A **manner of articulation** in which the airstream is audibly interfered with but not stopped entirely, as in the pronunciation of /f/ and /z/.

Front A position of **tongue advancement** used in the pronunciation of some vowels in which the tongue is extended to the front of the mouth, as in the articulation of /i/ and /e/.

Function word A word that has as its main function the specifying of grammatical relationships; for example, *the, to,* and *but* are function words, but *house, green,* and *happily* are not.

Genitive case The **case** specifying the possessor in a sentence, as in ***John's*** *teacher is tall* and ***My*** *wife is a lawyer* (compare **accusative case, dative case,** and **nominative case**).

Glide A **manner of articulation** in which a transition is effected between vowels or between a consonant and a vowel, as in the pronunciation of /w/ and /j/ (also **semivowel**).

Glottal A **place of articulation** involving a specific modification of the **glottis** (besides that required for **voiced** and **voiceless** sounds), as in the pronunciation of /h/.

Glottal stop* A **voiceless, glottal** speech sound articulated by the sudden separation of the **vocal cords,** which releases a small burst of air from the trachea, as occurs before the initial vowel sound in *eye*.

Glottis The space between the **vocal cords.**

Grammatical morpheme A **morpheme** that does not really have a sense in and of itself but that is used to express relationships between **lexical morphemes,** as with {of}, {and}, {re}, and {ful}.

Hard palate The hard, bony portion of the roof of the mouth behind the **alveolar ridge** and in front of the **velum.**

High A position of **tongue height** in which the tongue is raised to near the roof of the mouth, as in the pronunciation of /i/ and /u/ (compare **mid** and **low**).

High* A **distinctive feature** of speech sounds in which the tongue is raised to near the roof of the mouth, as in the pronunciation of /i/ and /g/.

Homorganic Used to describe two consecutive speech sounds that have the same place of articulation, as with the *-nd-* in *under* and the *-nk* in *ink*.

Inflection A morphological process that involves adding an **inflectional morpheme** to a word, as when the verb *kick,* inflected for the simple past tense, becomes *kicked,* or the noun *duck,* inflected for the plural, becomes *ducks*.

Inflectional morpheme An **affix** that, when added to a word, will not change the word's part of speech but will change such grammatical features as **tense** or **plurality,** as the *-ed* in *walked* and the *-s* in *desks;* the eight inflectional morphemes used in English are {plural}, {possessive}, {present tense}, {past tense}, {present participle}, {past participle}, {comparative}, and {superlative} (compare **derivational morpheme**).

Intercostal muscles* The muscles between the ribs that, when flexed and relaxed, force air into and out of the lungs for speaking and breathing.

Interdental A **manner of articulation** in which the tongue is placed between the teeth, as in the pronunciation of /θ/ and /ð/.

International Phonetic Alphabet (IPA) An alphabet in which there exists a one-to-one correspondence between speech sounds and symbols; the IPA is used in **transcription** by linguists and others who study language.

Intonation A **suprasegmental** in which the movement of pitch corresponds to contrastive differences in the meanings of speech forms, as in *John kissed Mary* versus *John kissed Mary?*

Invention A method of word formation in which the new word is created without reference to any existing **morphemes**, as with *Kodak* and *Xerox*.

Juncture A **suprasegmental** consisting of a slight gap or pause in a string of speech sounds, as in the difference between *a name* and *an aim* or between *also* and *all so*.

Labialized* Describes the articulation of a sound that has been altered to include lip rounding in anticipation of a following rounded segmental, as with the initial /t/ of *token*.

Labiodental A **place of articulation** in which the lower lip comes near or touches the upper front teeth, as in the pronunciation of /v/ and /f/.

Labiovelar A **place of articulation** in which the base of the tongue is raised near the **velum** and the lips are rounded, as in the pronunciation of /w/.

Larynx* The cartilage and muscle structure in which the vocal cords are located.

Lateral The speech sounds represented by /l/.

Lateral* A **distinctive feature** of speech sounds characterized by the sides of the tongue being lowered, as in the pronunciation of /l/.

Lax A way of pronouncing vowels in which the muscles of the tongue are unconstricted, as in the pronunciation of /ɪ/ and /æ/.

Lexical morpheme A morpheme that has an easily definable sense in and of itself, as with {cat}, {happy}, and {red} (compare **grammatical morpheme**).

Lip rounding A method of articulating vowels in which the lips are protracted, as in the pronunciation of /o/ and /u/.

Liquid A **manner of articulation** in which the airstream flows continuously through the mouth with less obstruction than that of fricatives, as in the pronunciation of /l/ and /r/.

Long* Describes the articulation of a speech sound that has been altered so that it is held for a proportionately longer period of time, as when a vowel is followed immediately in the same syllable by a consonantal segmental that is voiced and/or a fricative.

Low A position of **tongue height** in which the tongue is lowered to near the bottom of the mouth, as in the pronunciation of /a/ and /æ/ (compare **mid** and **high**).

Low* A **distinctive feature** of speech sounds characterized by the tongue being lowered to near the bottom of the mouth, as in the pronunciation of /a/ and /æ/.

Major class features* Phonological features that distinguish the major categories of sounds, as [**consonantal**] and [**obstruent**].

Manner of articulation How the flow of air from the lungs is modified by the speech organs during the production of sounds.

Mass noun Any noun that must be understood in terms of its mass rather than numerically; for example, *sand, water,* and *mustard* cannot be quantified numerically (unless "kinds of" or "quantities of" is understood)—and so are mass nouns (compare **count nouns**).

Metathesis An articulatory process in which the order of two sounds is reversed in certain phonetic contexts, usually resulting in an easier combination of sounds to pronounce; for example, many speakers often pronounce *ask* as /æks/.

Mid A position of **tongue height** in which the tongue is raised to the middle portion of the mouth, as in the pronunciation of /e/ and /o/ (compare **low** and **high**).

Minimal pair Two words that differ in only a minimal way—that is, by one sound—as in the initial sounds of *map* and *cap* (compare **minimal set**).

Minimal set Three or more words that differ in only a minimal way—that is, by one sound—as in the initial sounds of *bet, met, pet,* and *set* (compare **minimal pair**).

Monophthong The articulation of a single vowel in a single syllable, as in *tune* and *bit* (compare **diphthong**).

Morph An instance of a smallest unit of meaning in a language; for example, *house, -ed* (as in *walked*), and *un-* (as in *undo*) are all morphs.

Morpheme A category of semantically identical smallest units of meaning in a language; for example, {cat}, {past tense}, and {plural} are all morphemes, even though each may be represented in several phonetically different ways.

Morphologically conditioned Used to describe the occurrence of an allomorph when that occurrence is unpredictable and not determined by the phonology of the word to which the allomorph has been added; for example, nothing in the phonology of *child* predicts that the addition of {plural} will produce *children,* so the plural allomorph *-ren* is morphologically conditioned (compare **phonologically conditioned**).

Morphology The study of the smallest meaningful units in a language, including how those units combine to form words.

Morphophonemic rule A **descriptive rule** that accounts for the phonetic variation among the **allomorphs** of a given **morpheme.**

Narrow transcription A method of representing speech sounds using a phonetic alphabet in such a way that the major and minor characteristics of the sounds are accounted for (compare **broad transcription**).

Nasal A **manner of articulation** in which the airstream passes from the larynx through the **nasal cavity,** as in the pronunciation of /m/ and /n/.

Nasal* A **distinctive feature** of speech sounds characterized by the airstream passing from the **larynx** through the **nasal cavity,** as in the pronunciation of /m/ and /n/.

Nasal cavity The open area behind the nose through which the airstream must pass in the articulation of **nasals.**

Nasalized* Describes the articulation of a speech sound that has been altered so that part of the airstream exits through the nose rather than the mouth, as with the /æ/ in *pan.*

Natural class* A group of phonological sounds that have in common at least one property of production; for example, /m/, /n/, and /ŋ/ constitute a natural class because they are all [+ nasal].

Nondistinctive feature* An articulatory characteristic that does not contrast speech sounds; for example, [voice] is a nondistinctive feature of [v], [r], and [m], since all are voiced sounds (compare **distinctive feature**).

Number A grammatical category that marks distinctions between **singular** and **plural.**

Obligatory phonological process A **phonological process** that occurs for all the speakers of a given language or dialect (compare **optional phonological process**); for example, all speakers of English insert a vowel sound before the final /d/ when the past-tense morpheme is added to a word ending in /t/ or /d/.

Obstruent The category of speech sounds that includes all stops, fricatives, and affricates (compare **sonorant**).

Onomatopoeic word A word that mimics the sound for which it stands, as with *meow, quack, boom,* and *splash.* (Such words are created through **echoism.**)

Open class of words The category of words to which new members are easily added; for example, nouns, adjectives, and adverbs are open to new additions in English (compare **closed class of words**).

Optional phonological process A **phonological process** that occurs for some but not all the speakers of a given language or dialect (compare **obligatory phonological process**); for example, some speakers of English metathesize the /s/ and /k/ in the pronunciation of *ask* (thus producing /æks/), but not all do.

Palatal A place of articulation in which the **blade** of the tongue touches or comes near to the **hard palate**, as in the pronunciation of [ž] and [č].

Palatalized* Describes the articulation of a speech sound that has been altered so that the front of the tongue rises toward the palate, as with the /i/ in *key*.

Passive voice The form of sentence in which the receiver of the action expressed by the verb is encoded as the grammatical subject, as in *A pie was baked by John* and *$4,000 in cash was stolen from the bank by Angela* (compare **active voice**).

Past participle A verbal form that, when used with *have* in an **active sentence** or *be* in a **passive sentence**, denotes an action or state that has already occurred; in English, past participles most often end in *-en* (*spoken, eaten*) or *-ed* (*walked, nailed*) (compare **present participle**).

Past tense The grammatical category within **tense** that describes actions or states that have already occurred (compare **present tense**).

Periphrasis The formation of the **comparative** and **superlative** forms of adjectives and adverbs through the addition of *more* and *most* to the adjective, as in *more beautiful* and *most magnanimous*.

Person A grammatical category that marks distinctions between **first person, second person**, and **third person.**

Pharynx* The part of the throat extending between the mouth and the **larynx.**

Phone An instance of a speech sound, as with [b], [s], and [o] (also **segmental**).

Phoneme A category of speech sounds that all the speakers of a given language or dialect perceive as more or less identical; for example, speakers of English hear both [t] and [t^h] as instances of /t/.

Phonemic inventory All the **phonemes** contained in a given language or dialect.

Phonetic environment The speech sounds (or lack of same) immediately preceding and following another speech sound; for example, the phonetic environment of the vowel in *cat* is "following /k/ and preceding /t/," and the phonetic environment of the /t/ in the same word is "word-final, following /æ/."

Phonetic inventory All the **phones** contained in a given language or dialect.

Phonetics The study of speech sounds (see also **acoustic phonetics** and **articulatory phonetics**).

Phonological process The precise mechanism of sound change specified by a **descriptive** (phonological) **rule.**

Phonologically conditioned Used to describe the occurrence of an **allomorph** when that occurrence is predictable and determined by a sound in the word to which the allomorph has been added; for example, {plural}, when added to most words ending in a voiced sound that is not a **sibilant,** produces the phonologically conditioned allomorph [z] (compare **morphologically conditioned**).

Phonology The study of the sounds and sound patterns in a language.

Phonotactics The system and study of the arrangement of phonemes in a language.

Place of articulation The place(s) at which the airstream is modified in the throat and/or mouth to become speech sounds.

Plural The grammatical category within **number** which, in English, marks the meaning "more than one" (compare **singular**).

Prescriptive rule A subjective statement of how forms in a language should be rendered, such as: You should never split an infinitive and Never end a sentence with a preposition (compare **descriptive rule**).

Present participle A verbal form that, when used with *be,* denotes an action or state that is in the process of occurring; in English, present participles end in *-ing,* as in *running* and *sleeping* (compare **past participle**).

Present tense The grammatical category within **tense** that describes actions or states that are presently occurring or that habitually occur (compare **past**).

r-colored schwa The vowel and following /r/ sounds in words such as *bird* and *work* and the phonetic symbol used to describe them, [ɚ].

Reading pronunciation A method of pronunciation in which all and only the sounds in a word or string of words are articulated precisely in the order in which they appear (compare **connected conversation pronunciation**).

Reduced* A **distinctive feature** of the speech sound /ə/ characterized by the sound most often appearing as an unstressed variant of a vowel that is ordinarily stressed, as in the initial vowel of *opinion* (/əpɪnjɪn/).

Reduplication A method of word formation in which a morpheme is repeated or nearly so, as with *yo-yo, hanky panky,* and *tick tock.*

Retroflex The speech sounds represented by /r/ in English. (In other languages, some varieties of /r/ may be nonretroflex, as with the Spanish trilled *r* or the German uvular *r*.)

Root The morpheme or morphemes that remain after all the affixes have been stripped away; for example, *cat* is the root of *cats, happy* is the root of *unhappily,* and *corn* and *flake* are the roots of *cornflakes* (compare **stem**).

Round* A **distinctive feature** of speech sounds characterized by the lips protruding, as in the pronunciation of /u/ and /w/ (compare **unrounded**).

Rounded A characteristic of (especially vowel) articulation in which the lips protrude, as in the pronunciation of /u/ and /o/ (compare **unrounded**).

Second person The listener(s)—as opposed to the speaker(s) and outsider(s)—in the delineation of verbs and pronouns; for example, *you sleep* and *you travel* are both second person (compare **first person** and **third person**).

Segmental A speech sound (also **phone**; compare **suprasegmental**).

Semivowel A **manner of articulation** in which a transition is effected between vowels or between a consonant and a vowel, as with /w/ and /j/ (also **glide**).

Shifting A method of word formation in which an existing word is merely adapted to a new grammatical category; for example, the verb *father* represents shifting from the noun *father* (also **zero-conversion, zero-derivation**).

Sibilant Any of the six categories of speech sounds /s/, /z/, /š/, /ž/, /č/, and /ǰ/.

Simple word A word that consists of a single **morpheme**, such as *hat* and *eat* (compare **complex word**).

Singular The grammatical category within **number** which, in English, marks the meaning "one and only one" (compare **plural**).

Soft palate The soft, fleshy area near the rear of the roof of the mouth, directly behind the **hard palate** (also **velum**).

Sonorant The category of speech sounds that includes all nasals, liquids, and glides (as well as vowels; compare **obstruent**).

Sonorant* A **distinctive feature** of speech sounds characterized by the ability of the sound to be protracted or sung, as in vowels, glides, liquids, and nasals.

Stem A unit to which a morpheme is added; for example, *cat* is the stem of *cats* and *predictable* is the stem of *unpredictable* (compare **root**).

Stop A **manner of articulation** in which the airstream is stopped briefly but completely before it exits the vocal tract, as in the pronunciation of /d/, /t/, and /g/.

Stress A **suprasegmental** consisting of added emphasis being given to part of an utterance; for example, the first syllable of *paper* contains the main stress of that word.

Strident* A **distinctive feature** of speech sounds in which proportionately greater noise accompanies the articulation, as in the pronunciation of /s/ and /z/.

Stylistically conditioned When the formality of one's speech is influenced by the context in which one is speaking (also **contextually conditioned**).

Superlative The inflectional morpheme that, when added to adjectives and adverbs, conveys the meaning "most of all"; for example, *happiest* and *most beautiful* are both inflected with {superlative} (compare **comparative**).

Suprasegmental The nonsegmental, intrinsic properties of **phones**, such as **intonation, juncture, pitch, stress,** and **tone.**

Syllabic* 1: Describes the ability of a consonant segmental (usually a liquid or nasal following an obstruent) to stand alone as a syllable. (English syllables typically require a vowel to be present.) 2: Used to indicate that a consonant can serve as the nucleus of a syllable, as the /l/ in *bottle* and the /n/ in *button.*

Systematic gap A gap in a language's inventory of forms that corresponds to an impossible sequence of phonemes for that language; for example, *btpgle* and *msxo* both violate the **phonotactics** of English and thus could never be English words (compare **accidental gap**).

Tense 1: A grammatical category that marks the time of an occurrence relative to the moment of speaking, as in **present** and **past.** 2: A way of pronouncing vowels in which the muscles of the tongue are constricted, as in the pronunciation of /i/ and /e/.

Tense* A **distinctive feature** of speech sounds in which the muscles of the tongue are constricted, as in the pronunciation of /i/ and /e/.

Third person The outsider(s)—as opposed to the speaker(s) and listener(s)—in the delineation of verbs and pronouns; for example, *he/she/it sleeps* and *they travel* are both third person (compare **first person** and **second person**).

Tip* The end of the tongue nearest the front of the mouth, in front of the **blade.**

Tone The **suprasegmental** consisting of pitch differences that signal meaning within words. (English is not a tonal language, though Chinese, Korean, and many others are.)

Tongue advancement The position of the tongue in the mouth relative to the horizontal axis during the articulation of vowels, as in **front, central**, and **back**.

Tongue height The position of the tongue in the mouth relative to the vertical axis during the articulation of vowels, as in **high**, **mid**, and **low.**

Tongue tenseness The measure of how flexed the muscles in the tongue are during the articulation of vowels, as in **tense** and **lax.**

Trachea* The tubes connecting the **larynx** to the **bronchi.**

Transcribe To translate a language's alphabetic symbols into the symbols of a phonetic alphabet, based on the sounds the alphabetic symbols represent in a given word.

Transcription The process of translating a language's alphabetic symbols into the symbols of a phonetic alphabet, based on the sounds the alphabetic symbols represent in a given word.

Underlying form In phonology, a hypothetical, abstract form (the **phoneme** or **morpheme**) from which phonetic variants are derived by **descriptive rule.**

Unreleased* Describes the articulation of a speech sound that has been altered so that none of the airstream escaping the mouth or nose, as with the /t/ in sentence-final *cat.*

Unrounded A characteristic of (especially vowel) articulation in which the lips do not protrude, as in the pronunciation of /ɪ/ and /e/ (compare **rounded**).

Uvula* The small flap of tissue that dangles from the velum; the uvula is used to produce speech sounds in some languages (such as the uvular *r* in German) but not in English.

Velar The **place of articulation** corresponding to the **velum,** as in the pronunciation of /g/ and /k/.

Velarized* Describes the articulation of a speech sound that has been altered to include the body of the tongue being raised toward the velum, usually in anticipation of a following velar segmental, as with the /l/ of *milk.*

Velum The soft, fleshy area near the rear of the roof of the mouth, directly behind the **hard palate** (also **soft palate**).

Virgules The linguistic notation that encloses phonemes (//).

Vocal cords The muscles that line the inner wall of the **larynx** and that are used to produce speech sounds; the length and thickness of the vocal cords determine the pitch of one's voice.

Vocalic* A **distinctive feature** of speech sounds characterized by the sound being either a vowel or a nonvowel.

Voice* A **distinctive feature** of speech sounds characterized by the vocal cords either being brought together and allowed to vibrate (in which case the resulting sound is [+ voice]) or being separated and allowed to relax (in which case the resulting sound is [– voice]).

Voiced Used to describe any sound made with the vocal cords vibrating, as in the pronunciation of /z/, /v/, and /i/ (compare **voiceless**).

Voiceless Used to describe any sound made without the vocal cords vibrating, as in the pronunciation of /s/, /f/, and /t/ (compared **voiced**).

Voiceless* Describes an articulation in which a consonant segmental, usually a liquid, is pronounced with less than complete vibration of the vocal cords. Voicelessness usually occurs in a sound when the preceding sound (typically a stop) is **voiceless.**

Voiceless bilabial glide* Speech sound produced by articulating the sequence of [hw], as in (for some speakers) the initial sound of *where, white,* and/or *which.*

Voicing A characteristic of articulation in which the vocal cords are either brought together and allowed to vibrate (in which case the resulting sound is **voiced**) or separated and allowed to relax (in which case the resulting sound is **voiceless**).

Zero-conversion A method of word formation in which an existing word is merely adapted to a new grammatical category; for example, the verb *father* represents zero-conversion from the noun *father* (also **shifting, zero-derivation**).

Zero-derivation A method of word formation in which an existing word is merely adapted to a new grammatical category; for example, the verb *father* represents zero-derivation from the noun *father* (also **shifting, zero-conversion**).

Zero plural A **plural** formed with no resulting phonological change in the singular form of the word; for example, *sheep* + {plural} is still *sheep.*

Index

Note: Boldface numbers indicate the page(s) on which a term is identified as a key term. The letter *f* following a page number indicates a figure; the letter *t* indicates a table.